Under Milk Wood Revisited

The Wales of Dylan Thomas

Mark Davis & Tony Earnshaw

Foreword by Sally Burton

AMBERLEY

To my father, Trevor
In fond remembrance of
our Welsh road trip, 2009 (Tony Earnshaw)

To Dylan Thomas, for being the
inspiration behind my creation.
(Mark Davis)

First published 2014

Amberley Publishing
The Hill, Stroud
Gloucestershire, GL5 4EP

www.amberley-books.com

ISBN 978 1 4456 0755 9 (print)
ISBN 978 1 4456 3738 9 (ebook)

British Library Cataloguing in Publication Data.
A catalogue record for this book is available from the British Library.

Typesetting by Amberley Publishing.
Printed in the UK.

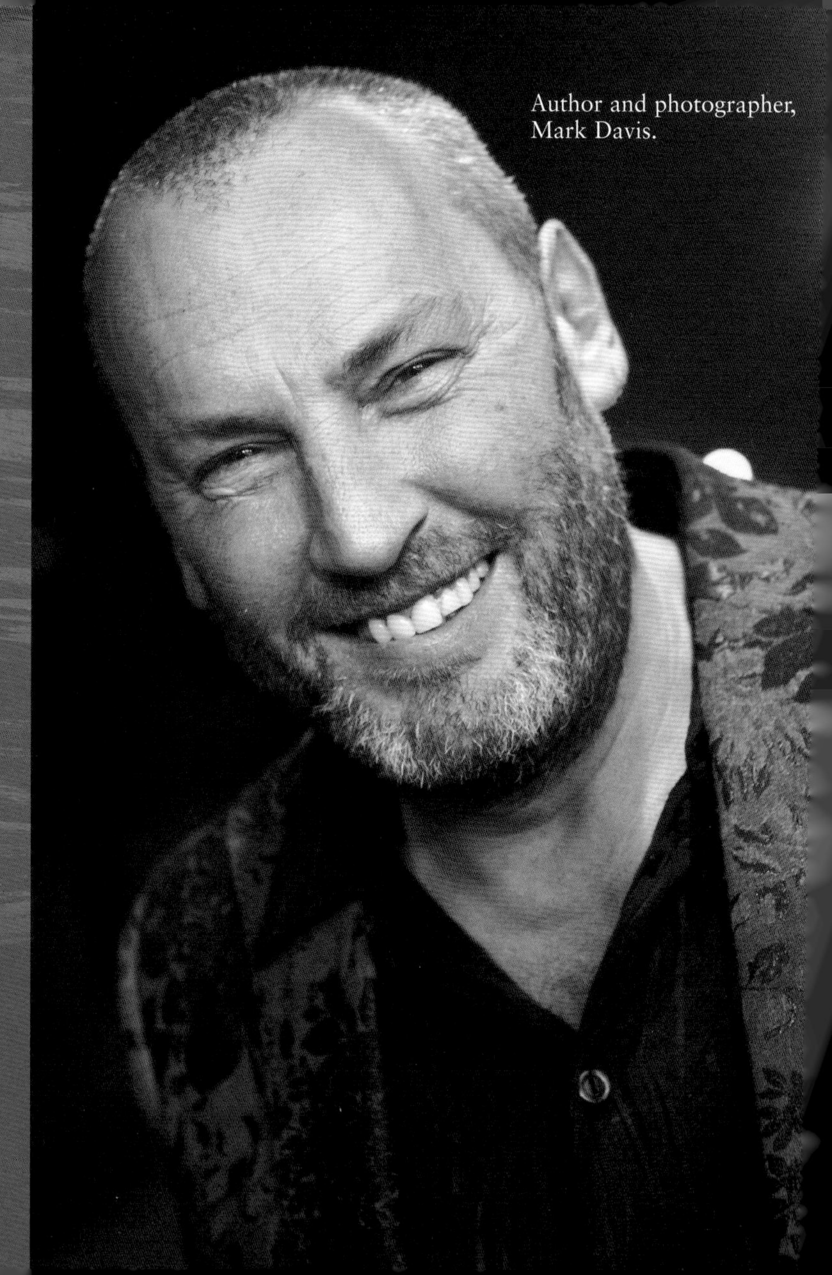

Author and photographer,
Mark Davis.

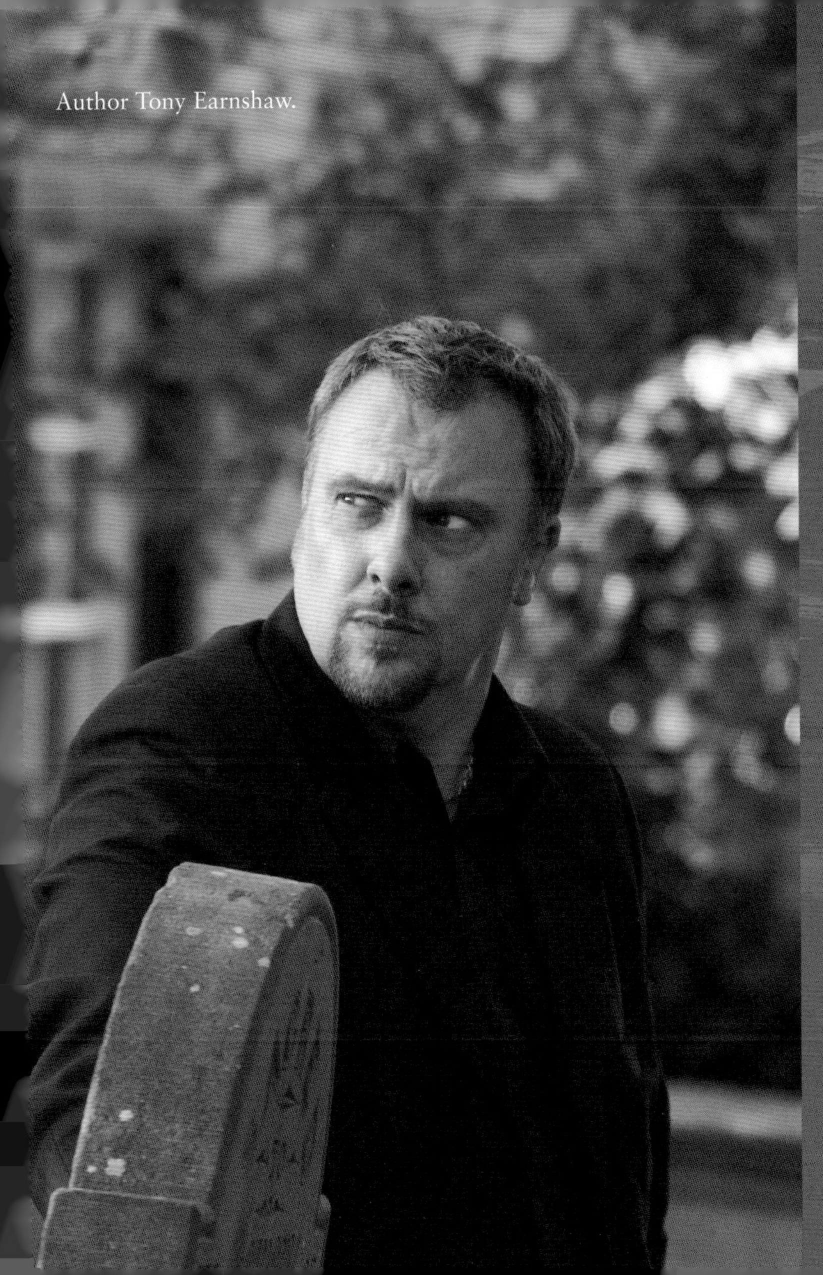
Author Tony Earnshaw.

Contents

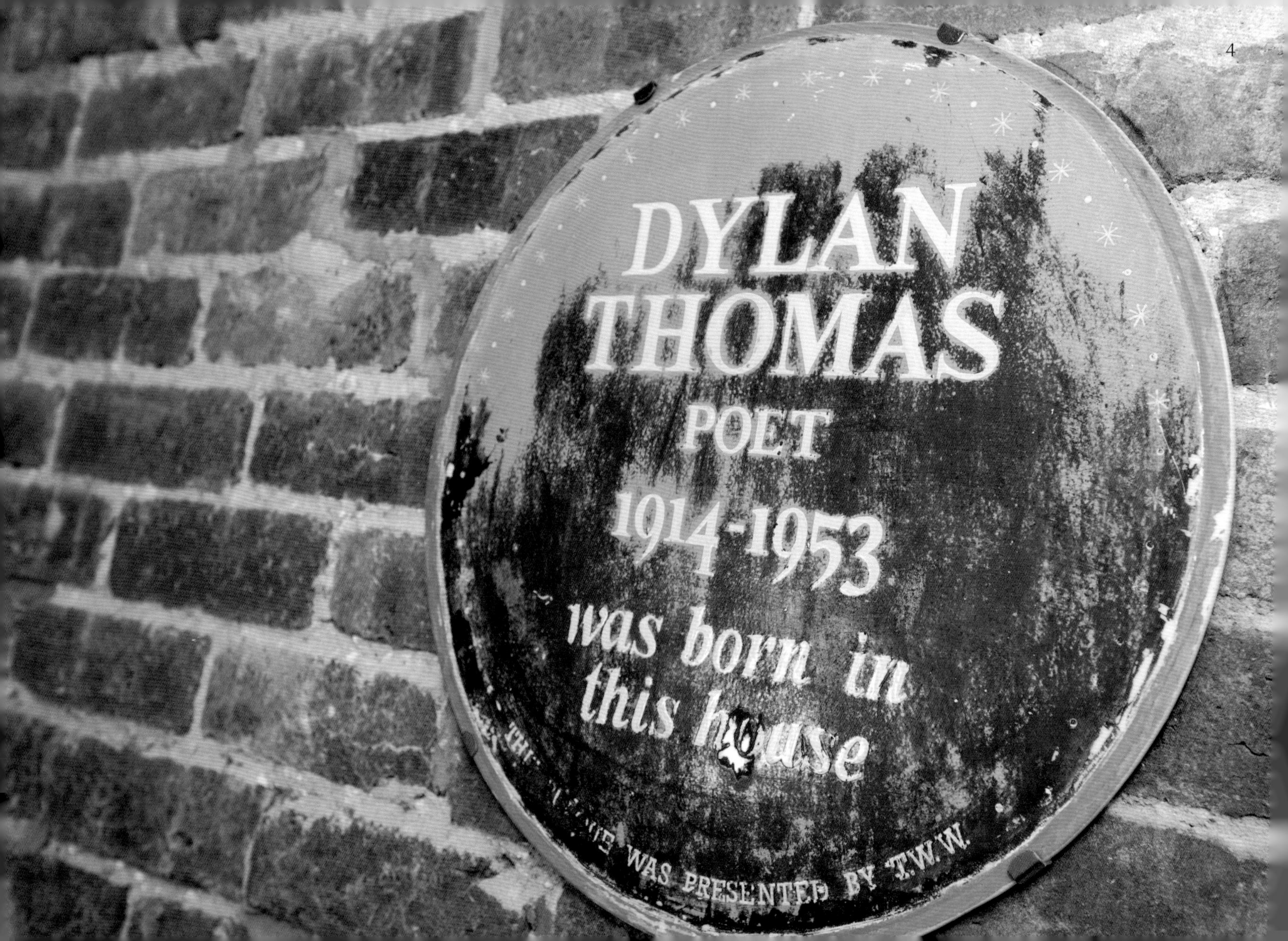

DYLAN
THOMAS
POET
1914-1953
was born in
this house
WAS PRESENTED BY T.W.W.

Acknowledgements

Very special thanks to Sally Burton for her foreword and to Dr Andrew Sinclair for his introduction and the generous use of images from his personal archive.

Production photographs from the film of *Under Milk Wood* are by Keith Hamshere and are reproduced by kind permission of Andrew Sinclair and Timon Films Ltd.

Grateful thanks are due to the following individuals and organisations: Vic Allen, Gareth Bailey, Emma Bangham, David Benedict, Laura Brown, Martin Grimes, (Headmaster of Dyffryn School, Taibach), Brian Gascoigne, Sally Griffiths (Chapter Arts Centre, Cardiff), Gemma Hargest (Tourism Development Coordinator, Neath Port Talbot County Borough Council) Bill Lawrence, Robin Lyons, Sian Owen, Tony Palmer, Siân Phillips, Caroline Rauter (Swansea University), Reel Solutions, Peter Shillingford, Betty Smith, Timon Films Ltd., The Tony Earnshaw Collection, and Professor Chris Williams of Cardiff University. Thanks also to Tom Furby at Amberley Publishing for all his help in producing this publication.

Sources:

Earnshaw, Tony, 'Gone for a Burton', Yorkshire Post, 4/3/13
Jenkins, David, *Richard Burton, A Brother Remembered* (London: 1994)
Jenkins, Graham, *Richard Burton, My Brother* (London: 1988)
McKenna, Rollie, *Portrait of Dylan* (London: 1982)
Misstear, Rachael, 'When Hollywood took over the seaside town of Fishguard', Wales Online, 16/6/14
Sinclair, Andrew, *The Screenplay of Dylan Thomas' Under Milk Wood* (New York: 1973)
Sinclair, Andrew, *Dylan Thomas: No Man More Magical* (New York: 1975)
Sinclair, Andrew, *Dylan the Bard* (London: 1999)
Sinclair, Andrew, *Under Milk Wood and Dylan on Dylan* (London: 2003)
Sinclair, Andrew, *Down Under Milk Wood* (London: 2012)
Thomas, Dylan, *Under Milk Wood* (London: 1972)
Williams, Chris (ed.), *The Richard Burton Diaries* (New Haven and London: 2012)

Dylan Thomas, 1961, directed by Jack Howells
A Child's Christmas in Wales, 1961, directed by Bruce Minnix
Under Milk Wood, 1972, directed by Andrew Sinclair
In From the Cold? 1988, directed by Tony Palmer

Extract from *Richard Burton's Diaries* by kind permission of rights holder: Swansea University, Information Services & Systems (ISS).

Foreword by Sally Burton

Richard Burton must have been around thirteen when he realised the importance of financial independence. He found many ways of making a bit of extra cash and one of those was collecting old newspapers from his neighbours and taking them to the fish and chip shop for use as wrapping paper. With bundles of newspapers tucked under his arms, he would manage to read what he could. As Welsh was Richard's first language it was a way of extending his use and understanding of English. He was thrilled when he discovered a poem printed in one of the old papers and even more thrilled when he realised he understood its meaning: so began Richard's lifelong love and rich interpretation of poetry.

It was during his teenage years that he discovered Dylan Thomas and his work. He was to admire and cherish his memories of Dylan Thomas throughout his life. One thing Richard worried about was the fact that when Dylan asked him for a loan of £200 he simply did not have the cash to fulfill the request. Dylan went to New York and died. Richard wondered if had he managed to find the £200 Dylan's fate would have been different. Probably not, but it was enough to be of lingering concern to Richard.

Dylan Thomas did not have Welsh as a first language, he spoke English, but he did have the rich and playful adventure the Welsh have with the English language. *Under Milk Wood*, if it were to be translated into Welsh, would simply not be as funny as it is in English.

Richard admired Dylan Thomas greatly and was thrilled to work with him and to become his friend in the early '50s in London. It was Richard's idea of perfect bliss to spend a Sunday afternoon at the BBC recording work for the Third Programme with a gaggle of eccentric actors. Richard would describe them as 'a melodrama of English actors'. Note that he describes them as 'English' actors. He and Dylan were different, they were Welsh, and they had the bond of being outsiders. Among the group – and Richard frequently referred to those days with abiding humour and affection – were Esme Percy, Andrew Cruikshank, Ernest Thesiger, Michael Hordern and Dylan Thomas. In his diaries Richard wrote:

> 'So there you are in my drab paradise of magnificent language for the speaking of which you were actually paid money, on a Sunday in Studio 8 of the BBC Portland Place, the Sunday papers strewn hither and thither and much chat between the boys who matched story after story and, because the competition is so intense, no one person was able to hold the floor for too long even if Dylan was there, for Dylan – the most compelling talker I've ever met – was oddly constricted by these precise cold English actors with their impeccable accents.'

After rehearsal they would break. Some went to the canteen but the drinking men would go to The George. They were ordered to be back at 6.30 p.m. for a run through. The red live transmission light went on at 8 p.m. sharp. The company of Dylan – who Richard described as an actor of exploding force – and the notable drinking with Dylan meant great times for the two of them and lots to remember and recall for Richard. They were tremendous, rollickingly good times but as Richard said, 't was the work itself that was the wonder.'

And part of that wonder was Dylan Thomas.

Introduction by Andrew Sinclair

On Laugharne and Lower Fishguard

If there ever was a bard who wrote odes for places, that was Dylan Thomas.

The poems ranged from Heaven to Satan, from dew to nightfalls, from Fern Hill to the end of his classic 'play for voices', when 'the suddenly wind-shaken wood springs awake for a second dark time this One Spring day'.

The sea-town most dear to Dylan was Laugharne, where he used to hole up in his Boathouse and compose his last verses on seascape and hillside. But when I was given the magic opportunity to film *Under Milk Wood* some fifty years ago, I found that the estuary there was a mudflat between high and low tide. So after trawling the whole Welsh coastline, already spoilt by caravan parks and genteel conversions, I found only Lower Fishguard miraculously preserved with a quay, the traditional pre-war houses stretching alongside to an inland village stone square, where the women could go about their gossip and errands.

When the three stars had finally signed their non-committal two paragraphs each, stating that they might well turn up to make the film, and the money began to flow, I found that Elizabeth Taylor would only play for two days, Richard Burton for five and a half days, and Peter O'Toole for five. And time was very short, given our schedule. Only three weeks to prepare to rebuild and equip Lower Fishguard.

With an excellent designer, Geoffrey Tozer, we built false fronts on the dock cottages and constructed a whole whaler's ship side on the first floor of Captain Cat's home. Quay Street was transformed into Cockle Row, and five stone cottages at Glyn-y-mel were moulded into a town square around a village pump. The pièce-de-resistance was to create in front of the public lavatories the undertaker's parlour of Evans the Death. So all seemed well.

Our stand-by was a deserted Rank stone flour store, which provided us with a dozen small sets, even if a tempest raged outside. We worked on the run, with the heavies from Lee Electrics humping the Brute lights and tracks and Mitchell camera equipment as if these were as light as mortars or machine-guns. Most of them had been in the Armed Forces, and a film crew on location is a pirate raid. I knew their reputation well enough to ask them to remove the eyesore in my main period set on the dock, a concrete lamp-post that defiled the sea-view.

'How much to lose that?' I asked Jake, the head gaffer.
'Four bottles of whiskey, guv.'
'Done.'

The next morning, the excrescence had vanished, as though it had never been there. And nobody seemed to notice or to care. I did not know then that the Lee Brothers had also rewired all the digs except The Sailors' Arms, so as to save the energy bills on the budget. Raiders, indeed. And as for the four bottles of whiskey, alas, I would have to deal with them later, and try to get back on set next morning.

Two other tricks I had learned from the old lags in the film trade. The first was the essential bit of dingle – in my case, two pieces, a flowering plastic cherry tree and a blossoming yellow gorse bush. As we were shooting in March in a Welsh winter, whenever the blooming plants were seen, one might believe that all was happening in the required spring. That was when those real buds burst out. And the dingle also blocked the sight of the ferryboat crossing to Dublin, or whatever intruded on a good angle.

The other wheeze was the movable cornerpiece. End the Action with the actor moving from the chosen set, Cut and shift the set to wherever, start shooting it and Pull Back to the actor moving in, and Bingo! The player was transported from Piccadilly to Timbuktu as though he or she had just turned the corner. Our ticket to four different graveyards was to start on the tomb of NORMA JANE, the wartime romance of the Two Voices. Anyway, because Elizabeth Taylor could not come to the Welsh cemetery, and Richard Burton's short schedule did not allow it, we had to bring a cemetery to them.

In one sense, where you make a film makes the film. And the Gwaun Valley with its pagan cairns and bleeding yew trees was supernatural, let alone a near quarry that had transported prehistoric astronomical rocks to Stonehenge. The drowning of an onlooking boy during the shooting made me pay his photographer father to bring back cliff shots of dancing Welsh seals coming back from the sea; their singing voices are meant to be the drowned dead, like the five sailors who back to Captain Cat in his dreams.

So I filmed a nightmare dance in the pouring rain, with a gale blowing the roofs away, while the actors playing the people of Llaregyb caracoled around the town pump and pranced away into the waves, and they were dissolved into seals, and Satan's jester walked back from the wild drowned caper he had led from the back of a squealing pig to the black Milk Wood, where the Satan of Richard Burton was waiting, crossing himself and smiling darkly, with his last incantation sounding, that begins:

'The Wood, whose every tree-foot's cloven in the black glad
sight of the hunter of lovers …'

And so the film had an end, a magical end, that had grown out of its words and its making, out of the life of the welcoming town and the death of the boy that had its sad meaning to us all, out of the rich deep words of the Welsh poet of poets.

And yet after his untimely death in New York, Dylan was buried in Laugharne, where, in the Boathouse, he had penned his supreme poetry, also a description of the town:

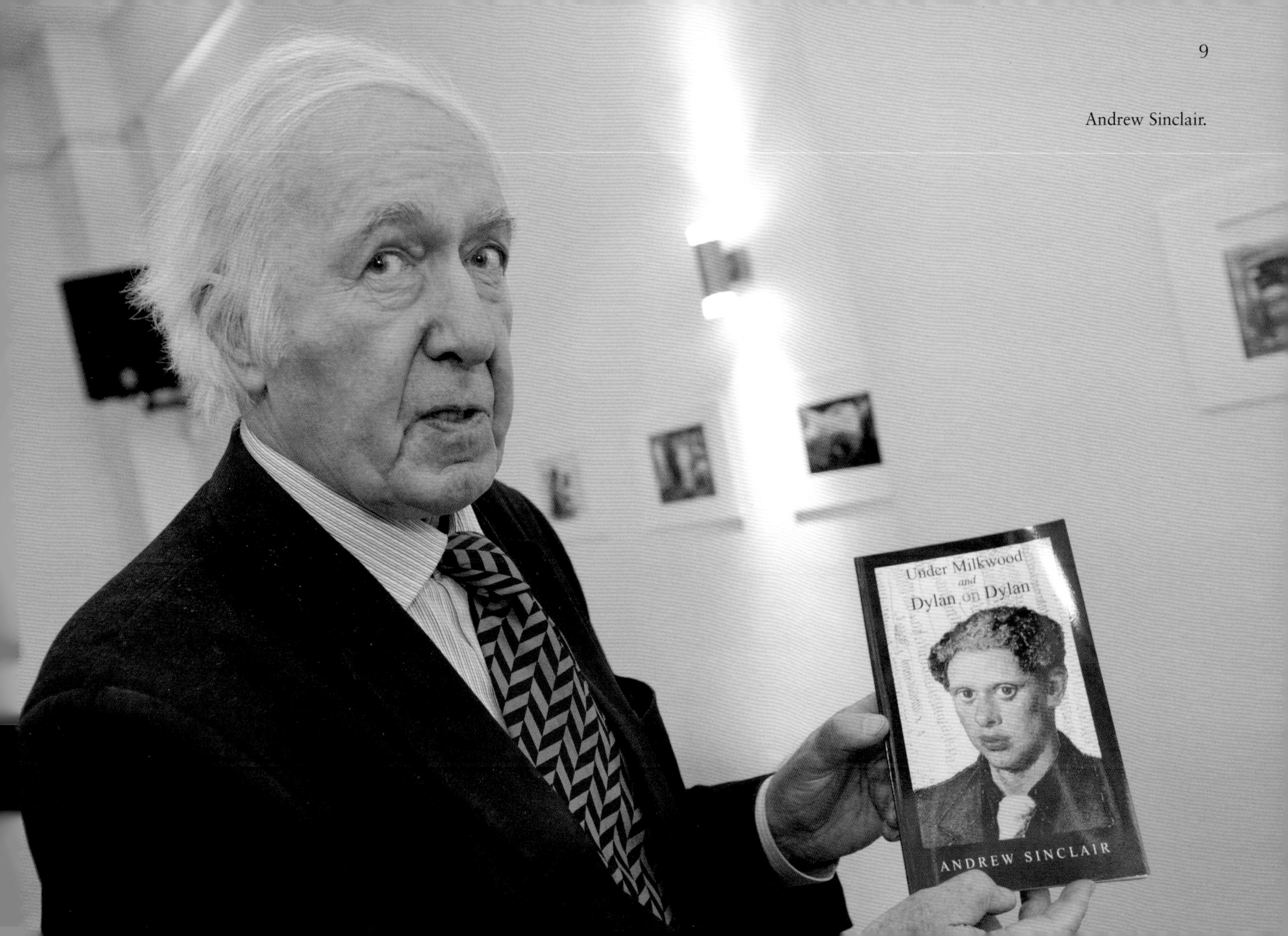

Andrew Sinclair.

> O to sit there, found, along in the universe, at home, at last, the people all with their arms open! ... you climb the stones to see river, sea, cormorants nesting like thin headstones, the cockle-women webfoot, and the undead, round Pendine Head, streaming like trippers up into seaside sky, making a noise like St Giles Fair, silent as all the electric chairs and bells of my nerves as I think, here, of the best town, the best house, the only castle, the mapped, measured, unhabited, drained, garaged, townhalled, pubbed and churched, shopped, gulled and estuaried one state of happiness!

Yet the verses came hard to him:

> In my craft or sullen art
> Exercised in the still night
> When only the moon rages
> And the lovers lie abed
> With all their griefs in their arms,
> I labour by singing light
> Not for ambition or bread
> Or the strut and trade of charms
> On the ivory stages
> But for the common wages
> Of their most secret heart.

His words will always sing and peal as bells, as long as we have ears to hear them. For Dylan knew:

> And death shall have no dominion.
> Dead men naked they shall be one
> With the man in the wind and the west moon;
> When their bones are picked clean and the clean bones gone,
> They shall have stars at elbow and foot;
> Though they go mad they shall be sane,
> Though they sink through the sea they shall rise again;
> Though lovers be lost love shall not;
> And death shall have no dominion.

In the Welsh language, Dylan means the Son of the Wave. Ceaseless as the flow of the seas, we shall hear his words for ever.

Andrew Sinclair,
London, July 2014

Ugly, Lovely Town

The Swansea of Dylan Thomas

'This sea-town was my world.
And the park itself was a world within the world of the sea-town.'
– Dylan Marlais Thomas

The view from the top of Cwmdonkin Drive is one of tile roofs and terraced houses. In the distance, the Mumbles and the shore. Dylan Marlais Thomas was born at Number 5 on 27 October 1914.

Across the street is Cwmdonkin Park, a magical place for a young lad, full of imagination and stories. In 'Twenty Four Years' Dylan wrote of his childhood 'when there were wolves in Wales'. Doubtless he saw them in his imagination in Cwmdonkin Park, 'a world within the world of the sea-town ... full of terrors and treasures'. He called it 'an ugly, lovely town ... crawling, sprawling by a long and splendid curving shore'.

The reservoir, once open, was covered over long ago. Today's children cannot sail upon it or pursue the swans like Dylan and his friends did ninety years ago. Then it was a land of uncultivated jungles, manicured greenery, ponds, bandstands, playgrounds and a fountain with chained cups where a hunchback drank.

As a young man he and a friend climbed and scrambled out to the giant rock of the Worm's Head. Triumphant on its top they shared their triumph with the wind and the gulls. 'Why don't we live here always?' he asked. 'Always and always. Build a bloody house and live like bloody kings!'

Carmarthen Bay, Rhossilli sands, the Gower and Swansea. All fruit for Dylan's words, memories crashing headlong into emotive nostalgia, nostalgia becoming longing, longing becoming hiraeth, that melancholy mood that affects the Welsh and the south Welsh most of all. 'Time held me green and dying,' he wrote in 'Fern Hill', 'Though I sang in my chains like the sea.'

Thomas' memories of an idyllic childhood form the core of *A Child's Christmas in Wales*. In 1961 it was presented on American TV for *Camera Three*. Richard Burton, then appearing in *Camelot* on Broadway, hosted the piece and read the story on camera.

'The beginning was in Wales, my country, and the town of Swansea close to my own village,' said Burton. 'Dylan Thomas was a Welshman whose work took him far from home but there were times when he ached to be back in the house he kept at Laugharne. He suffered acutely from homesickness and he was

To begin at the beginning...

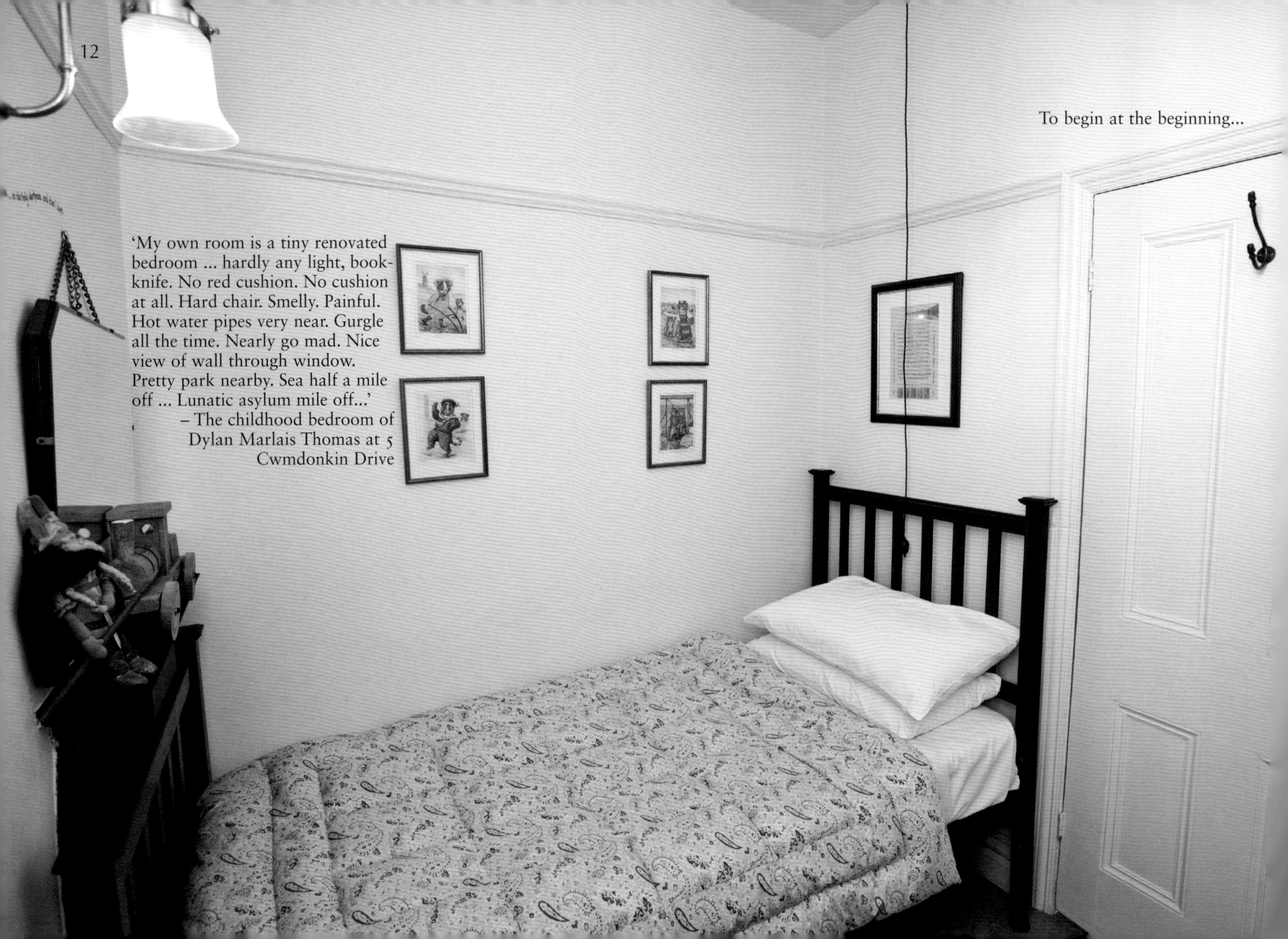

'My own room is a tiny renovated bedroom ... hardly any light, book-knife. No red cushion. No cushion at all. Hard chair. Smelly. Painful. Hot water pipes very near. Gurgle all the time. Nearly go mad. Nice view of wall through window. Pretty park nearby. Sea half a mile off ... Lunatic asylum mile off...'
– The childhood bedroom of Dylan Marlais Thomas at 5 Cwmdonkin Drive

never really happy away from Wales. Wherever he was he made straight for the sea or the river or whatever water there was. He would walk down and stare at the water, throw a cigarette in and watch it whirl around and brood over the fact that between Pier 90 and Wales there is nothing but water.'

Burton and Thomas first 'met' when the seventeen-year-old was already an established poet. His first poem was printed in the local newspaper, which said, 'Brilliant local boy has written a poem, which we now put in our columns.' Said Burton: 'You can imagine the lifted eyebrow of the editor who put it in because it was the poem "The force that through the green fuse drives the flower / Drives my green age". He must have wondered what it was all about.'

It was said that there were two men living inside Dylan Thomas. One who wrote and did not drink and hardly spoke – a painstaking craftsman of poetry. The other Dylan drank and talked and who made repeated trips to America between 1950 and 1953. He didn't care for New York or London or any other metropolis that drew him away from Wales, commenting, 'Every pavement drills through your soles to your scalp, and out pops a lamp-post covered with hair.'

Dylan wrote warmly of his childhood and his youth. Two later incidents remained with him all his short life. He went down to the Mumbles and a red-headed girl changed partners. For that his then-fiancée, Pamela Hansford Johnson, left him for boasting about it. That was a true story. He wrote another short story called 'Just Like Little Dogs', which, again, centred on a girl swapping between two men. In Andrew Sinclair's film of *Under Milk Wood* the girl became Norma Jane, the plaything of two ghostly visitors. Said Sinclair, 'It's the dead coming back to life'– a running theme in a play about religion, sex and death.

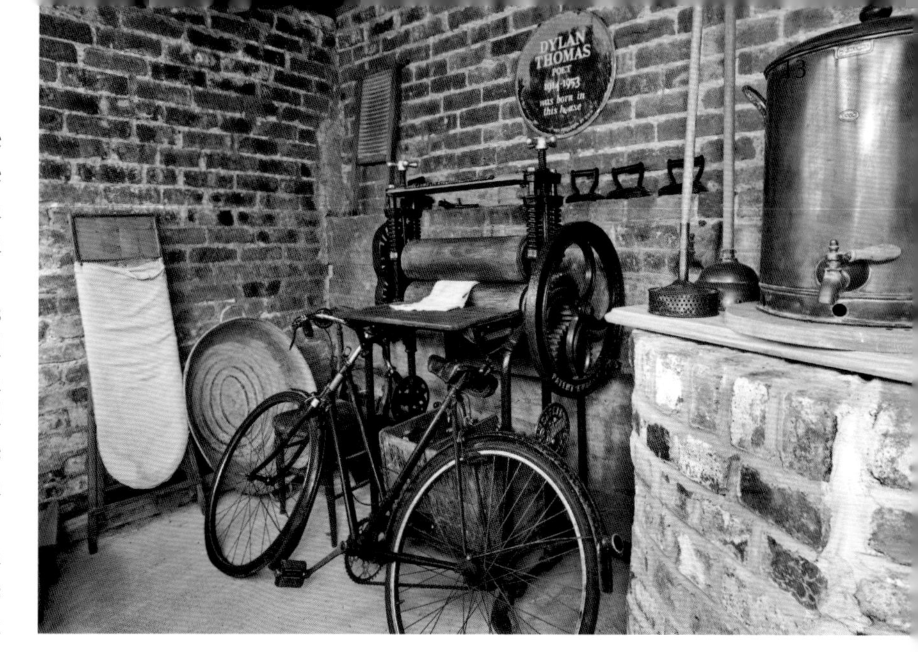

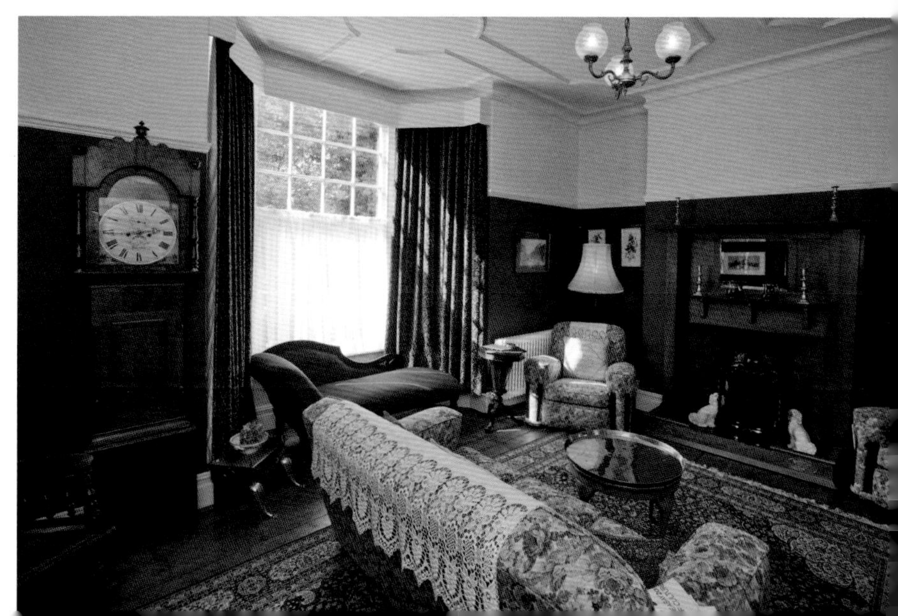

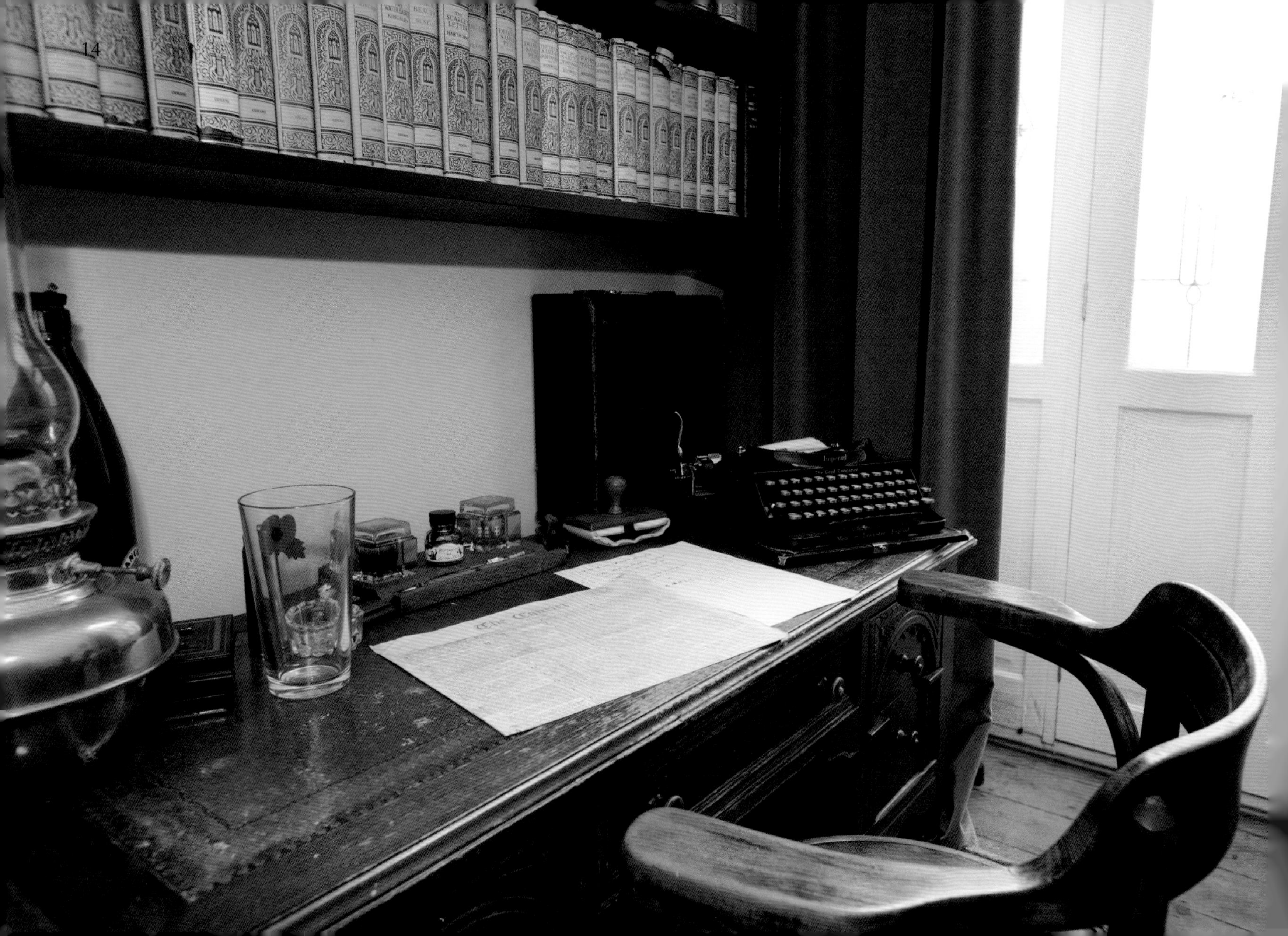

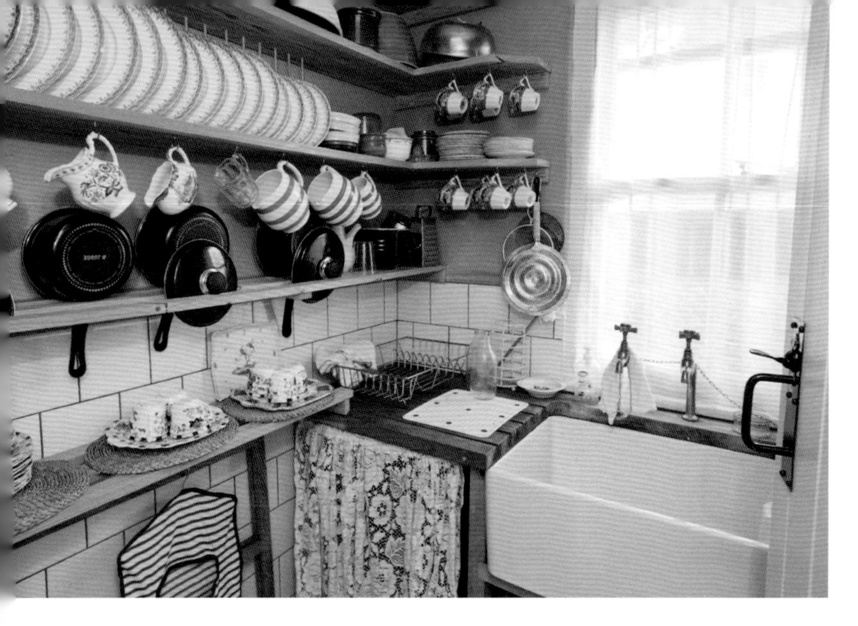

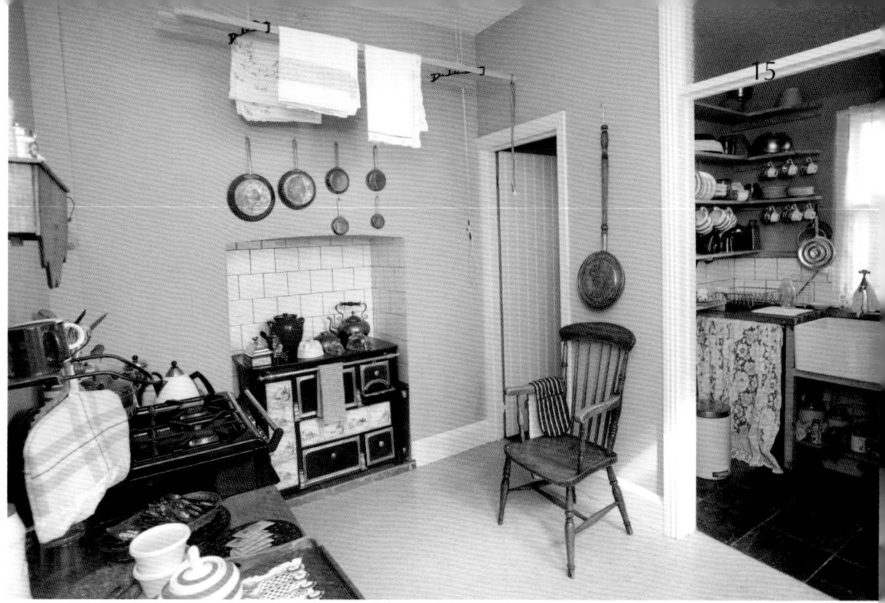

Over the past few years No. 5 Cwmdonkin Drive has been carefully restored by Geoff Haden to the condition it was in as a new house. It was bought by the Thomas family in 1914, just a few months before Dylan Marlais Thomas was born in the front bedroom, which can be seen bottom left. Geoff is the vice chairman of the Dylan Thomas Society and a founder and board member of the £30,000 Dylan Thomas Prize for young writers sponsored by Swansea University.

Above: Dylan's mother, Florrie, cooked twice a day with the help of a daily maid and a Monday maid to assist with the washing. Off the kitchen is the pantry or larder, which is where food was kept cool, and the scullery with its deep sink and storage for everyday crockery, pots and pans.

Opposite: DJ's study. This room was the domain of DJ Thomas (Dylan's father) – a very male room that would now be called his 'personal space'. DJ was a Welsh speaker, an academic, a piano player, a smoker, a drinker and an Anglophile. He surrounded himself with the classics and kept abreast of contemporary books from the Boot's lending library.

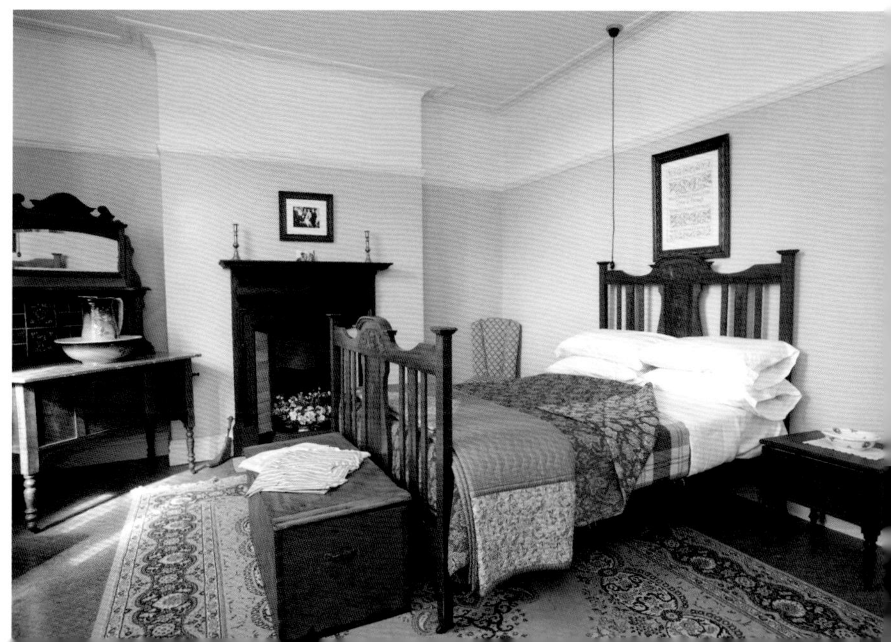

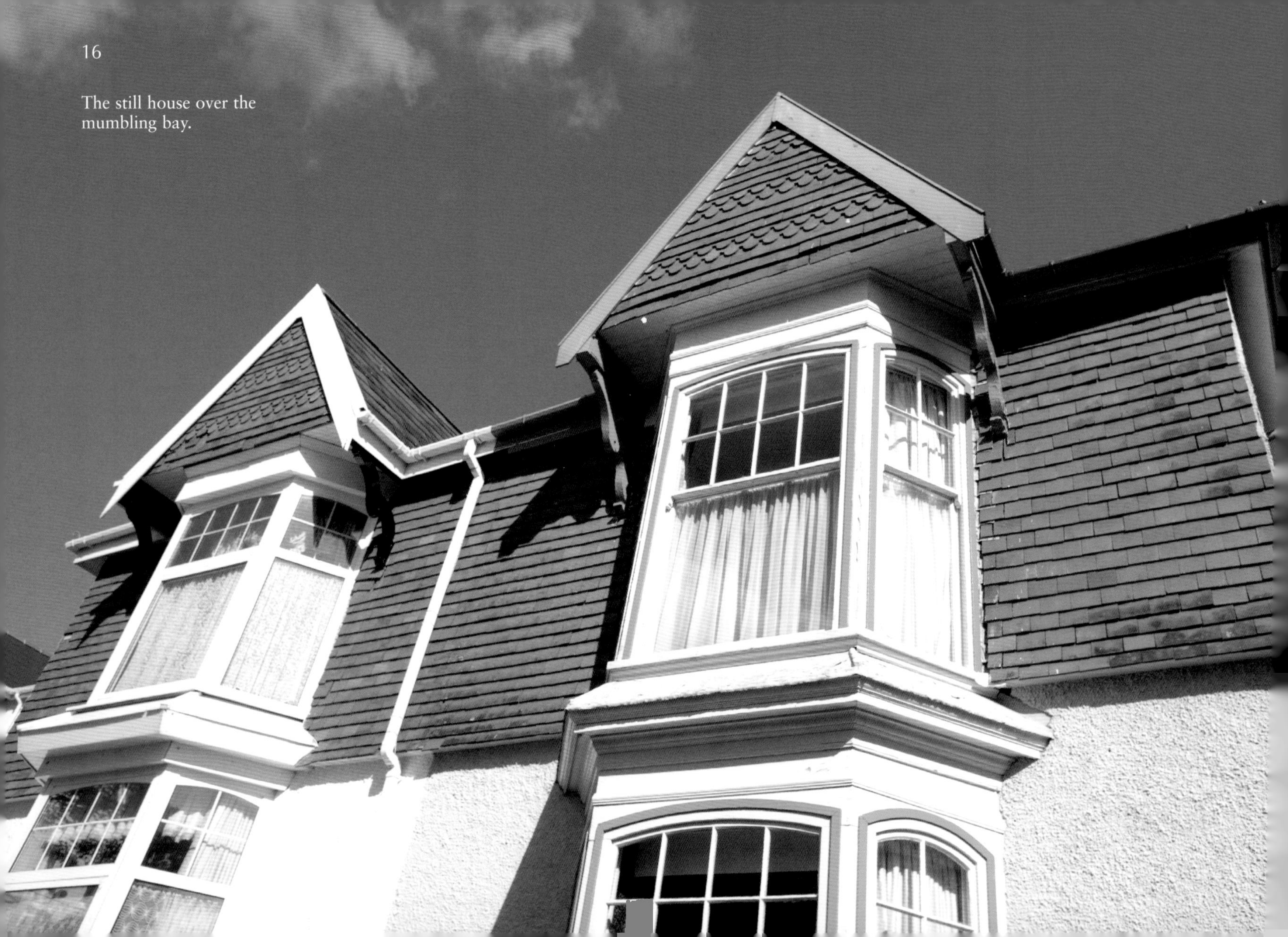

The still house over the mumbling bay.

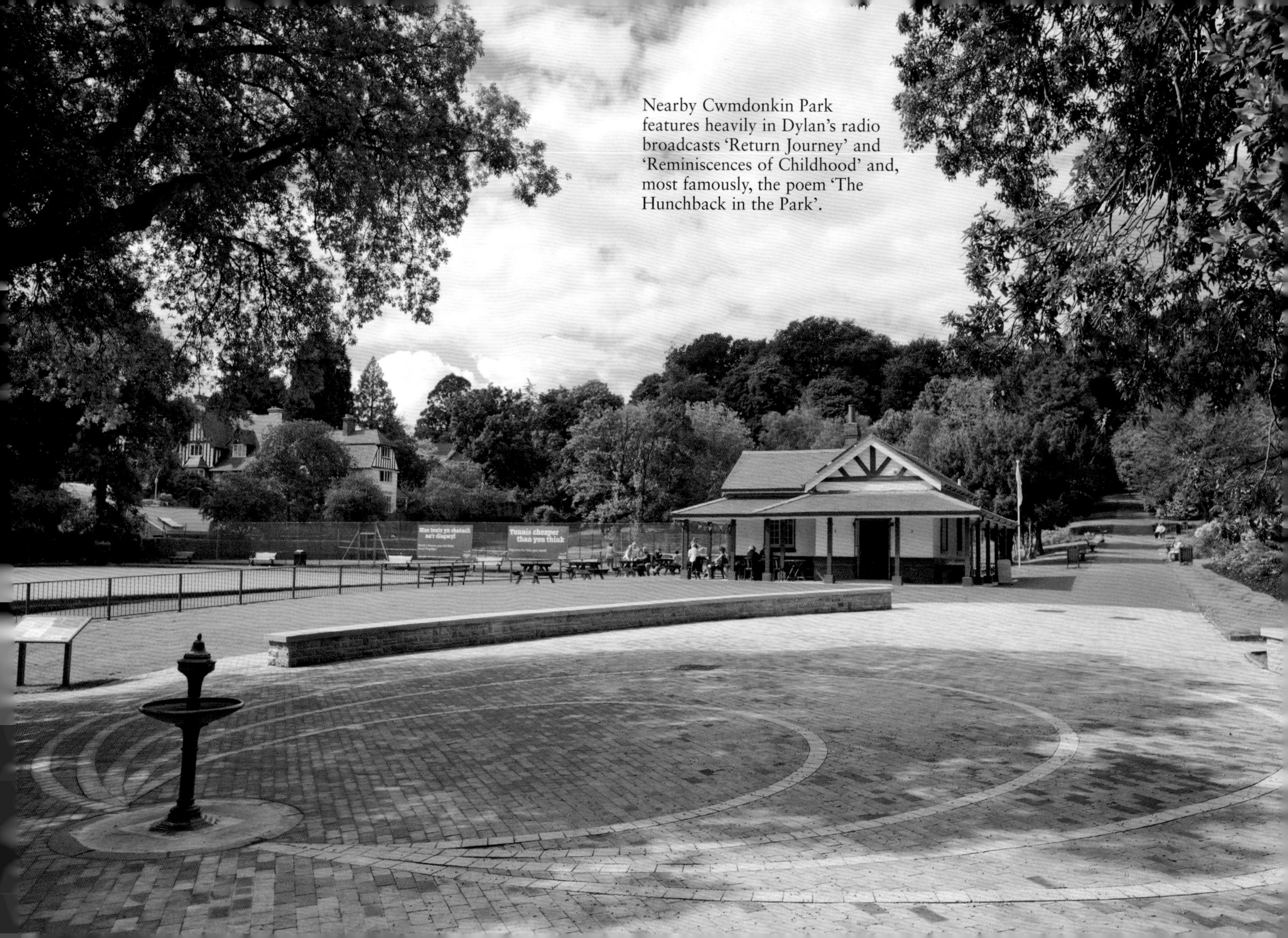

Nearby Cwmdonkin Park features heavily in Dylan's radio broadcasts 'Return Journey' and 'Reminiscences of Childhood' and, most famously, the poem 'The Hunchback in the Park'.

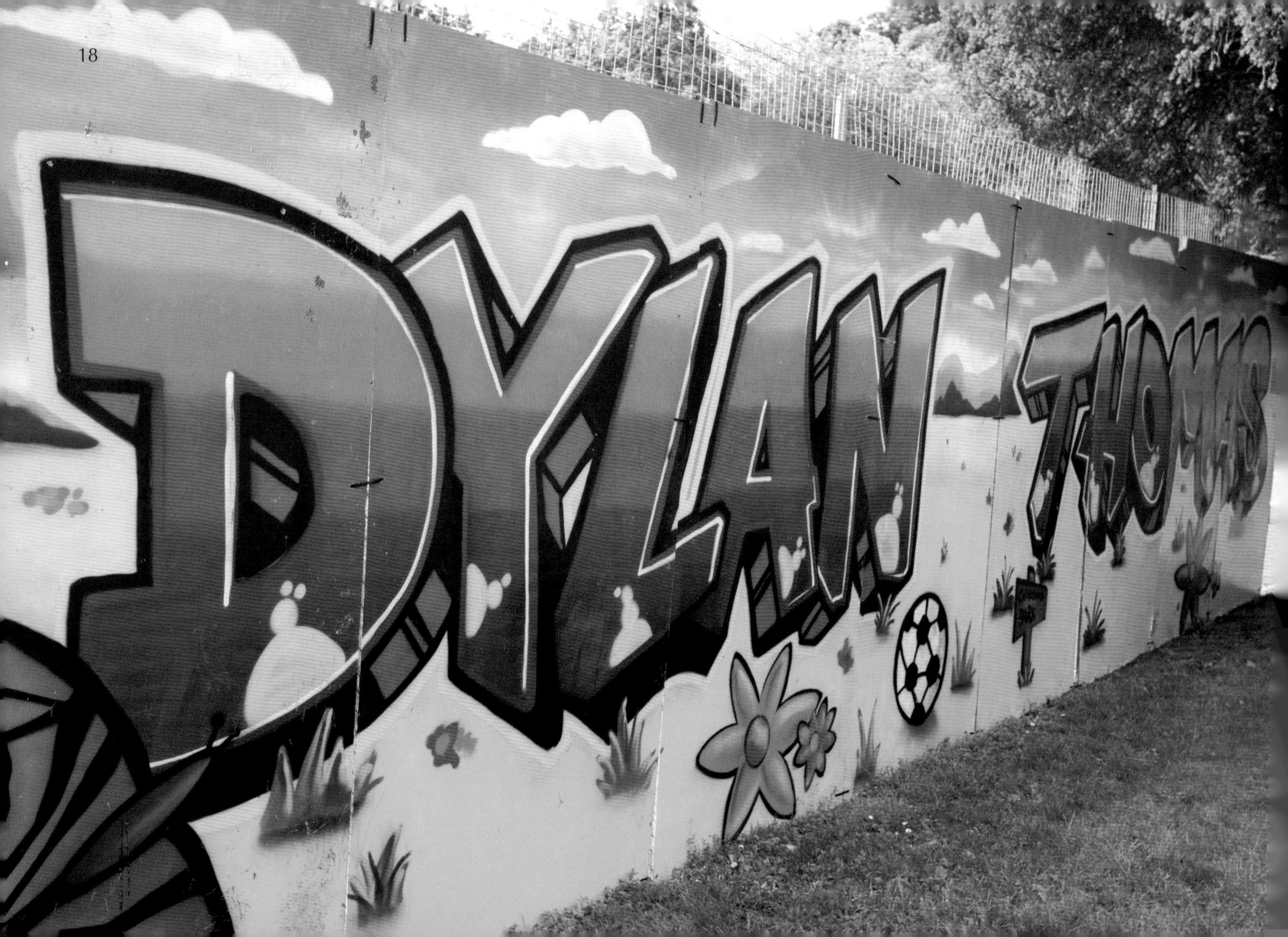
DYLAN
THOMAS

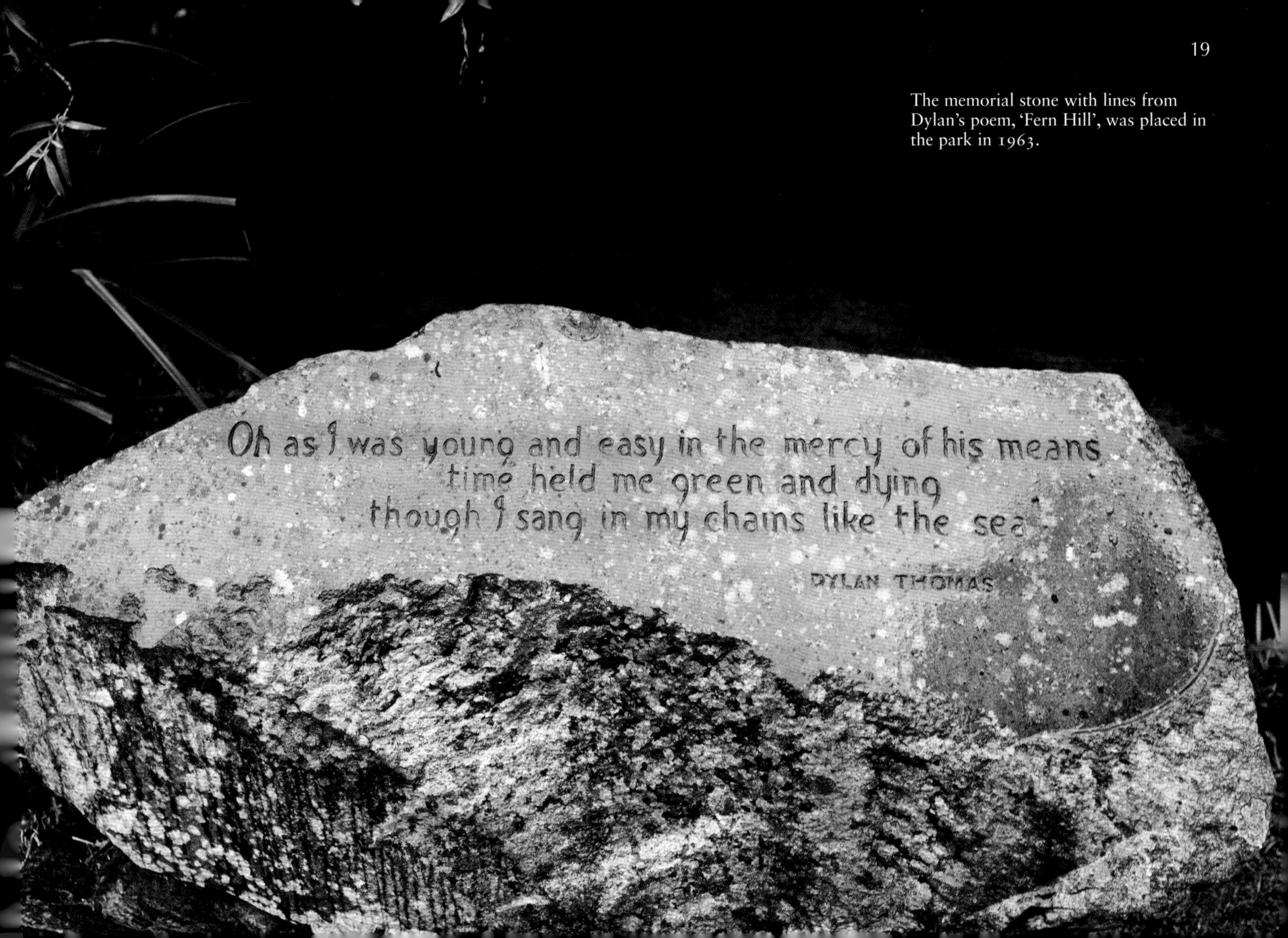

The memorial stone with lines from Dylan's poem, 'Fern Hill', was placed in the park in 1963.

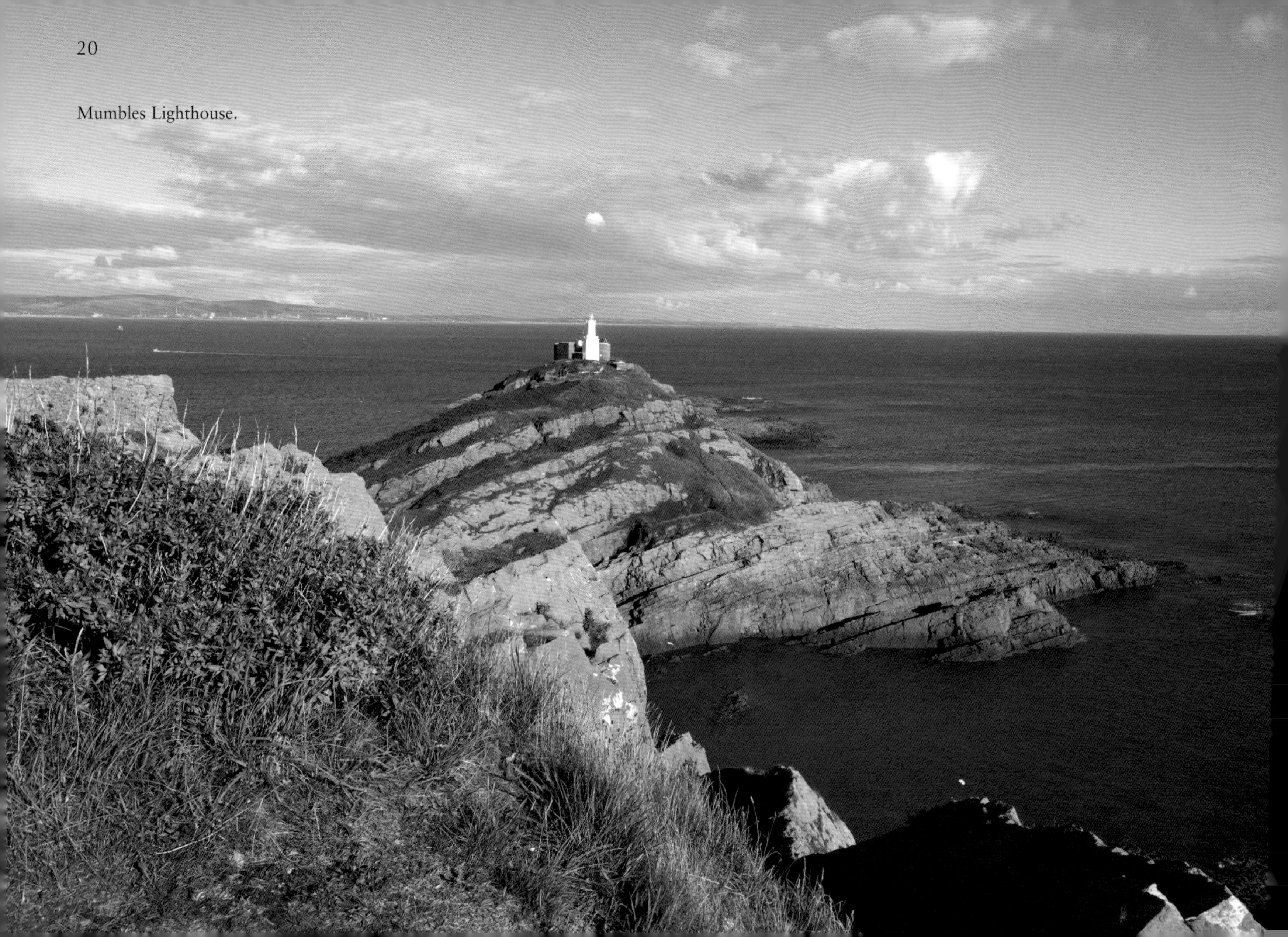

Mumbles Lighthouse.

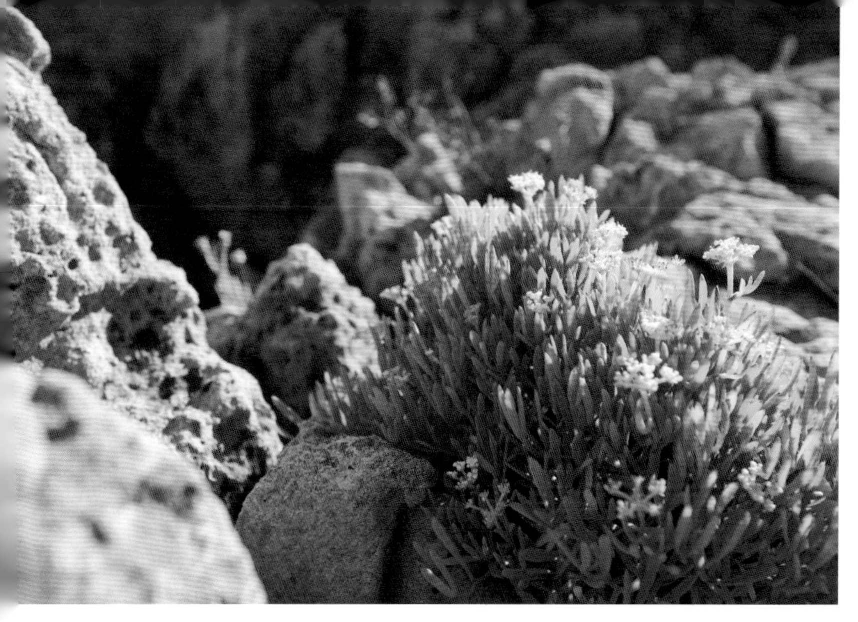

'A rather nice village, despite its name,' was how Dylan described this small, increasingly up and coming fishing village situated on the Gower Peninsula.

The Mumbles is mentioned in *Under Milk Wood* when the fourth drowned sailor introduces himself as 'Alfred Pomeroy Jones, sea lawyer, born in Mumbles, sung like a linnet, crowned you with a flagon, tattooed with mermaids, thirst like a dredger, died of blisters.'

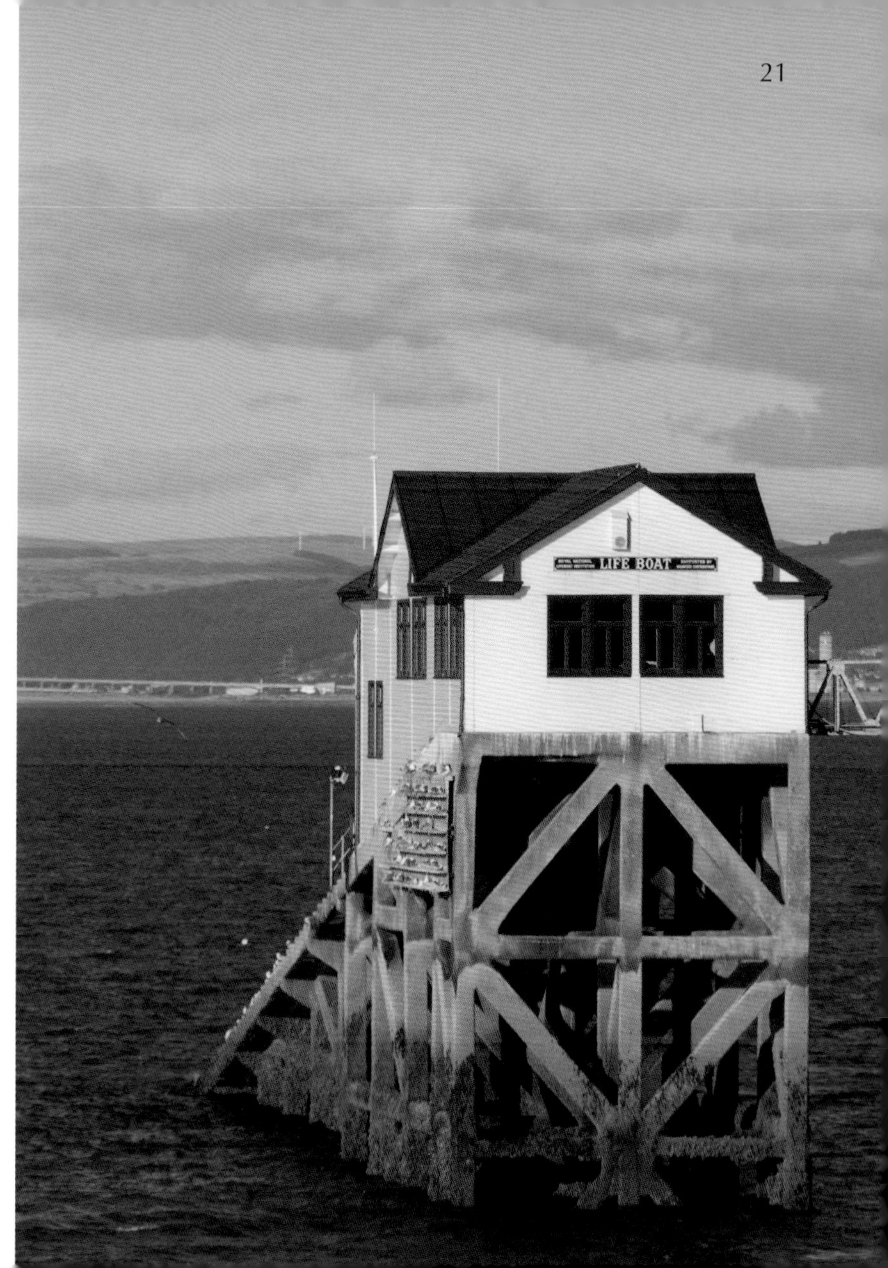

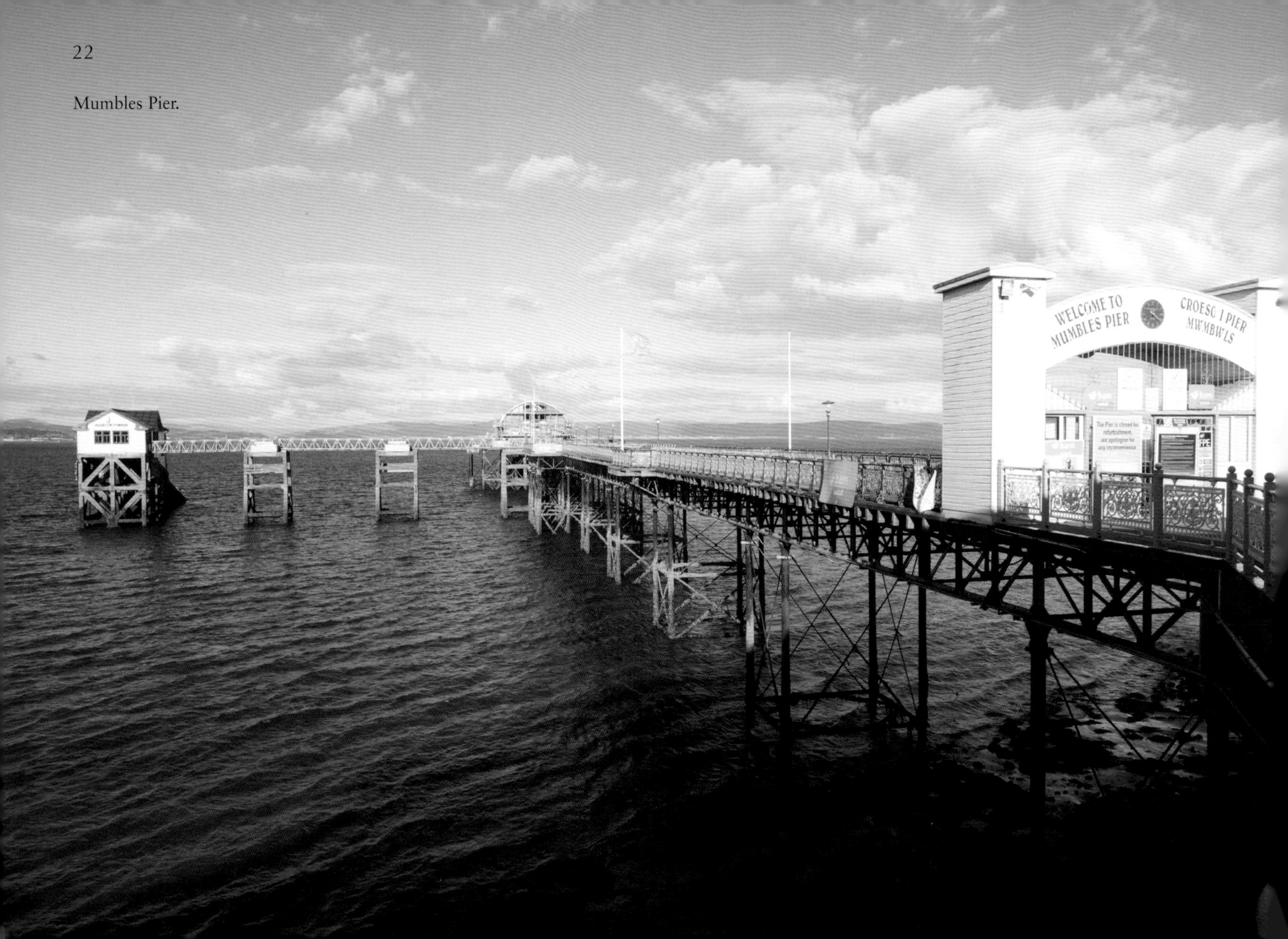

Mumbles Pier.

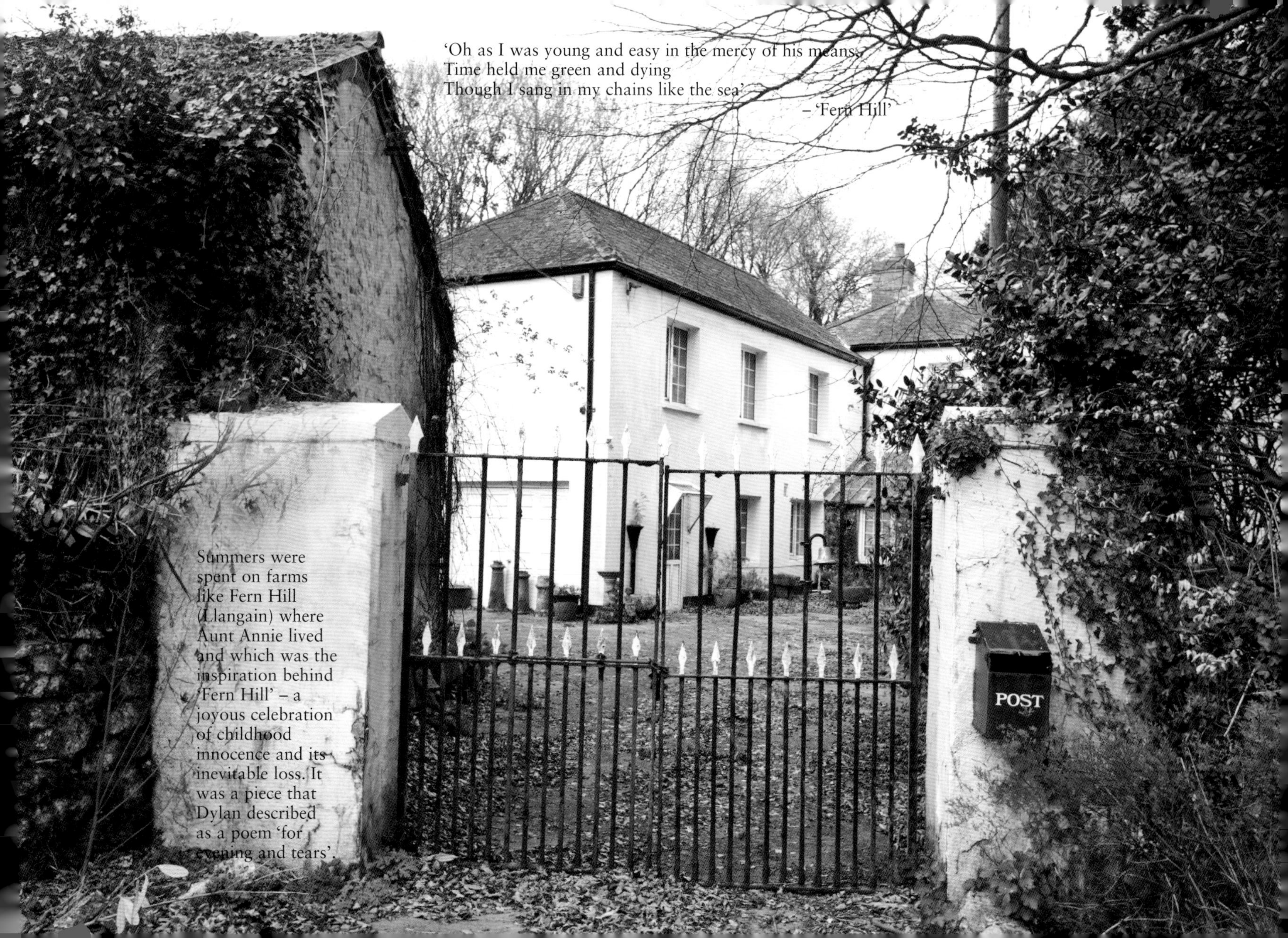

'Oh as I was young and easy in the mercy of his means,
Time held me green and dying
Though I sang in my chains like the sea'
– 'Fern Hill'

Summers were spent on farms like Fern Hill (Llangain) where Aunt Annie lived and which was the inspiration behind 'Fern Hill' – a joyous celebration of childhood innocence and its inevitable loss. It was a piece that Dylan described as a poem 'for evening and tears'.

'You may travel the world over but you will not find anything more beautiful; so restful, so colourful or so unspoilt' was how artist Augustus John described the West Wales town of Tenby. The town was the birthplace of two artists who affected Dylan throughout his life: Nina Hamnett (born Valentine's Day 1890 at Lexden Terrace, top right) and Augustus himself (in January 1878) at the nearby Esplanade. It was via Augustus John that Dylan met his Caitlin in London in April 1936.

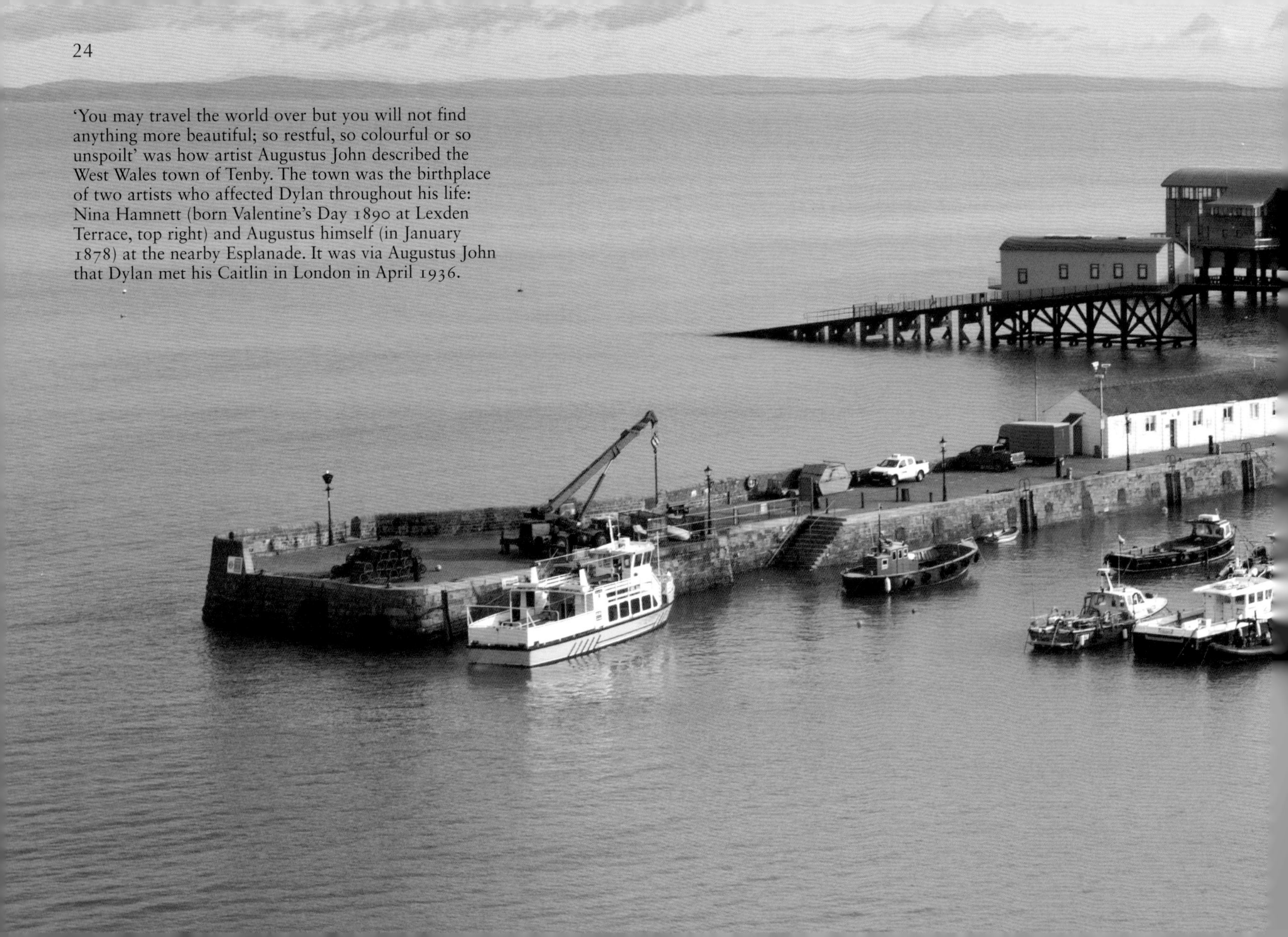

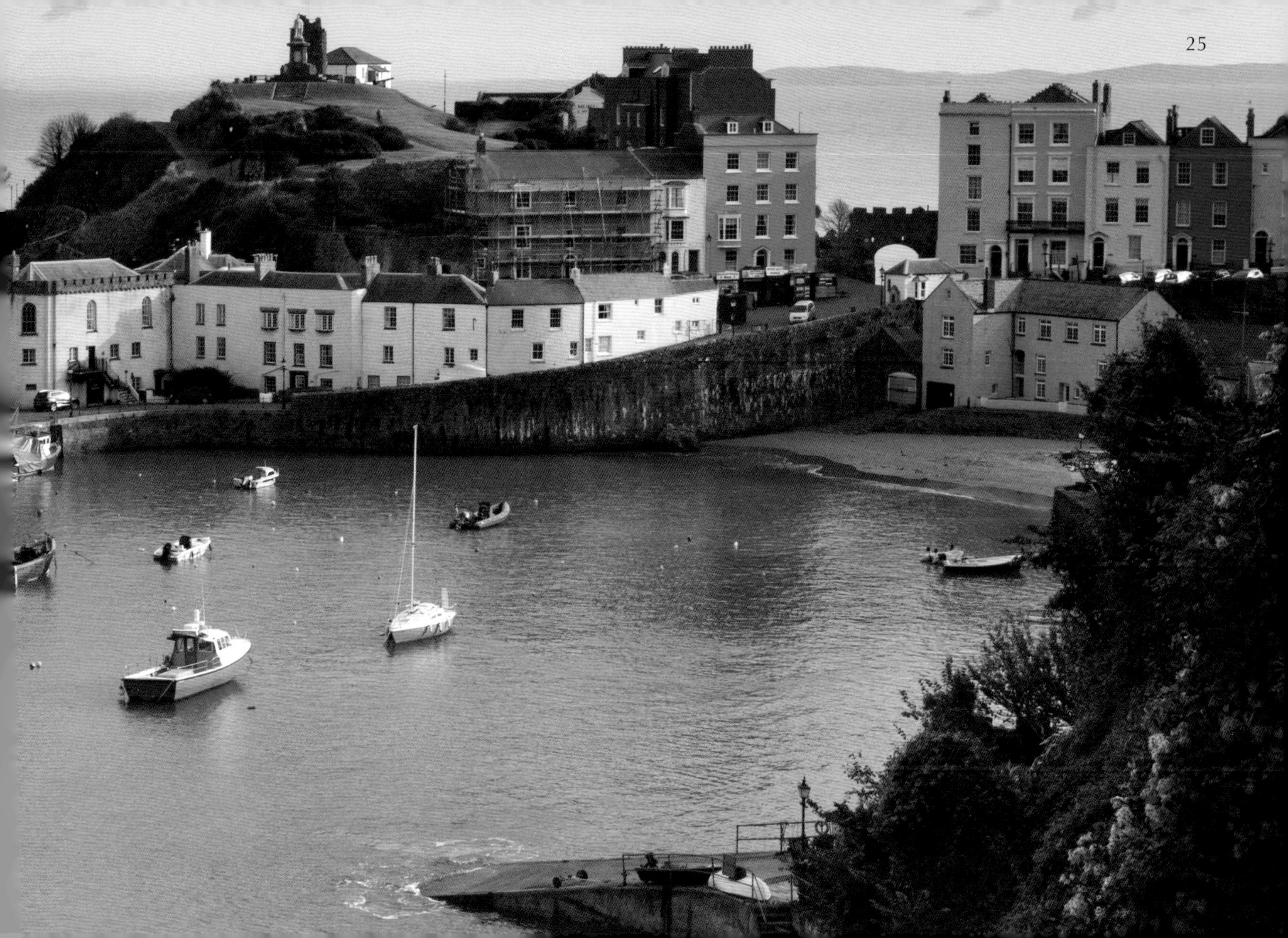

A Legend is Forged

The Taibach of Richard Burton

'I rather like my reputation, actually, that of a spoiled genius from the Welsh gutter, a drunk, a womaniser; it's rather an attractive image.'

– Richard Burton

The enduring legend of Richard Burton was built on a foundation of coal seams, pit props, beer, rugby and a deeply rooted sense of family and belonging.

Burton was born Richard Walter Jenkins Jnr in the poor South Wales mining village of Pontrhydyfen on 10 November 1925. Yet while young Richie was indeed the fifth son of a hard-drinking miner, he actually grew up not in the cramped family home but in the nearby town of Taibach.

His was a life forged by tragedy and familial dislocation. Richie's mother died when he was just two years old and he left Welsh-speaking Pontrhydyfen to live with his eldest sister, Cecilia, known as Cis, and her husband Elfed in English-speaking Taibach, a suburb of Port Talbot six miles down the Afan Valley. Thus it was that Richie's formative years were spent with an adoring older sister 20 years his senior.

Port Talbot then, as now, was an industrial town. Richie's life revolved around a compact square mile in Taibach that included houses, schools, chapels, cinemas, playing fields, pubs, fish and chips shops and the mighty Mynydd Brombil, a mountain (known to all as 'the Side') that overlooked parallel lines of streets.

Richie grew up in two homes prior to flying the nest. Both are on Caradoc Street. He first lived with Cis and Elfed at the bottom of the hill before moving up to the top. His school, Eastern Primary, was a few short yards round the corner on Incline Row and the Gibeon Chapel where he got his first inkling of drama is a minute or so away along a back lane.

It was here that Richie first came to understand and appreciate the power of drama – from the blood-and-thunder sermons of his preacher. 'I got his autograph,' he wrote in his 1940 diary.

A stone's throw away stood the Picturedrome, a fleapit cinema known to one and all as 'The Cach' (pronounced 'cack', which is what it stood for). In the early 1930s it was still showing silent films. Young Jenkins often watched two or three films a week. Today it is a nursing home.

At Port Talbot Secondary School (now Dyffryn Comprehensive) Richie was a rebellious teenager, albeit one who yearned to learn. He left in 1940 and reluctantly took a job in the haberdashery section of the Taibach Co-operative Wholesale Society. Jenkins the Co-op, they called him, and he hated it.

He was allowed back to school following a joint appeal by masters Meredith Jones, Philip Burton and others. It was at this point that his life dramatically changed.

In 1941, aged sixteen, Richie Jenkins moved into a room in a house on Connaught Street owned by 'Ma' Smith. One of the other lodgers was Philip Burton, a cultured man with a keen interest in drama and the arts. To satisfy what he later described as his 'Pygmalion complex' Burton took on Jenkins and tutored him in elocution, English, literature and acting.

The downstairs parlour where Burton smoothed the rough edges off Jenkins' Welsh accent is still there. Richie called it 'the room of terror'.

One day Richie burst into the house to show Burton a poem he had discovered. With gravity he read the line, 'The force that through the green fuse drives the flower.'

'What does it mean?' asked his mentor.

'I don't know,' replied his protégé, 'but isn't it *wonderful*?'

Burton was prevented from adopting young Jenkins because he was twenty days short of being twenty-one years older than his charge. Instead he became the lad's legal guardian. It was at this point that Richie took his guardian's name and Richard Burton was born.

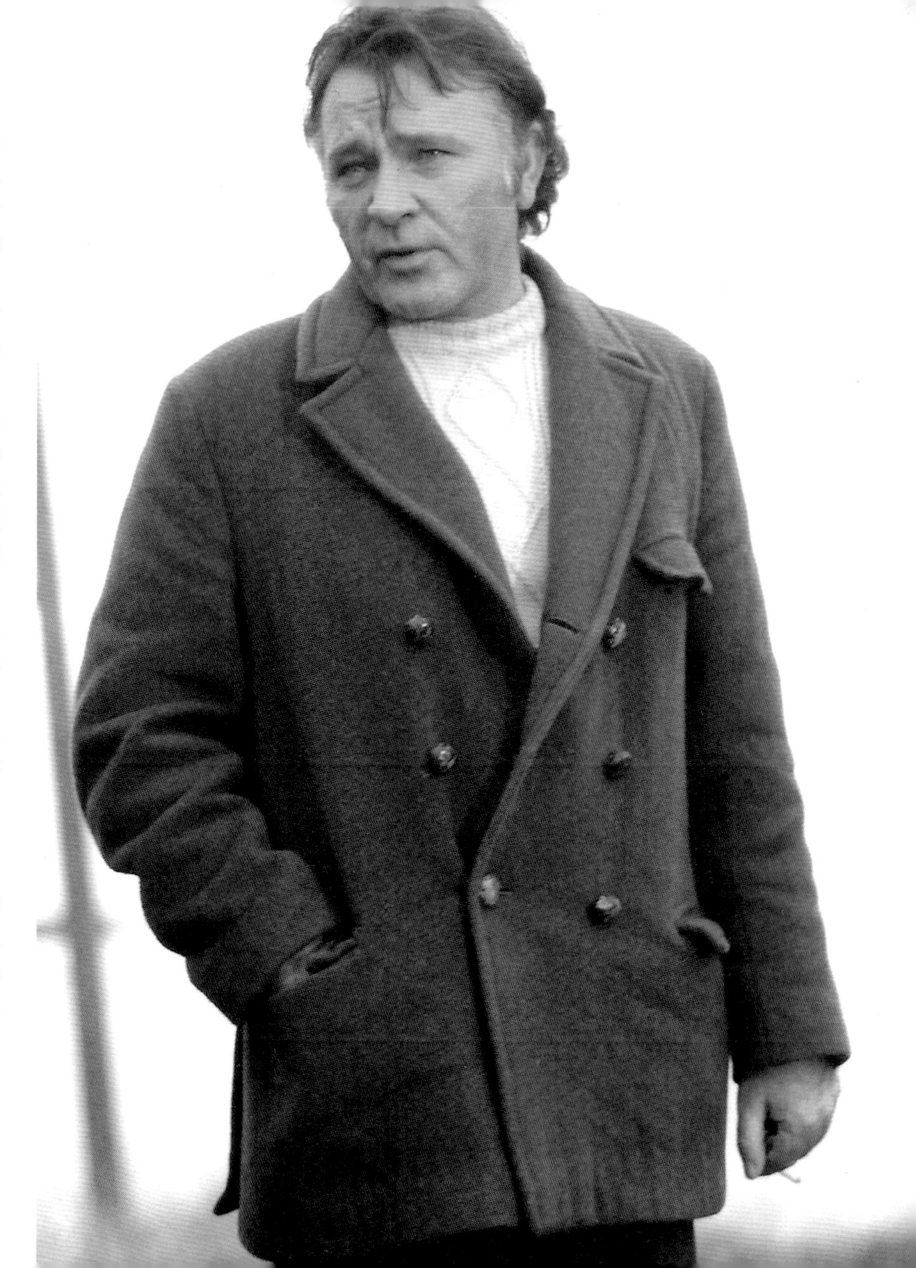

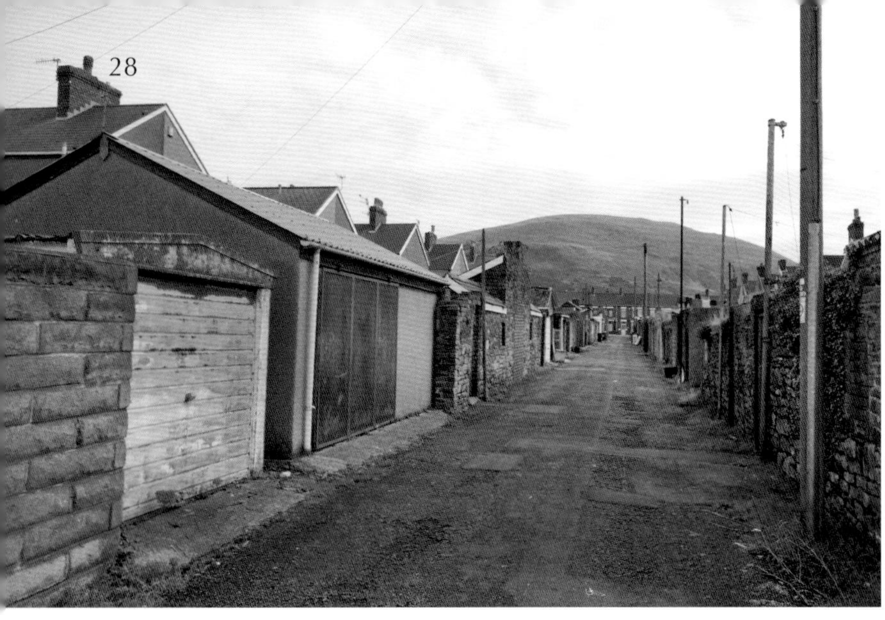

Richie lived with Cis and Elfed in Caradoc Street for fourteen years. It was not an easy life despite the unconditional love of his sister. In 1942, Richie abruptly left school and started work as a haberdasher's assistant at the local Co-operative store. Later, when he was accepted back at Port Talbot Secondary School, he moved to a house on Connaught Street where teacher Philip Burton was also a lodger. Richie's bedroom was 'a little, little, tiny room', according to Betty Smith. It is now her shower room. He stayed at Connaught Street for two and a half years until he was called up to the RAF.

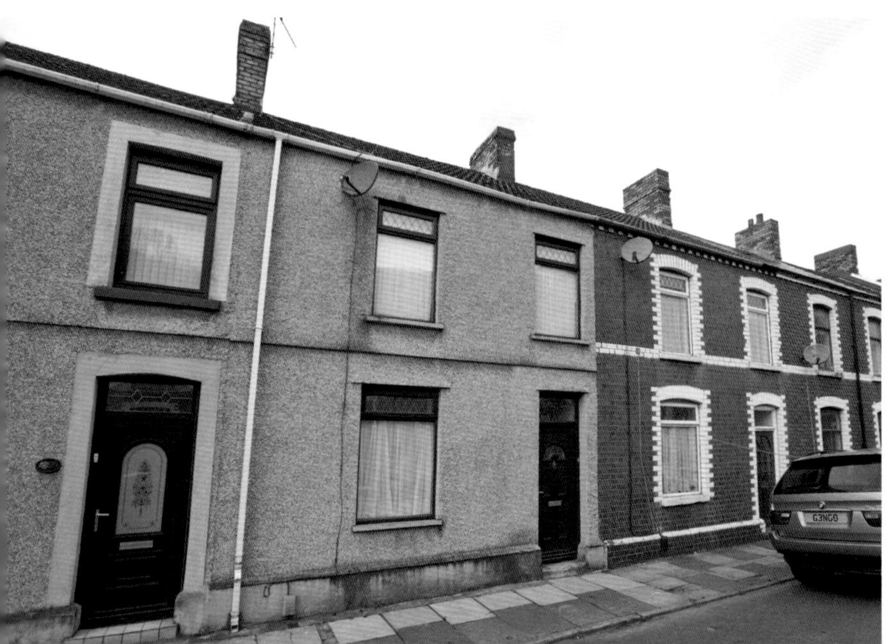

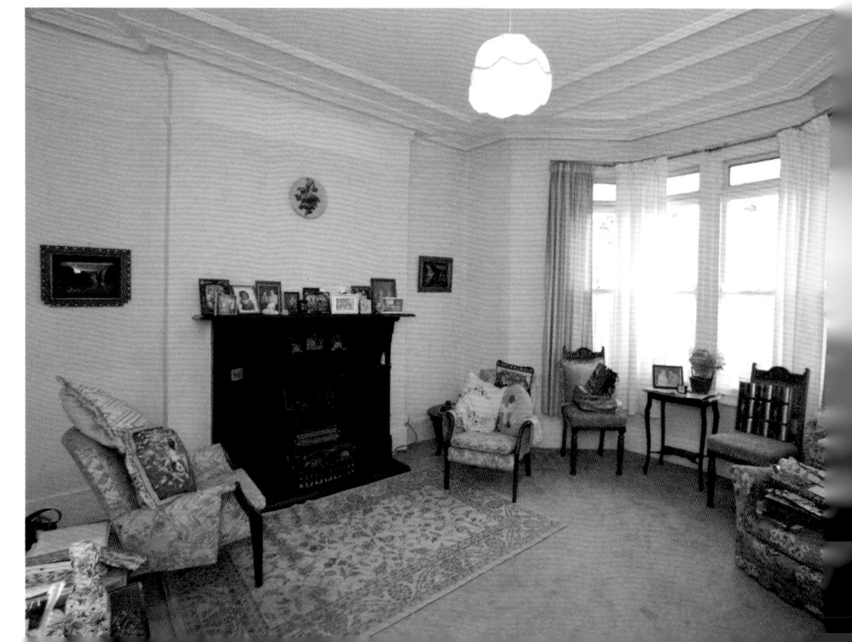

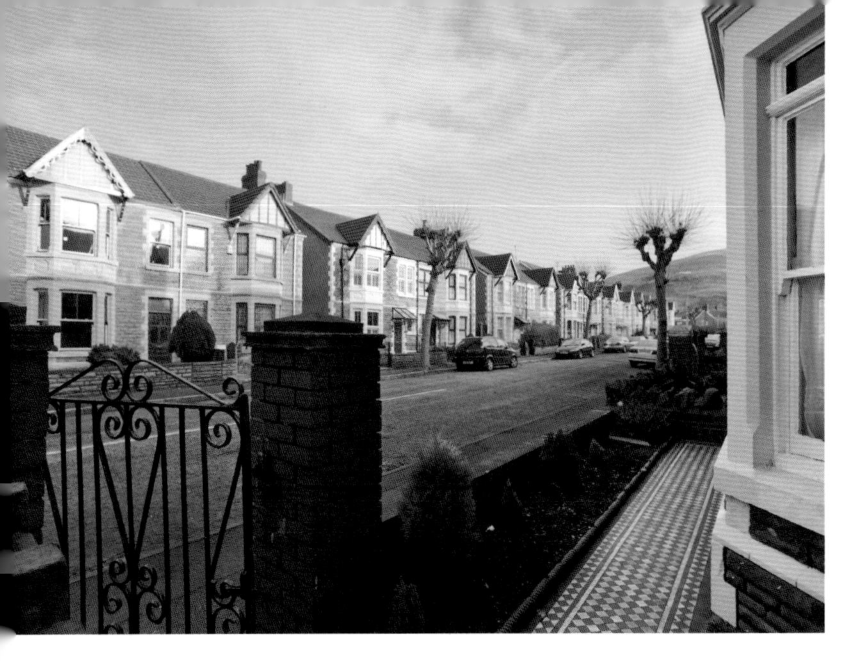

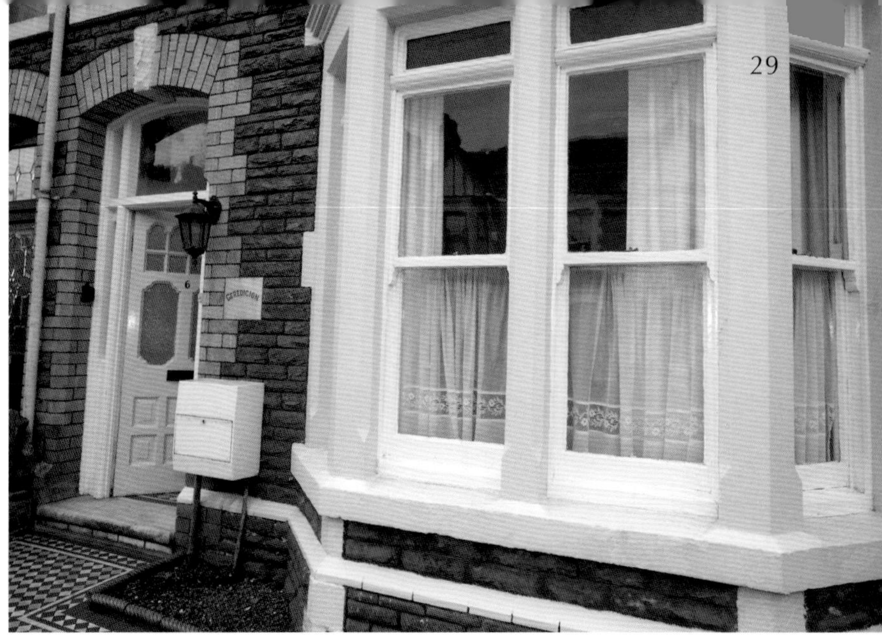

The house at Connaught Street, where Richie lodged with Ma Smith and her daughters, is remarkably unchanged despite the passage of time. One can imagine the young, wild Richie Jenkins bursting through the front door rushing to – or from – a game of rugby. Just a quarter of a mile from Caradoc Street it nonetheless represented a more genteel side to Taibach, and a new beginning for sixteen-year-old Richard Walter Jenkins. The front parlour became Richie's classroom. It can be entered via the door next to the walking stick hanging on the wall.

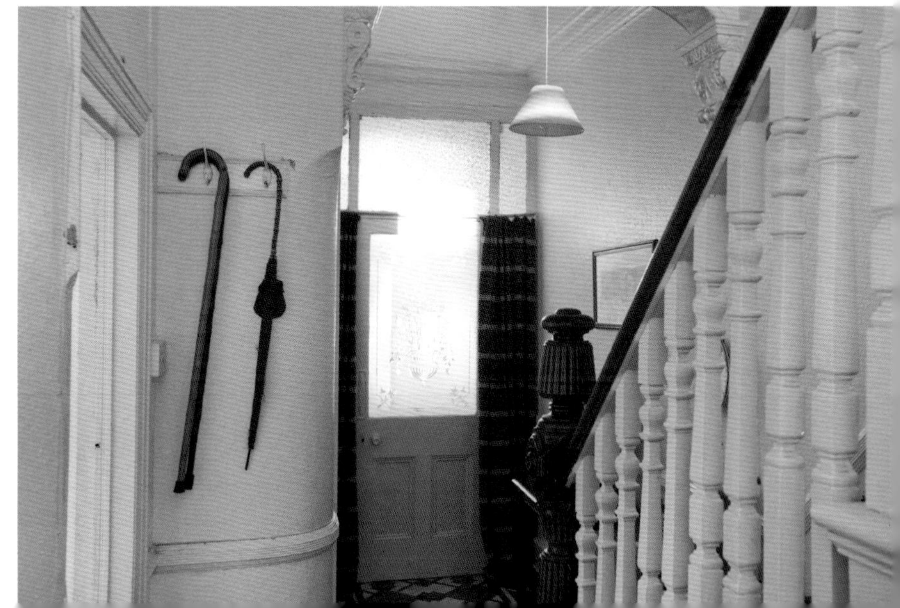

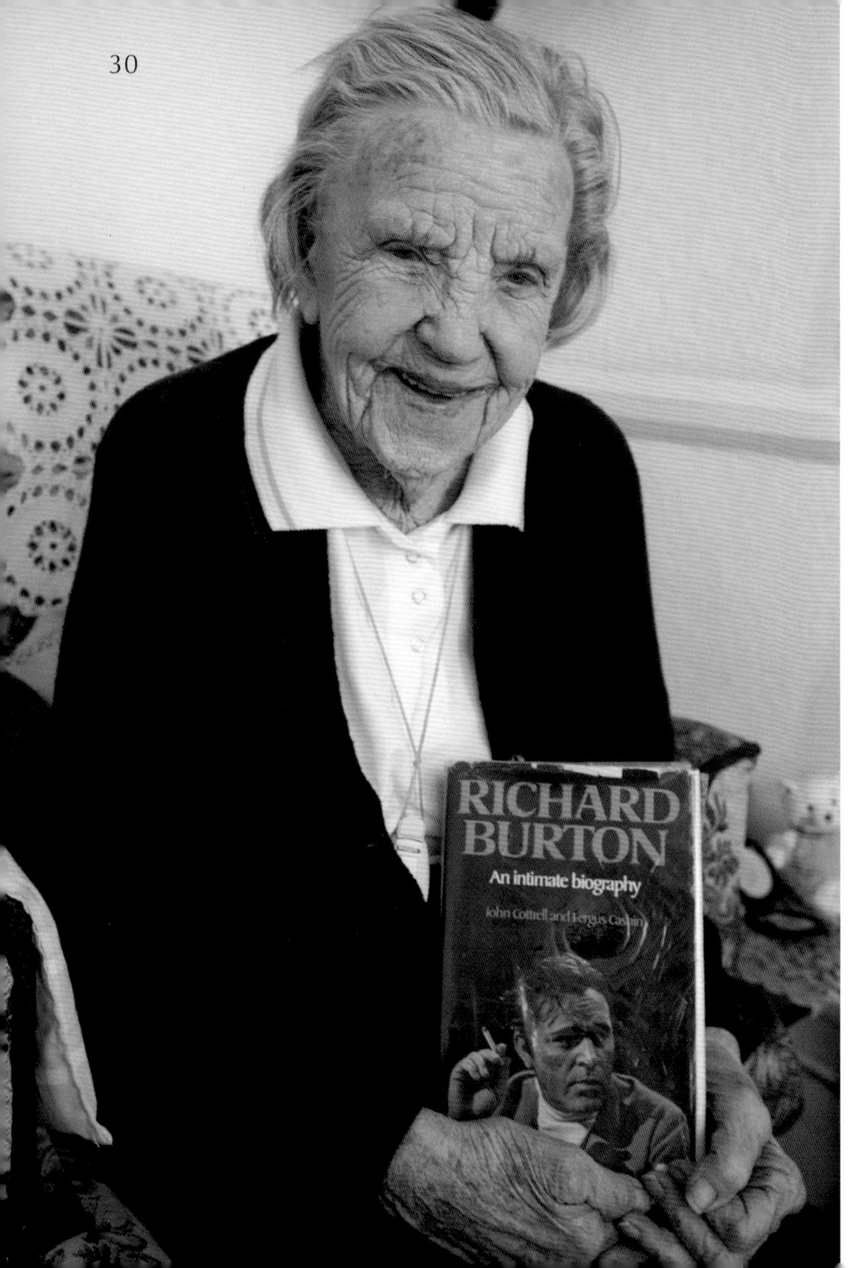

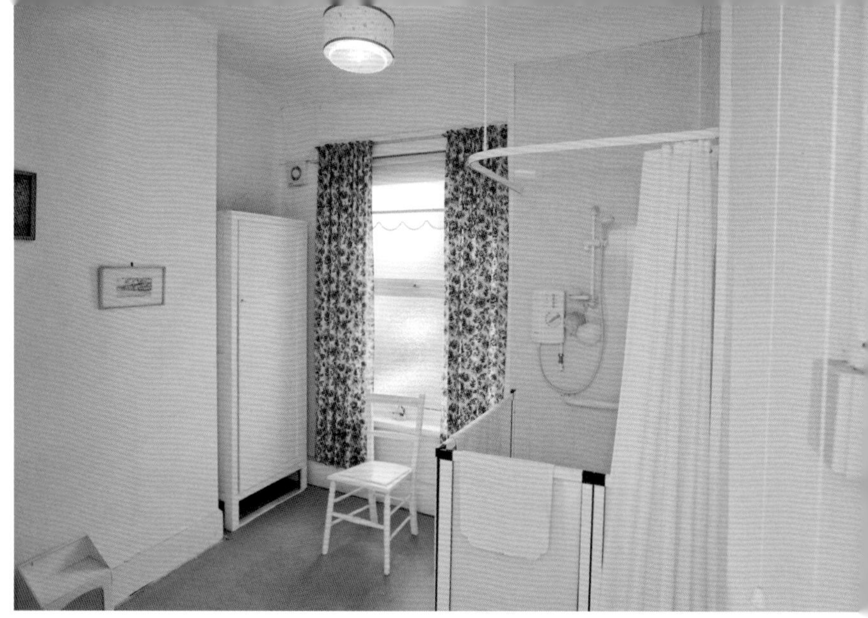

Miss Betty Smith, the 103-year-old daughter of landlady Ma Smith, remembered Richie with affection. 'We always called him Richie. Never called him Richard,' she said. 'Richie had good principles. Mother often used to offer him a couple of bob and he'd say, 'No, you can't afford it.' He did take it eventually. He had a very nice personality. With his first wages he bought my mother a picture of the Mona Lisa. I've still got it. His problem was drink. His father couldn't pass a pub and I think Richie inherited it. I don't know how he did all the shows he did.'

'Philip Burton took Richie under his wing. And, of course, Philip had a very good speaking voice. Richie went in for acting eventually and they did a lot of practising in my front room. He smoked, which Philip didn't like. He smoked in the bottom lavatory but there was a ventilator on the door and he could see the smoke coming out. Philip would say, 'Where's Richie?' and my mother would say, 'No idea.' But she knew he was having a cigarette. Philip was a schoolmaster and he lived with mother for twenty years. They would go up the mountain together to practise. He tried to get Richie's Welsh accent away. For most of the plays Richie did at the beginning they didn't want the Welsh accent. And Philip didn't ever speak Welsh.' – Betty Smith

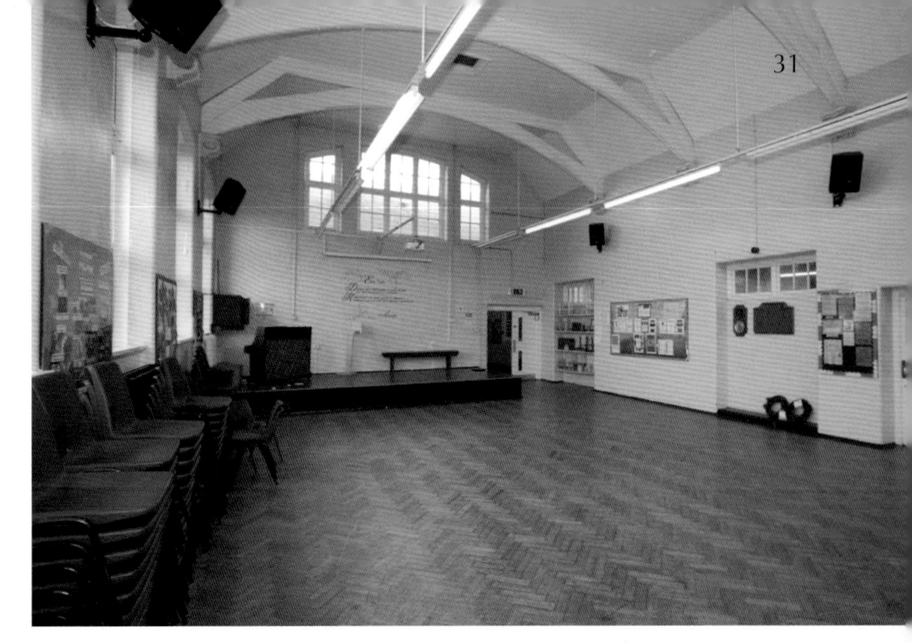

The hall at Richie's old school. When he was a pupil he was a member of Leisan house. Nowadays the house names have been changed to Burton, Emmanuel and Hopkins to celebrate Burton and fellow local legends Ivor Emmanuel (born in Pontrhydyfen like Burton) and Anthony Hopkins, who also grew up in Taibach.

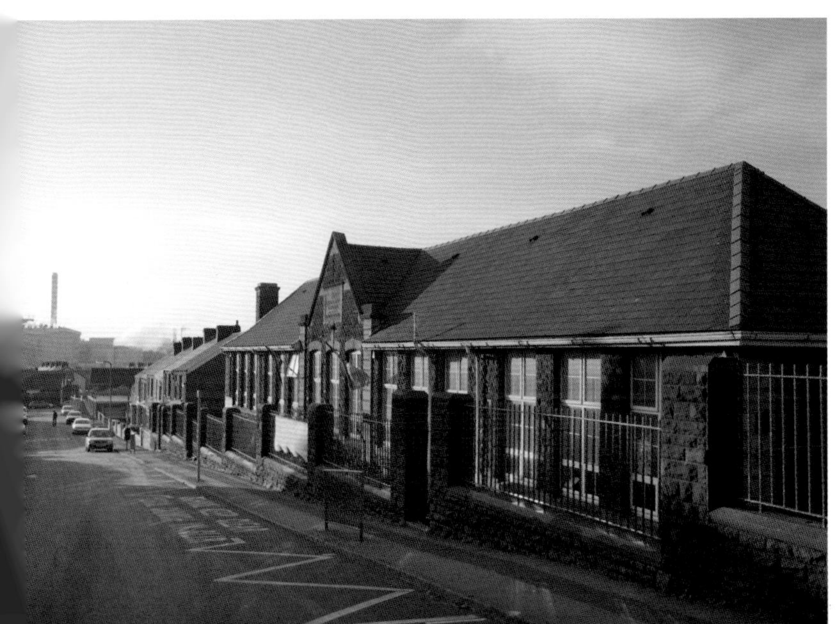

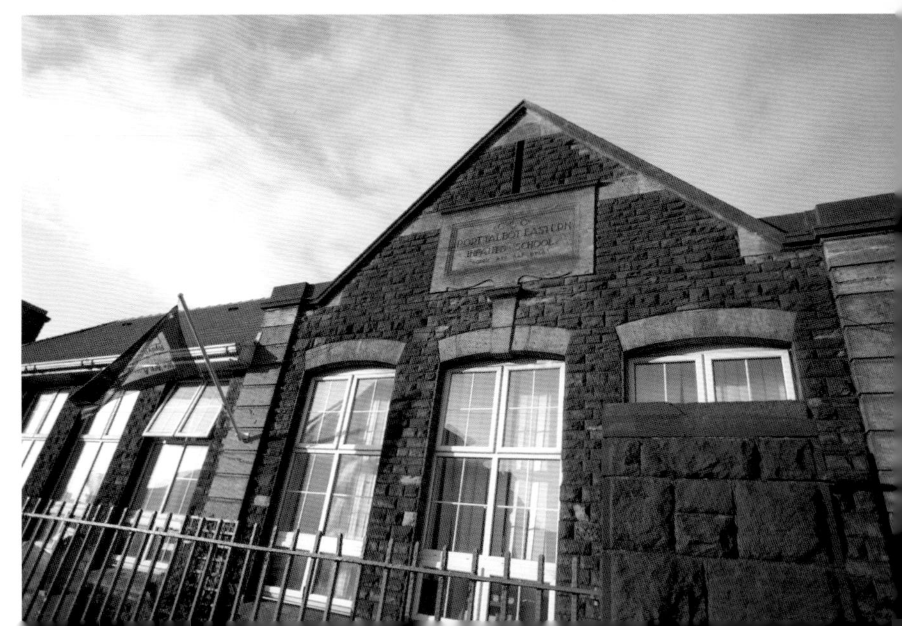

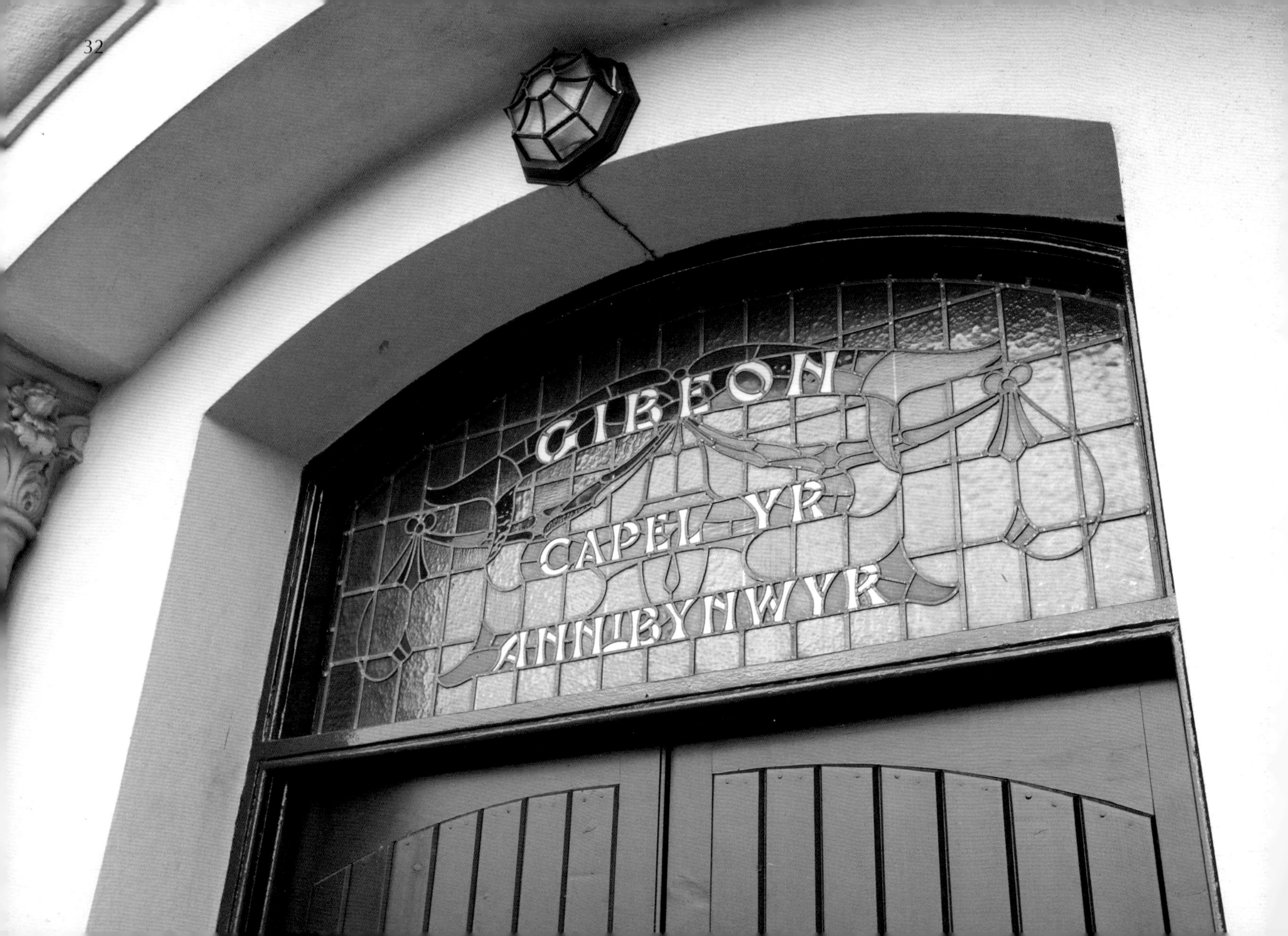
GIBEON
CAPEL YR
ANNIBYNWYR

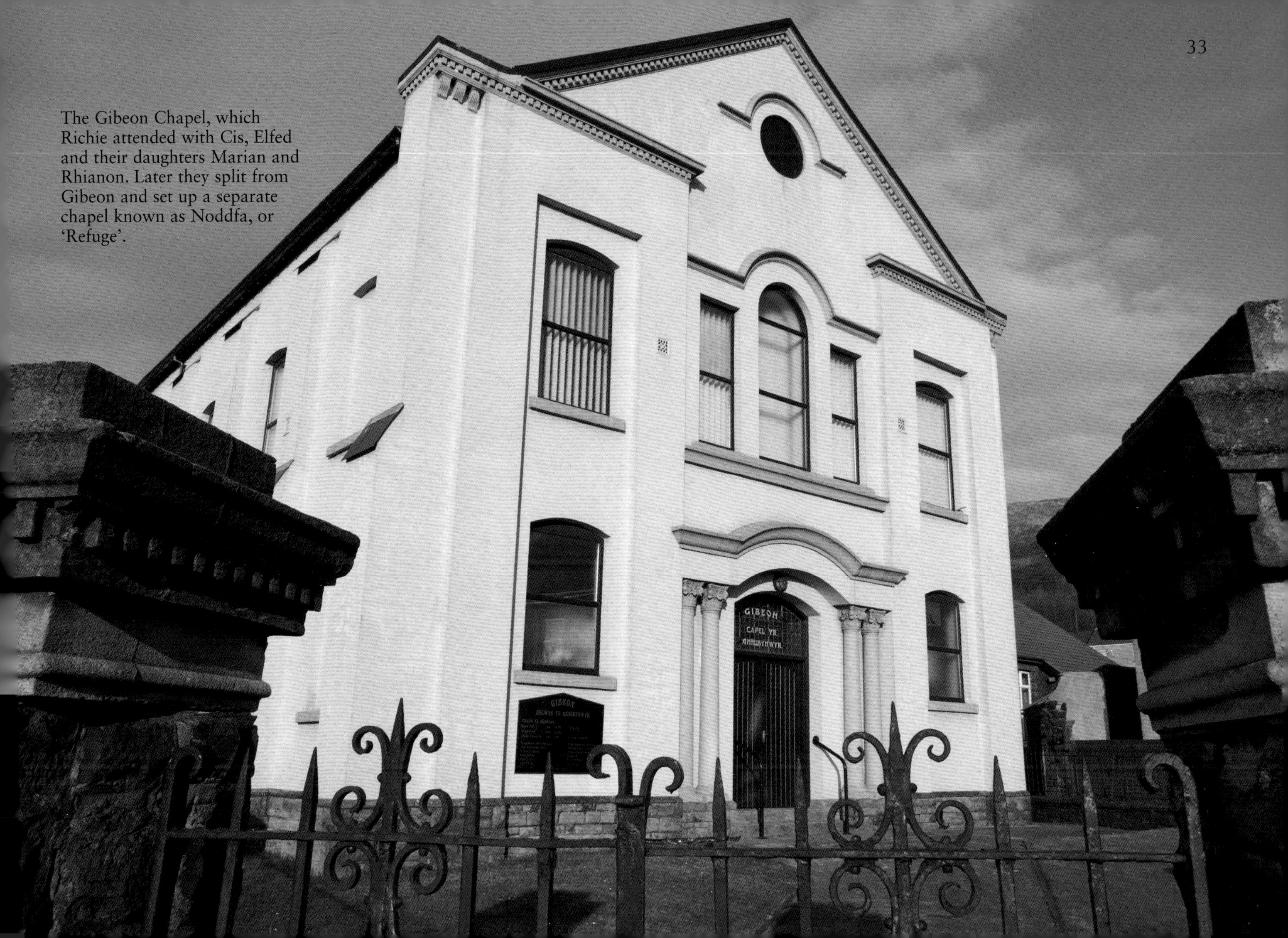

The Gibeon Chapel, which Richie attended with Cis, Elfed and their daughters Marian and Rhianon. Later they split from Gibeon and set up a separate chapel known as Noddfa, or 'Refuge'.

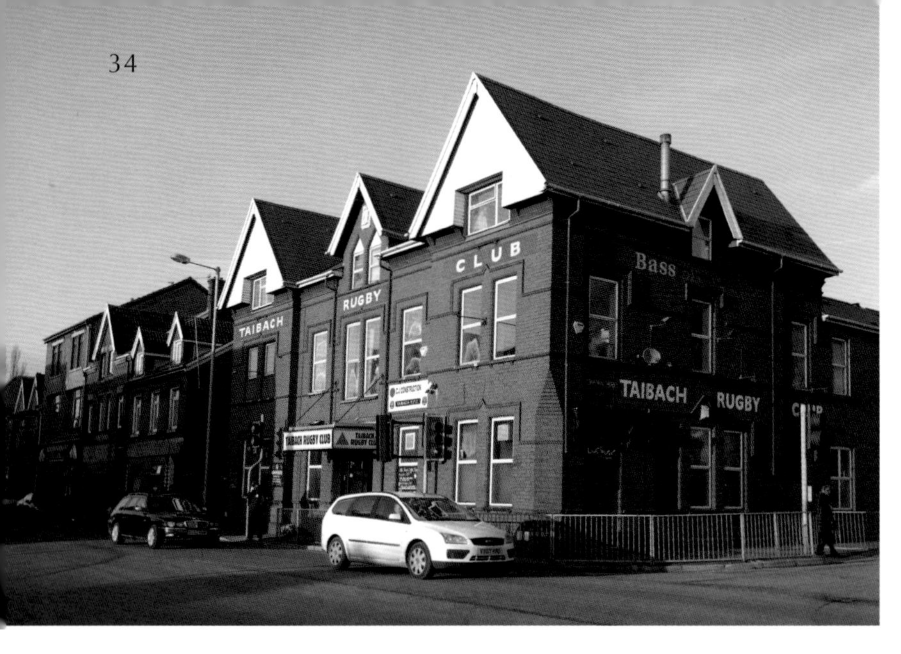

To train his voice Richie Jenkins would climb high up on 'the Side', where he would yell and scream until he somehow 'fixed' his voice at the level that suited him. Forty years later he would recall, 'it was primitive, but it worked'. In partnership with the disciplined vocal drilling he received from Philip Burton in the front room at their lodgings in Connaught Street it was here that he ground away his Welsh accent and learned to speak like the BBC performer he would soon become. The rehearsals could get quite loud with the result that landlady Ma Smith, who slept in the bedroom above, would bang on the floor to quieten the noise from below. Across the street from Taibach Library stands Filco's, formerly the Taibach Co-operative Wholesale Society, where he gloomily worked as a haberdasher's assistant.

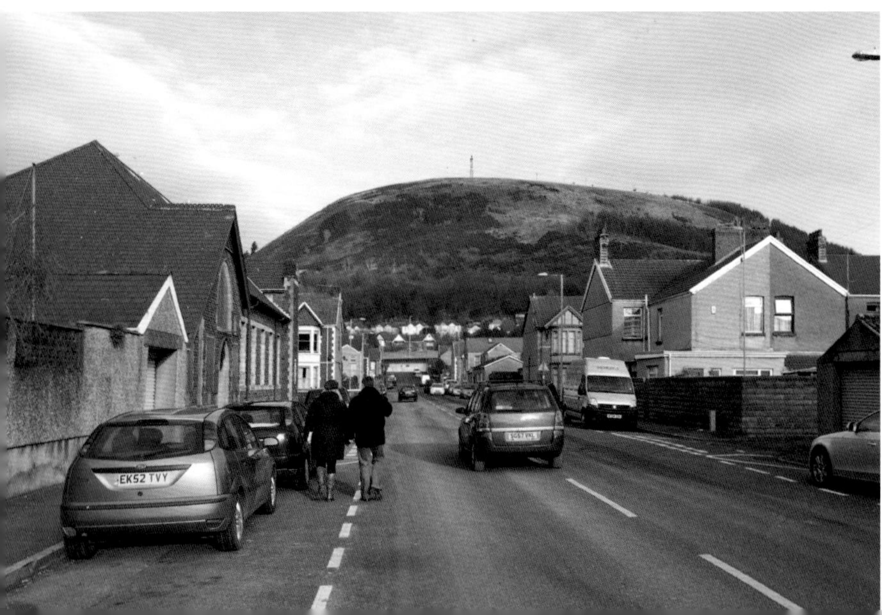

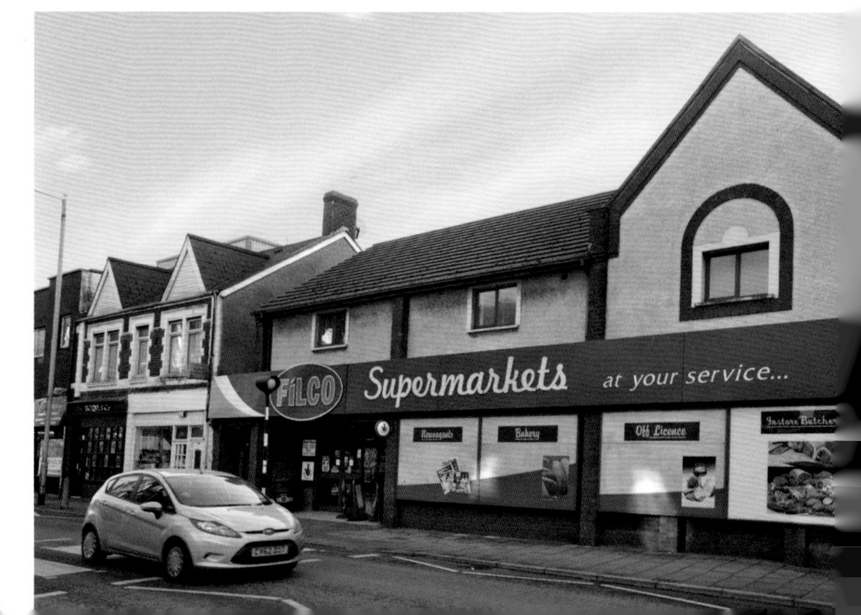

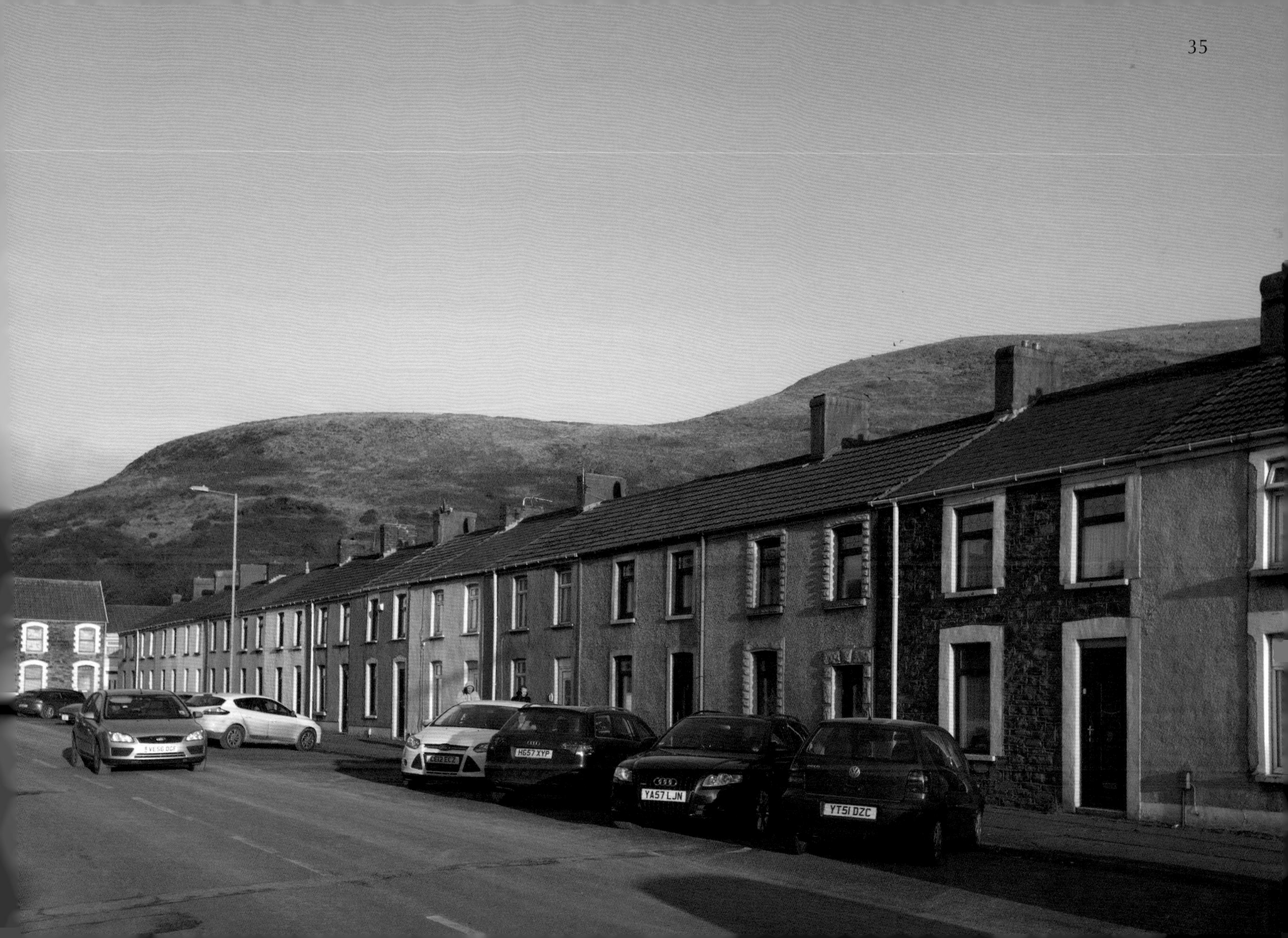
H657 XYP
YA57 LJN
YT51 DZC

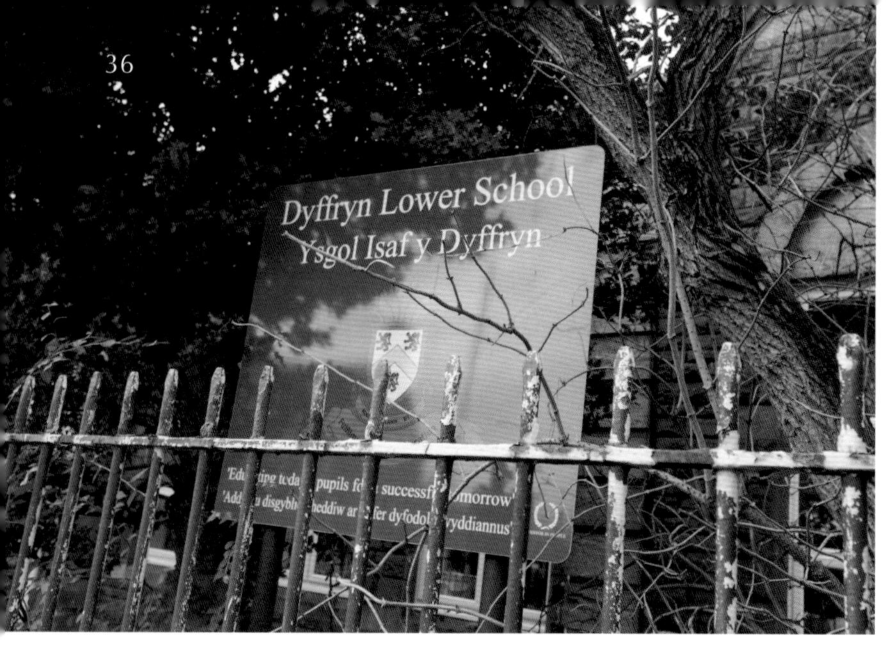

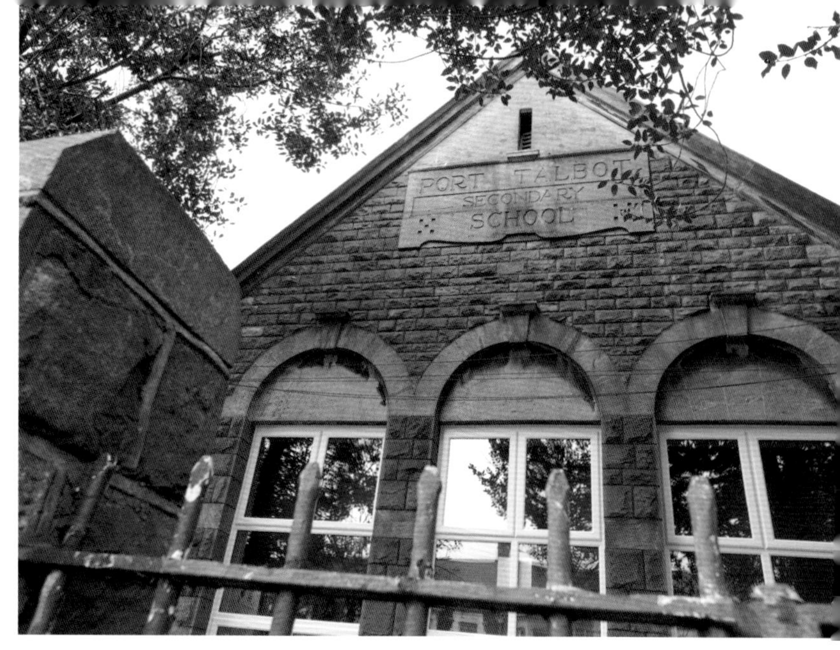

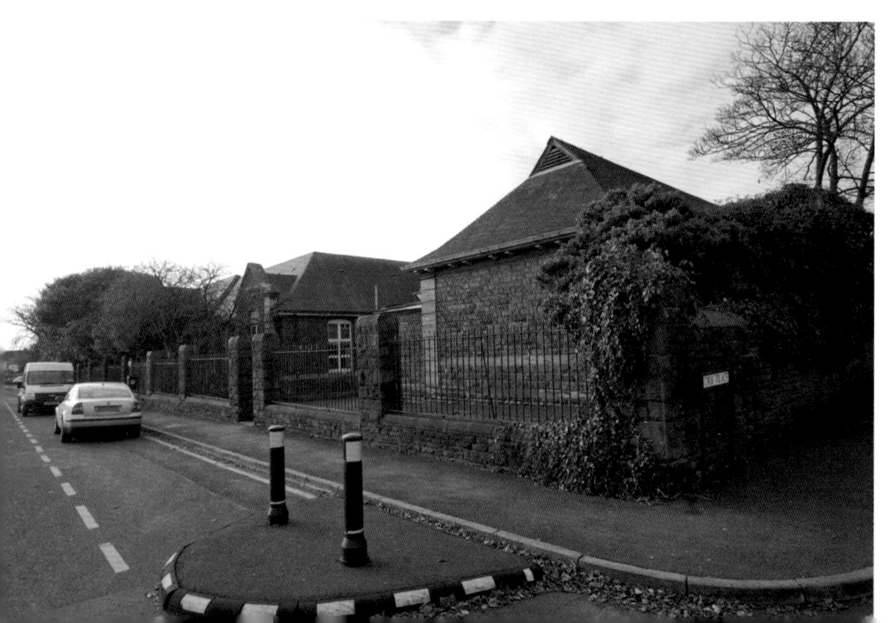

This page: As well as his name, Philip Burton gave Richie Jenkins a second chance. Now, seventy years later, pupils at Dyffryn Comprehensive (formerly Port Talbot Secondary School) have been involved in creating the Richard Burton Trail, helping produce a guide and designing a leaflet. Said headteacher Martin Grimes: 'It is proper that we acknowledge someone like Richard Burton. It's not something we've given any attention to until recently. The impetus came with the changing of our library. That was a happy coincidence. It's also an opportunity to exploit a another way into doing so many other things.' Burton, a man who loved words, would have appreciated that.

Opposite: Taibach Library, where Richie enjoyed an autodidact's education; he always had his nose in a book.

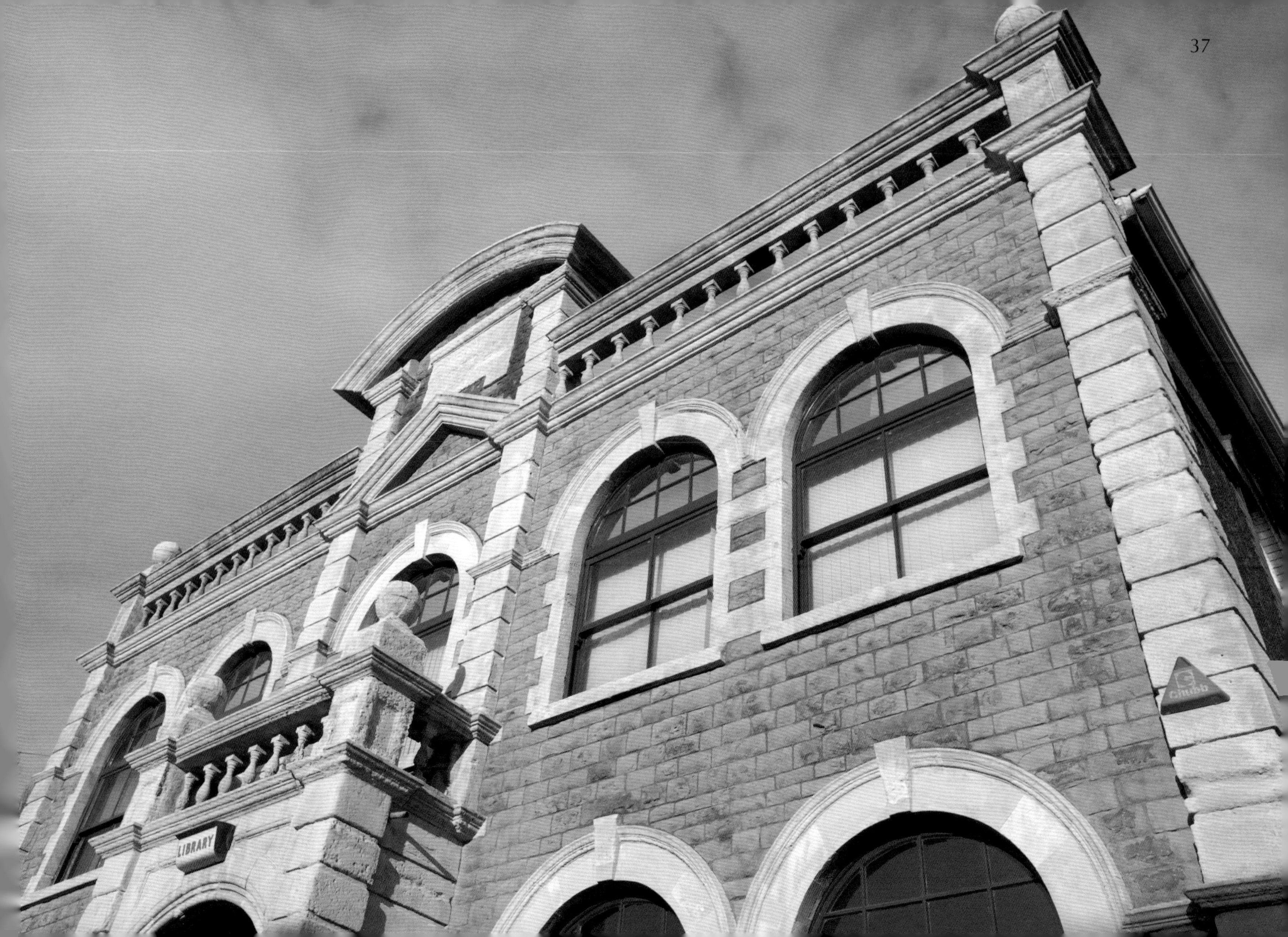
LIBRARY

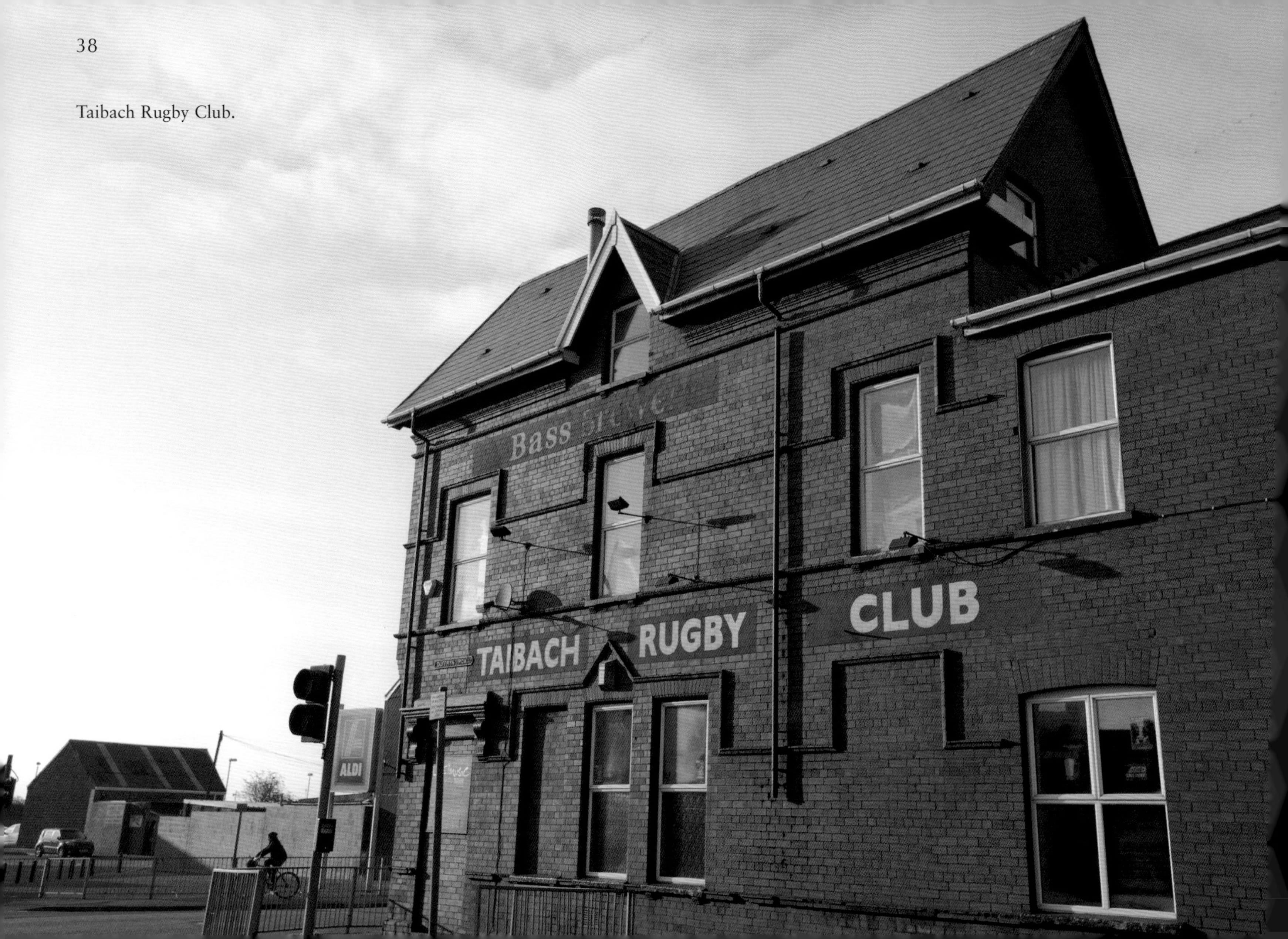

Taibach Rugby Club.

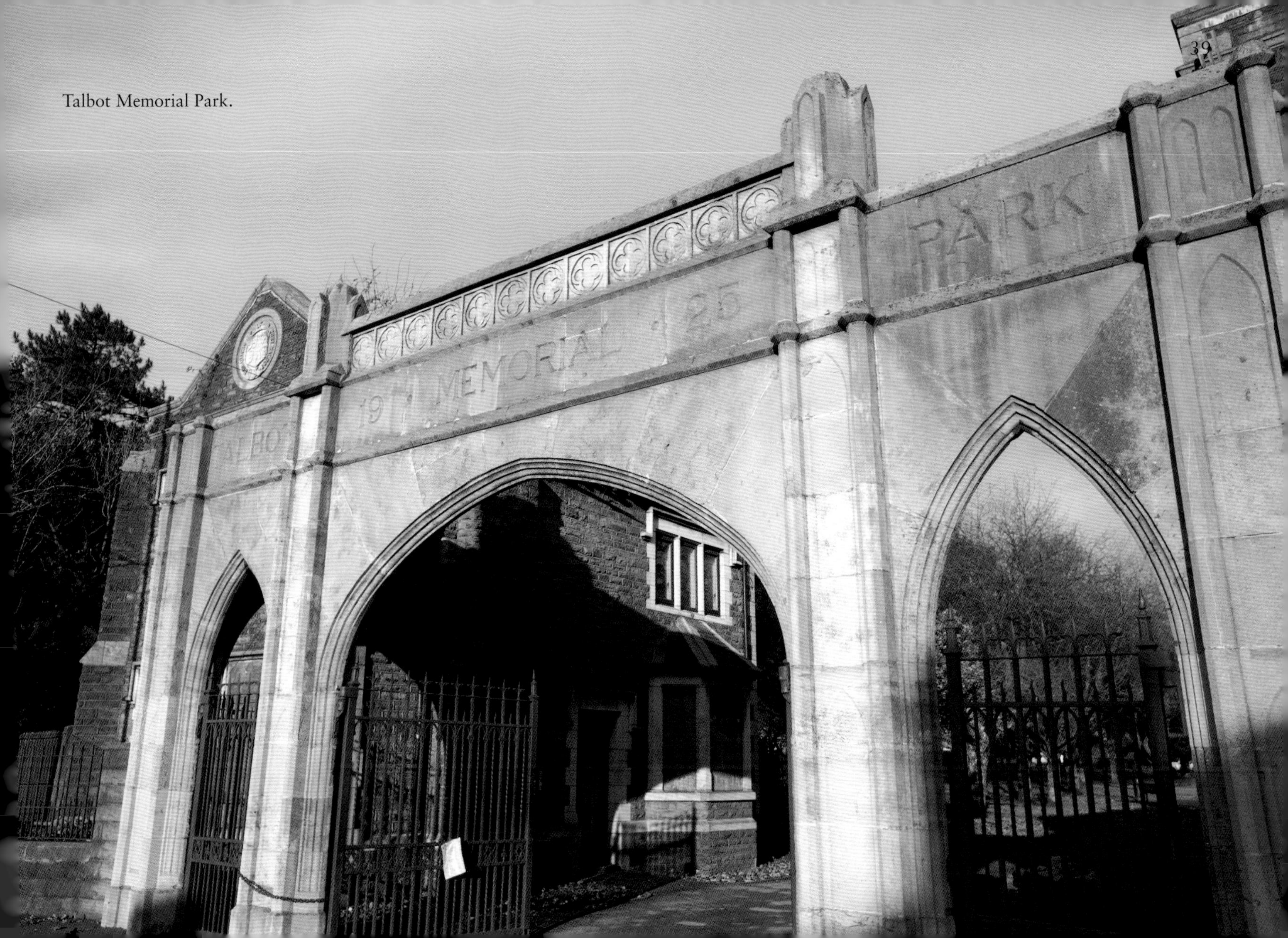

Talbot Memorial Park.

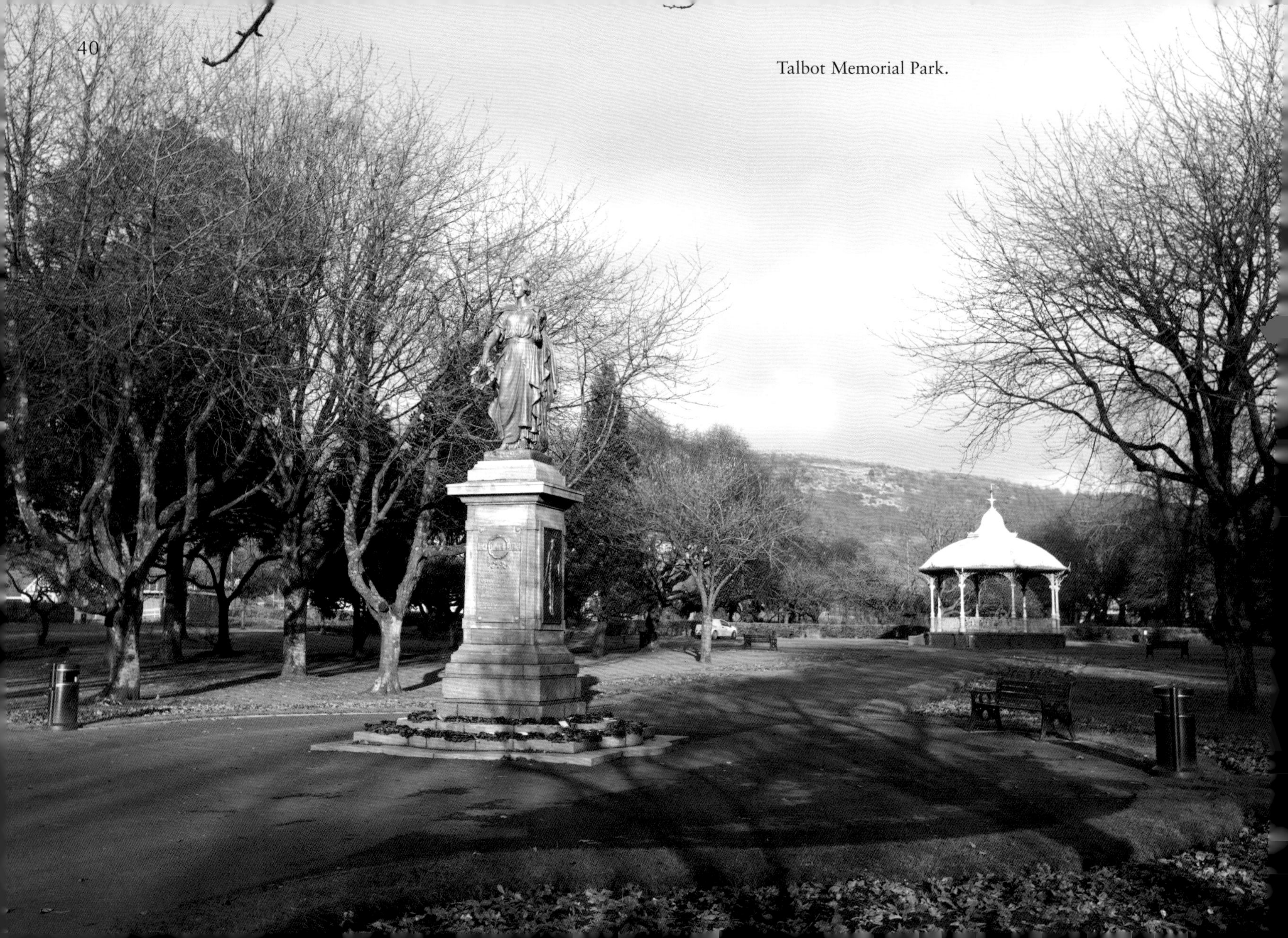

Talbot Memorial Park.

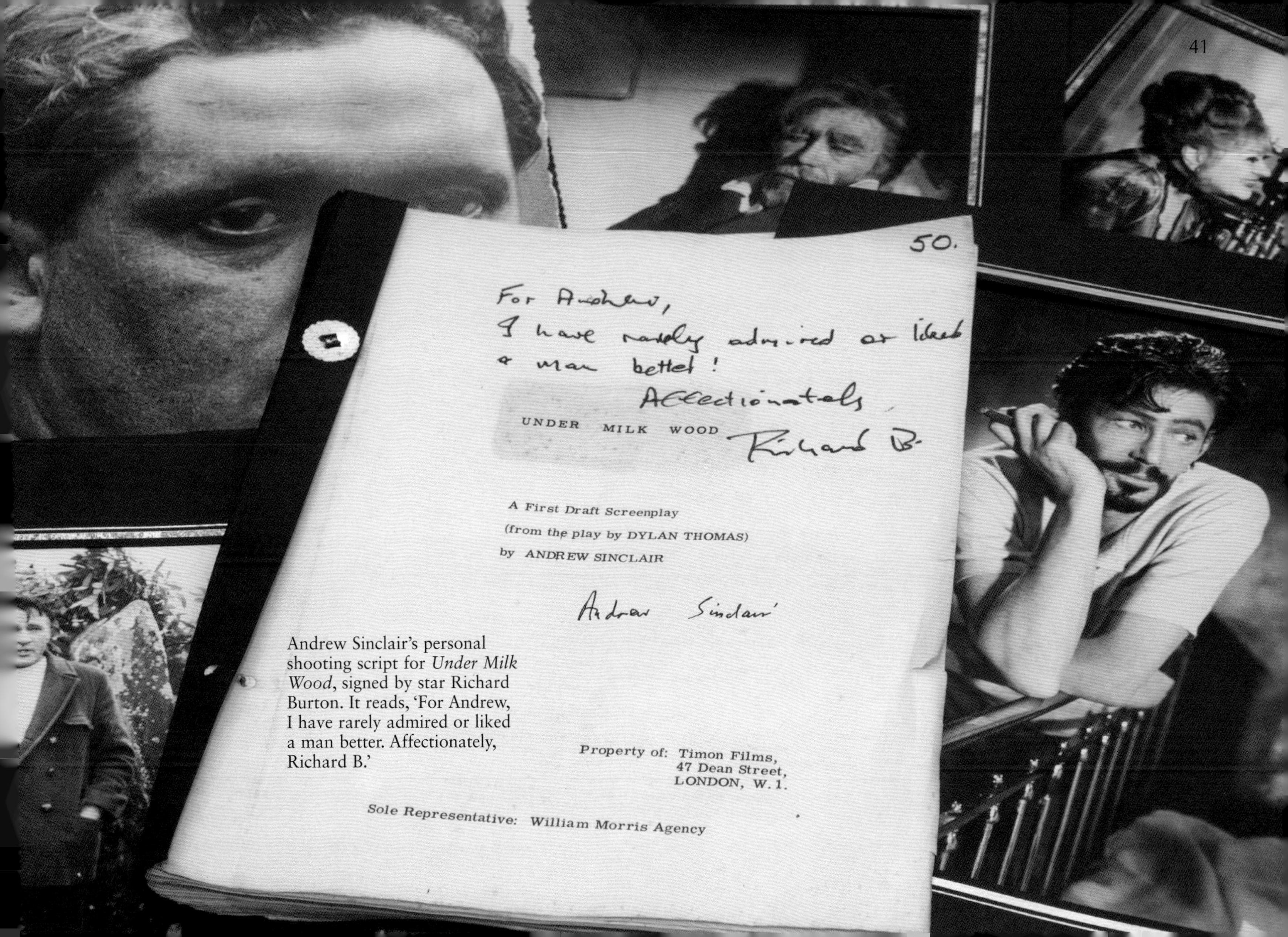

Andrew Sinclair's personal shooting script for *Under Milk Wood*, signed by star Richard Burton. It reads, 'For Andrew, I have rarely admired or liked a man better. Affectionately, Richard B.'

Wholly Bad or Good

Llareggub, Fishguard and the Film of Under Milk Wood

> '*Under Milk Wood* is all about religion, sex and death. It is also a comic masterpiece.'
>
> – Richard Burton as told to Andrew Sinclair

Richard Burton is inextricably linked with Dylan Thomas. It is invariably Burton's voice – rich, resonant, regal and robust – that echoes through the collective consciousness of the world whenever the Welsh bard's words are broadcast.

Young Burton first encountered Thomas as a teenager. Later they would become friends, sharing a microphone for the BBC and drinking in the pubs that bordered the august Corporation's London headquarters.

History tells us that Thomas intended Burton to partner him in his play for voices, *Under Milk Wood*. Thomas would be First Voice, Burton Second. Depression, isolation, strangers, drink and death prevented Thomas' plans from materialising. But in late January 1954, eleven weeks after Thomas died in New York, it was Burton who would read his friend's words in a radio adaptation that has since passed into legend.

The poetry of Dylan Thomas provides a literary spine for Richard Burton's career as an actor. He gave voice to his words on radio, on television, on record, on stage and on film.

Burton acted in two radio versions of *Under Milk Wood*, in 1954 and again in 1963. The latter would become a posthumous film credit when it was used as the basis for Robin Lyons' animated film in 1992. By then Burton had been dead for eight years.

Burton also appeared in Jack Howells' *Dylan Thomas*, trudging along the lonely shore at Laugharne as he recalled his dead friend in a short documentary that won an Oscar. And he was in *A Child's Christmas in Wales*, an American TV tribute, reading and reminiscing against a New York backdrop. There were also records and staged readings for charity. Burton was fond of Donne, Hopkins, Coleridge and Shakespeare, but it was Thomas he returned to time and again.

When Scots academic, author, dramatist and scriptwriter Andrew Sinclair daringly adapted *Under Milk Wood* for the cinema screen it was to Burton he turned to, to lead the nocturnal carousing in Llareggub. His fellow revellers included

Peter O'Toole, Elizabeth Taylor and a formidable ensemble of Welsh players led by Siân Phillips.

Thus Richard Burton is unique in being the only actor to have embraced Dylan Thomas across all art forms. It is a devotion haunting in its intimation of guilt (Burton carried with him a sense of regret that he had been unable to lend Thomas money, with the result that he voyaged to New York and his doom) and yet cloaked in a sense of immense Celtic pride.

Thomas was the self-styled bombastic adolescent provincial Bohemian, 'a gabbing, ambitious, mock-tough, pretentious young man'.

Nothing pretentious there, commented Burton. To understand Burton's dedication to his friend is to understand what Wales meant to each of them. Both Burton and Thomas are rooted in a Wales of nostalgia – a land that existed briefly in childhood and was forever etched in the memory.

One was a working class miner's son. The other was a middle class son of a teacher. But their partnership transcends class, just as Dylan Thomas' words transcend time.

Burton was fond of storytelling and would frequently rhapsodise about Thomas and other poets of his acquaintance such as Louis MacNeice. On one occasion they were drinking together after a BBC recording session. Thomas asked those present what they considered to be the most powerful and moving piece of poetry in the English language.

Burton recited a soliloquy from Shakespeare – possibly 'To be or not to be' from *Hamlet*. MacNeice offered up some of his own poetry. Thomas silenced them both.

'This,' he said, 'is the best poem in the English language,' and then spoke the following lines:

I am.
Thou art.
He, she, it is.
We are.
You are.
They are.

Sixty years later it is impossible to argue with the purity of his choice. Burton knew it, too: he told that story until the end of his days.

Had he lived Richard Burton would have enjoyed a much quieter life with Sally, away from private jets, motor yachts and million-dollar jewels. He would have become more accessible. His death, on 5 August 1984, aged fifty-eight, robbed his young wife and the wider world of that accessibility. For Burton was a sociable man. He enjoyed the talk, to tell stories, to recite Shakespeare and poetry.

And always his favourite poet was his long-dead friend, Dylan Thomas.

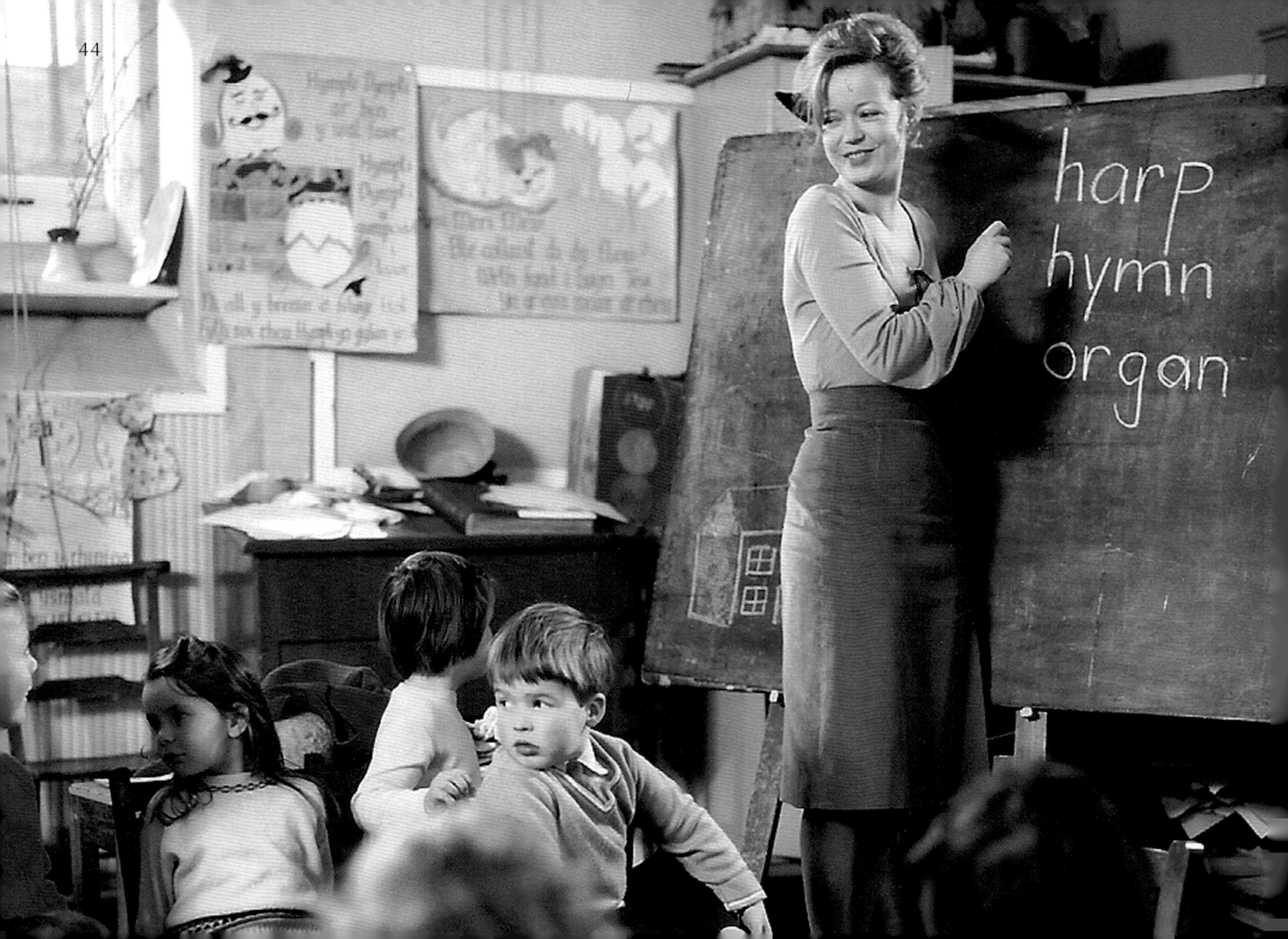
harp
hymn
organ

Blessed (or cursed) with three of the biggest stars of the era – he famously did not want to be saddled with Elizabeth Taylor, who worked for two days as 'Captain Cat's wet dream', Rosie Probert – writer/director Andrew Sinclair assembled a formidable Celtic ensemble. One critic accurately described it as 'the Debrett of Welsh acting talent'. The undercurrent of ribald sexuality that flows through Thomas' work is given physicality via a succession of perfectly cast female roles. Two are represented here: schoolteacher Gossamer Beynon (played by the late Angharad Rees), lusted after in comic fashion by publican Sinbad Sailors and Polly Garter (played by Ann Beach), martyred every night by a succession of men and who longs only for her one true love, Little Willy Wee, 'who is dead, dead, dead'. Beach's mournful singing as she scrubs the church floor is one of the high points of the film of *Under Milk Wood*.

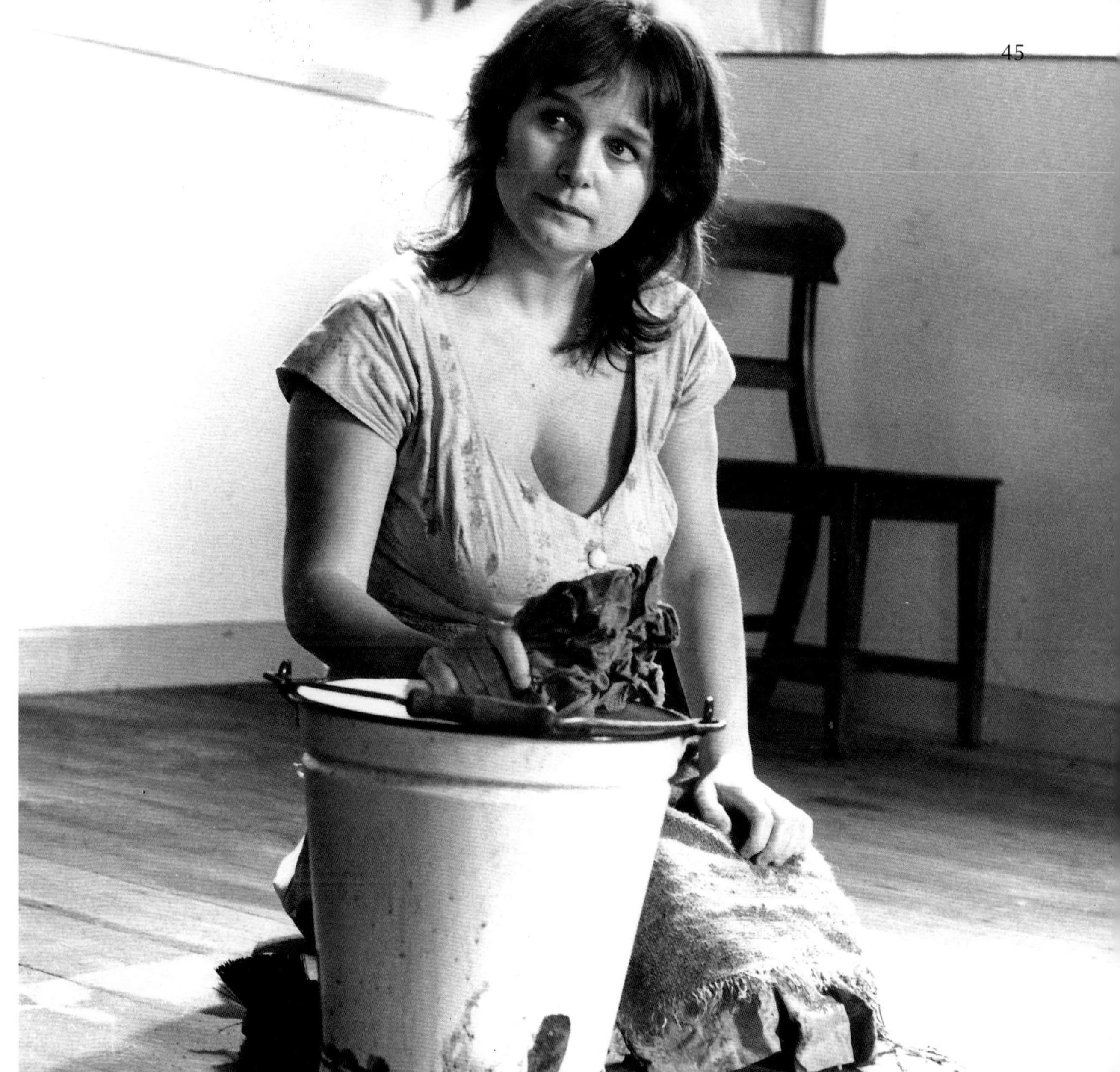

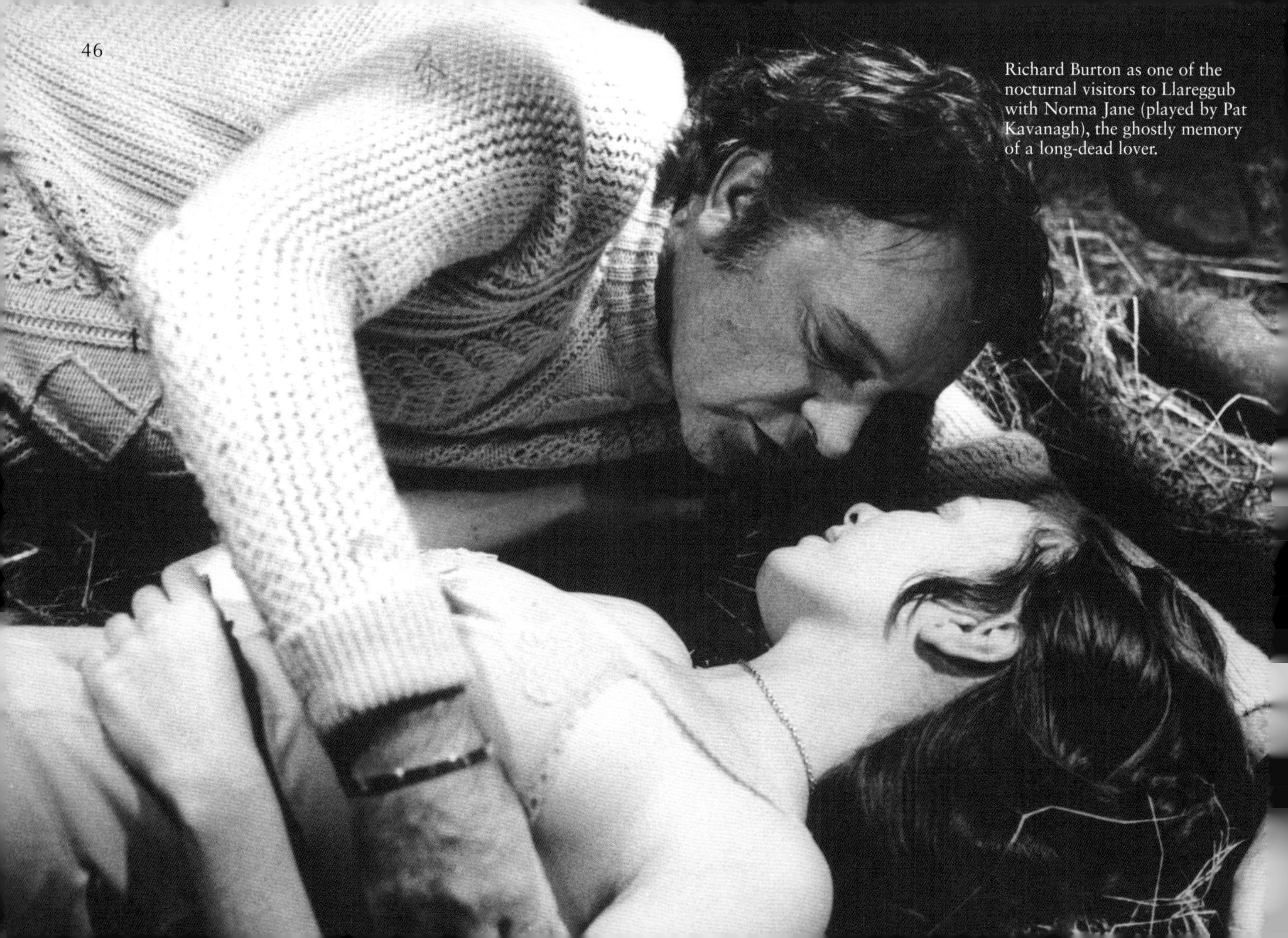

Richard Burton as one of the nocturnal visitors to Llareggub with Norma Jane (played by Pat Kavanagh), the ghostly memory of a long-dead lover.

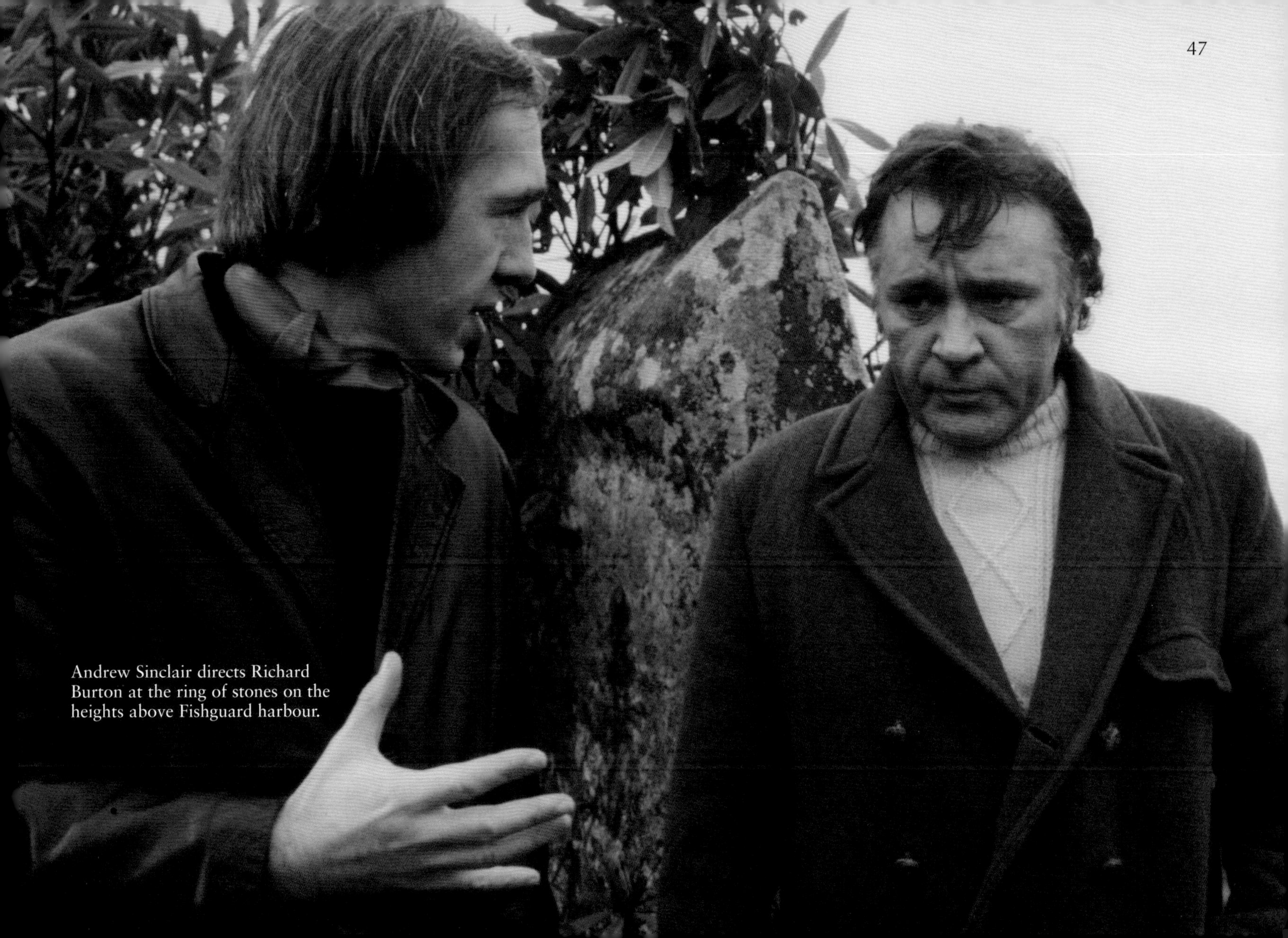

Andrew Sinclair directs Richard Burton at the ring of stones on the heights above Fishguard harbour.

A fearless and versatile performer who was equally at home playing soldiers, clerics or lusty rogues, Richard Burton was one of the screen's premier screen talents.

Born Richard Walter Jenkins in the tiny Welsh mining village of Pontrhydyfen on 10 November 1925, the twelfth of thirteen children, he was to escape the pit through the encouragement of his surrogate father, teacher Philip Burton, who also gave him his name.

Early theatre success in London was matched by success in films. His first, a Welsh drama entitled *The Last Days of Dolwyn*, was written and directed by Emlyn Williams, and starred Williams as the villain. Burton, then just twenty-three, took the juvenile lead. On the film he met his first wife, actress Sybil Williams.

Over the next four years he would move between the stage and the movie studio. He stormed the theatre in the '50s with a clutch of plays at The Old Vic, including *Hamlet*, *Coriolanus*, *King John*, *Henry V* and *Othello*, in which he alternated the roles of the Moor and Iago with John Neville. Movies included *The Robe* (the first picture in CinemaScope), *The Desert Rats*, *Alexander the Great* and *My Cousin Rachel*, for which he was nominated for his first Academy Award as Best Supporting Actor.

Throughout the 1950s his reputation as a stage performer grew while his film career stagnated. All that was to change in 1961 when he met Elizabeth Taylor on the set of *Cleopatra*. The story is well-trod: they fell in love, left their respective spouses and the world reeled from a love affair Burton was to call 'Le Scandale'.

They were together for more than twelve headline-grabbing years. They divorced and briefly remarried, eventually calling it a day in 1976. During that time they were, unquestionably, the most glamorous couple on the planet. Occasionally their charisma spilled over into their movies. They would make six largely indifferent films together, one enjoyable romp (*The Taming of the Shrew*) and one coruscating domestic drama: the multi-Oscar-nominated *Who's Afraid of Virginia Woolf?*

The '60s represented Burton's halcyon period as a film actor. The great movies – and equally great performances – included *Becket*, *The Night of the Iguana*, *Where Eagles Dare*, *Anne of the Thousand Days* and *The Spy Who Came in from the Cold*, arguably his most luminous performance and one for which he was again Oscar-nominated. He lost to Paul Scofield.

In the '70s he seemed to lose his way both professionally and personally. As his relationship with Taylor nose-dived so did his film performances. Who, for instance, remembers the likes of *The Klansman*, *Hammersmith is Out* or *Sutjeska*? *Under Milk Wood* represents a high point, albeit a quirky one. After an intense period of drinking he re-emerged in the mid-'70s with a new wife, Suzy Hunt, and roles in a number of key films including *The Wild Geese*. For his performance in Sidney Lumet's *Equus* he received his seventh and final Oscar nomination.

Burton's final years were happy ones. Now divorced from Suzy he met Sally Hay on the set of a mammoth nine-hour TV film on the life of Richard Wagner. They married in 1983. The following year he took a supporting role in Michael Radford's screen version of George Orwell's *1984* and, as the sinister, whispering inquisitor O'Brien, delivered one of the best performances of his career. He then appeared with his daughter, Kate, in a star-studded TV miniseries called *Ellis Island*. He was engaged to reprise his tough mercenary Colonel Allen Faulkner in *Wild Geese II* and was planning a film of *The Quiet American* when, on 5 August 1984, he died.

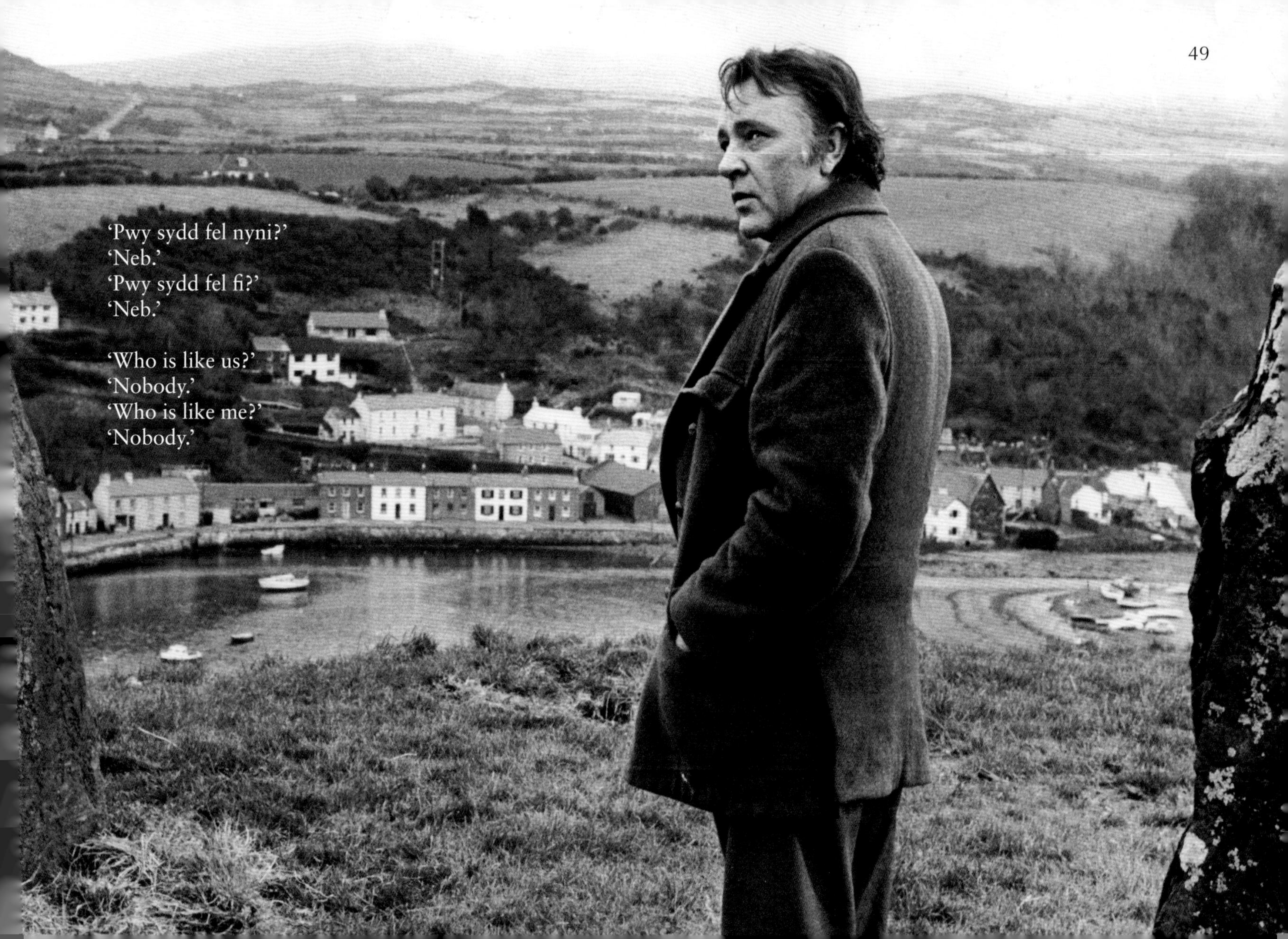

'Pwy sydd fel nyni?'
'Neb.'
'Pwy sydd fel fi?'
'Neb.'

'Who is like us?'
'Nobody.'
'Who is like me?'
'Nobody.'

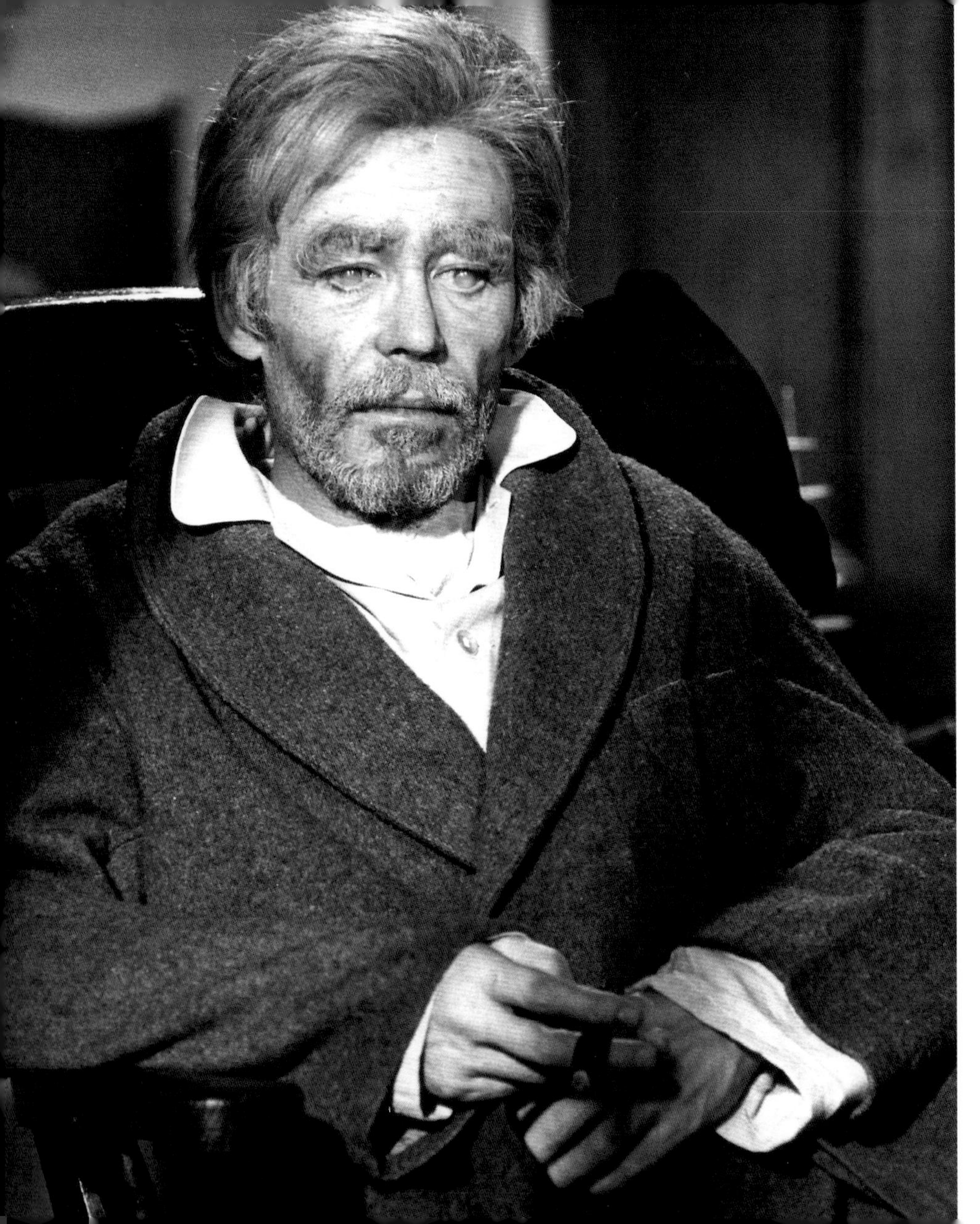

After a day's filming Peter O'Toole would retire to one of the local Fishguard pubs where he would lead the singing. Andrew Sinclair recalled a similar incident of drunken carousing in his flat as O'Toole loudly ran through his repertoire of Gaelic folk songs. Suddenly there was a thunderous banging on the door. Towards dawn a policeman came to stop us disturbing the peace. O'Toole persuaded him to drink whisky from his helmet and join in the choruses. He always had enough charm to steal the brass off a bobby's badge. Among all the stars I worked with, he was the meteor.'

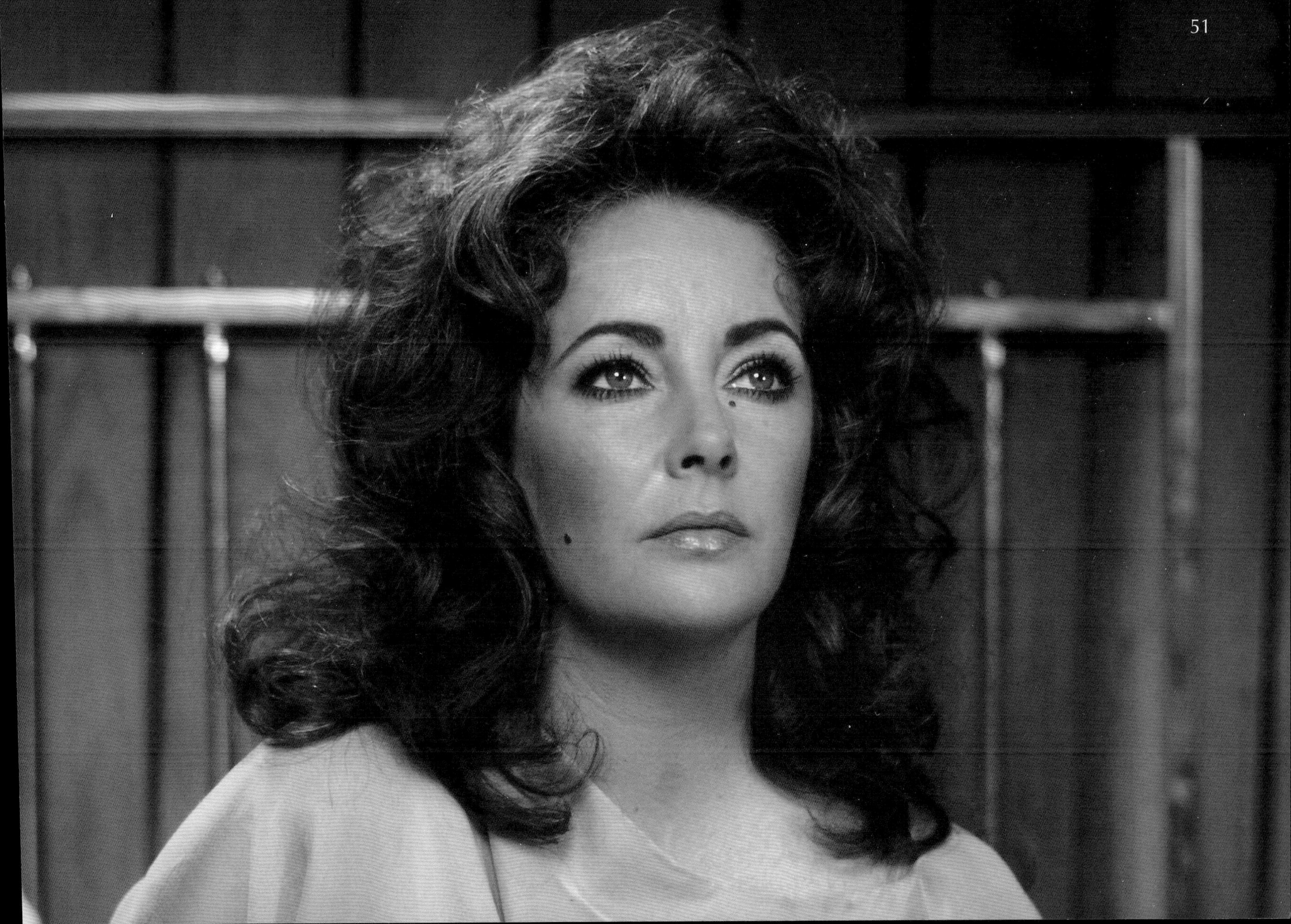

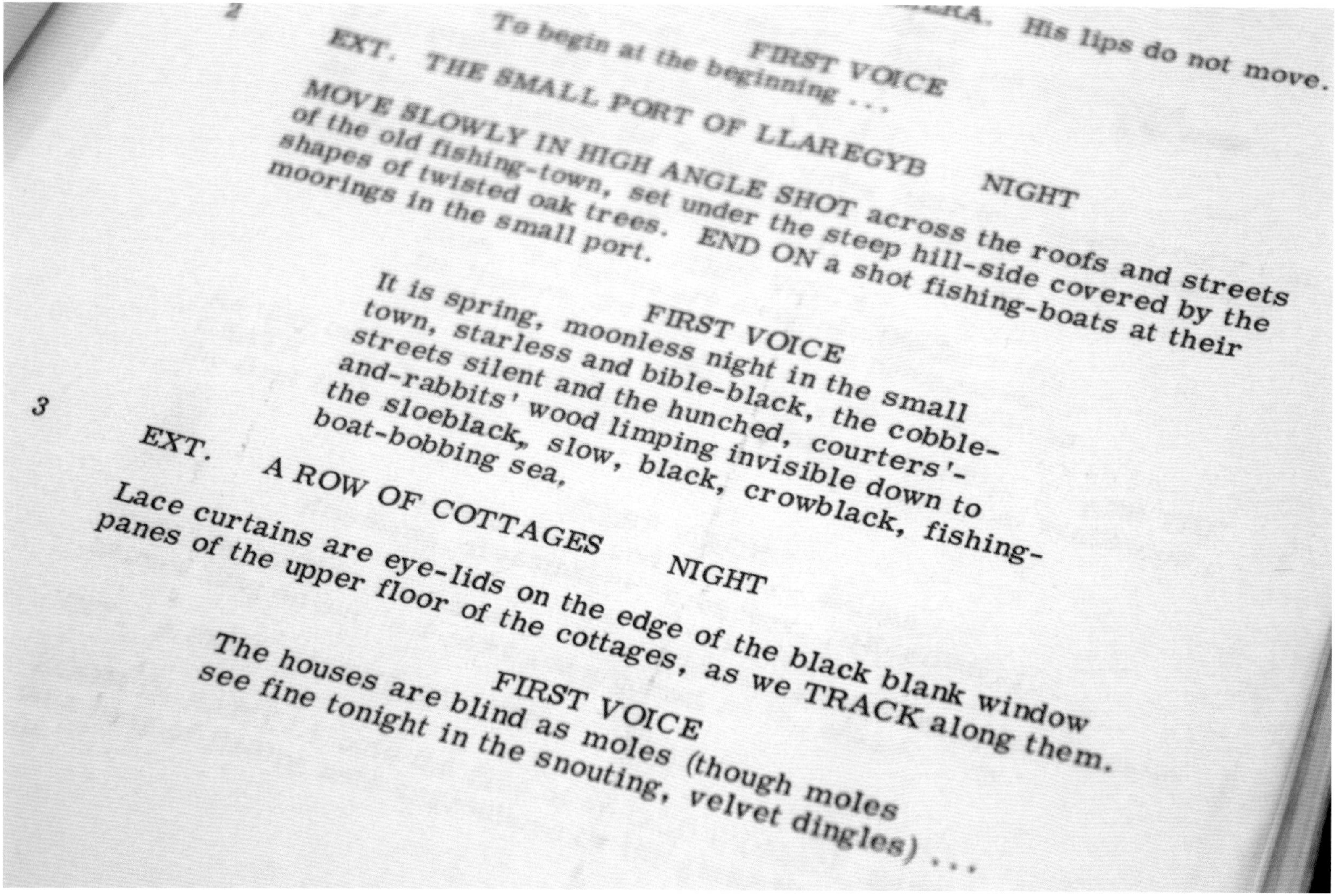

...ERA. His lips do not move.

2

FIRST VOICE

To begin at the beginning ...

EXT. THE SMALL PORT OF LLAREGYB NIGHT

MOVE SLOWLY IN HIGH ANGLE SHOT across the roofs and streets of the old fishing-town, set under the steep hill-side covered by the shapes of twisted oak trees. END ON a shot fishing-boats at their moorings in the small port.

FIRST VOICE

It is spring, moonless night in the small town, starless and bible-black, the cobble-streets silent and the hunched, courters'-and-rabbits' wood limping invisible down to the sloeblack, slow, black, crowblack, fishing-boat-bobbing sea.

3

EXT. A ROW OF COTTAGES NIGHT

Lace curtains are eye-lids on the edge of the black blank window panes of the upper floor of the cottages, as we TRACK along them.

FIRST VOICE

The houses are blind as moles (though moles see fine tonight in the snouting, velvet dingles) ...

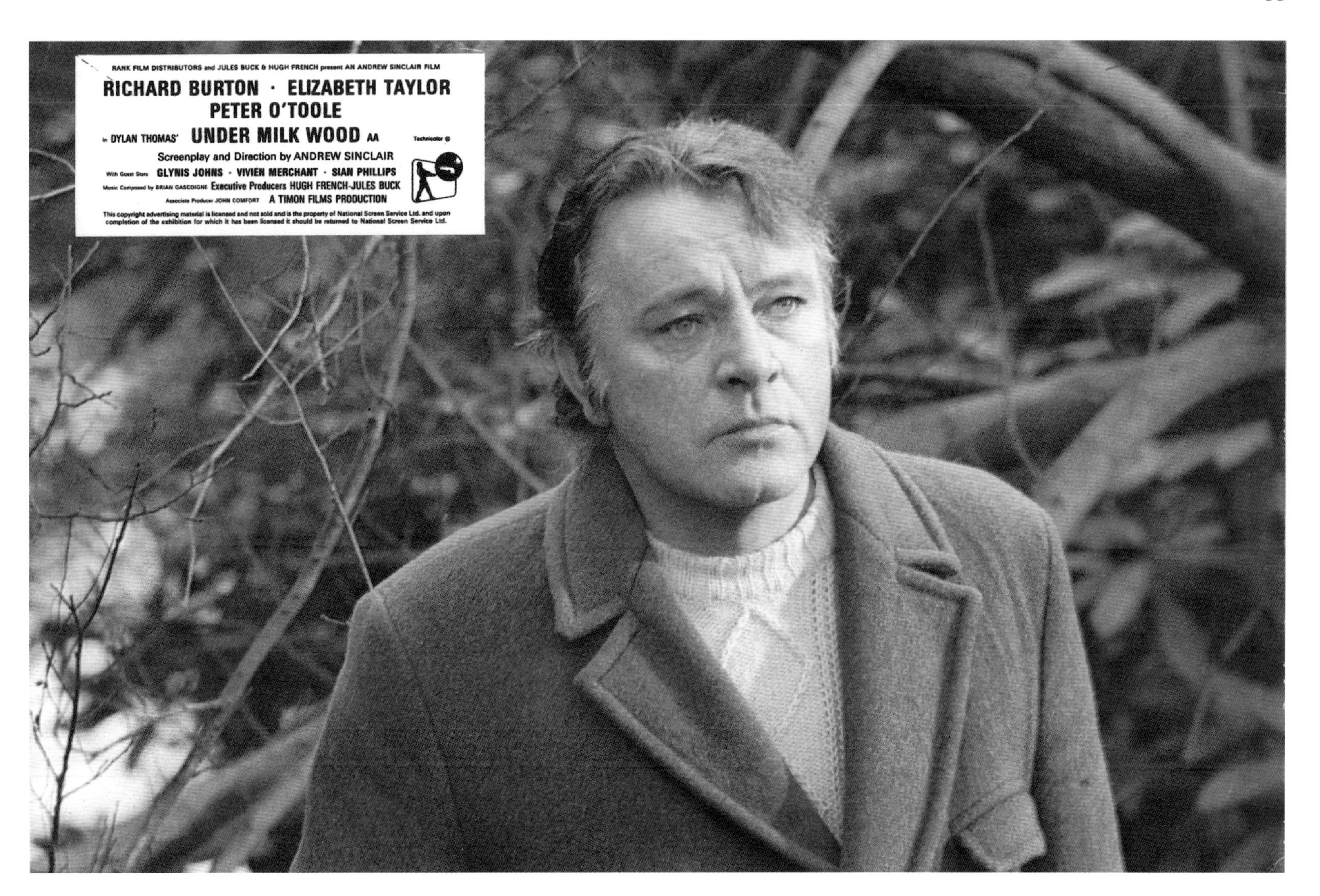
RANK FILM DISTRIBUTORS and JULES BUCK & HUGH FRENCH present AN ANDREW SINCLAIR FILM
RICHARD BURTON · ELIZABETH TAYLOR
PETER O'TOOLE
in DYLAN THOMAS' UNDER MILK WOOD AA
Technicolor ®
Screenplay and Direction by ANDREW SINCLAIR
With Guest Stars GLYNIS JOHNS · VIVIEN MERCHANT · SIAN PHILLIPS
Music Composed by BRIAN GASCOIGNE Executive Producers HUGH FRENCH-JULES BUCK
Associate Producer JOHN COMFORT A TIMON FILMS PRODUCTION
This copyright advertising material is licensed and not sold and is the property of National Screen Service Ltd. and upon completion of the exhibition for which it has been licensed it should be returned to National Screen Service Ltd.

Mr Cherry Owen
(Glynn Edwards)

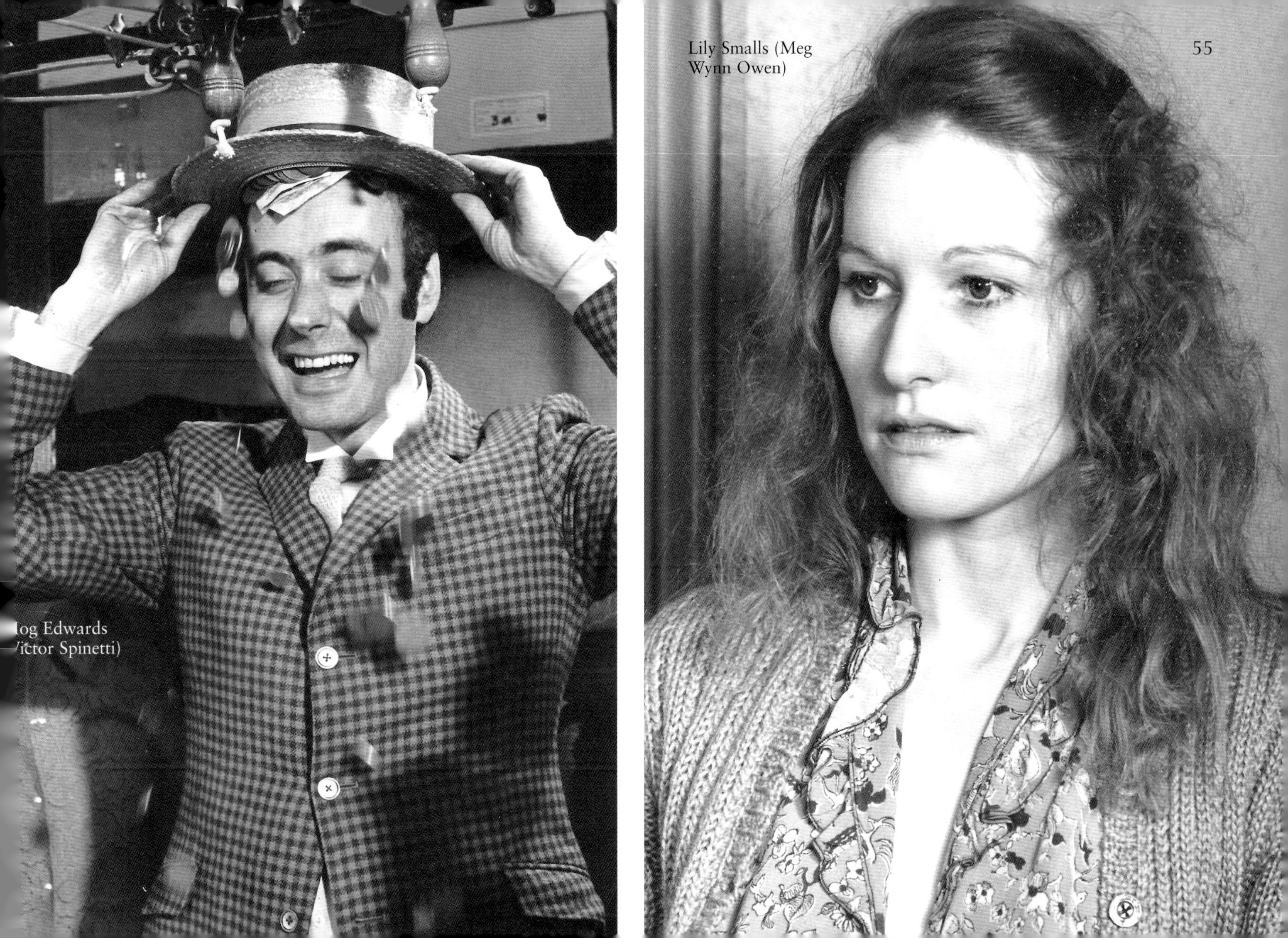

log Edwards
Victor Spinetti)

Lily Smalls (Meg
Wynn Owen)

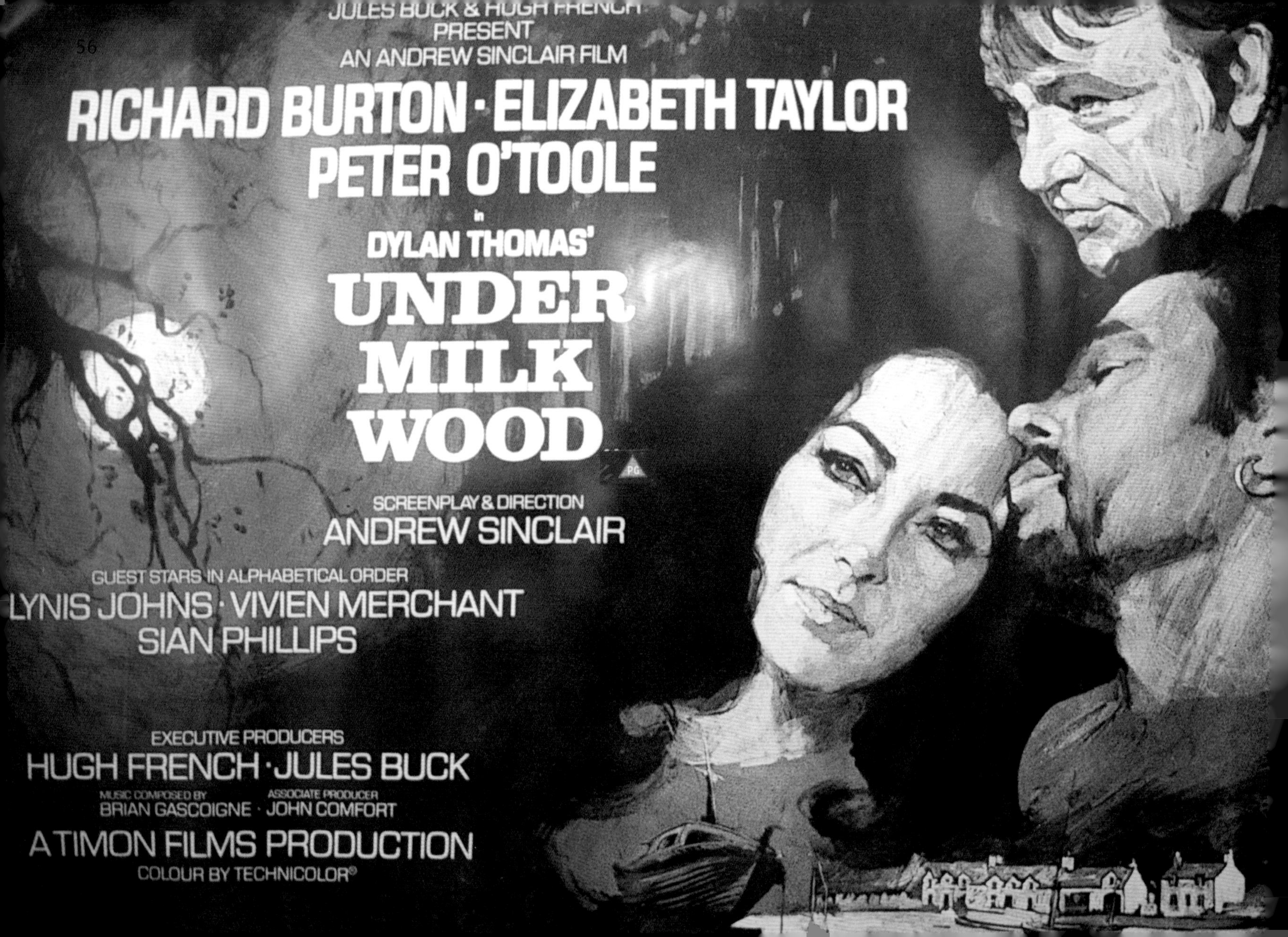
JULES BUCK & HUGH FRENCH
PRESENT
AN ANDREW SINCLAIR FILM
RICHARD BURTON · ELIZABETH TAYLOR
PETER O'TOOLE
in
DYLAN THOMAS'
UNDER
MILK
WOOD
PG
SCREENPLAY & DIRECTION
ANDREW SINCLAIR
GUEST STARS IN ALPHABETICAL ORDER
LYNIS JOHNS · VIVIEN MERCHANT
SIAN PHILLIPS
EXECUTIVE PRODUCERS
HUGH FRENCH · JULES BUCK
MUSIC COMPOSED BY
BRIAN GASCOIGNE
ASSOCIATE PRODUCER
JOHN COMFORT
A TIMON FILMS PRODUCTION
COLOUR BY TECHNICOLOR®

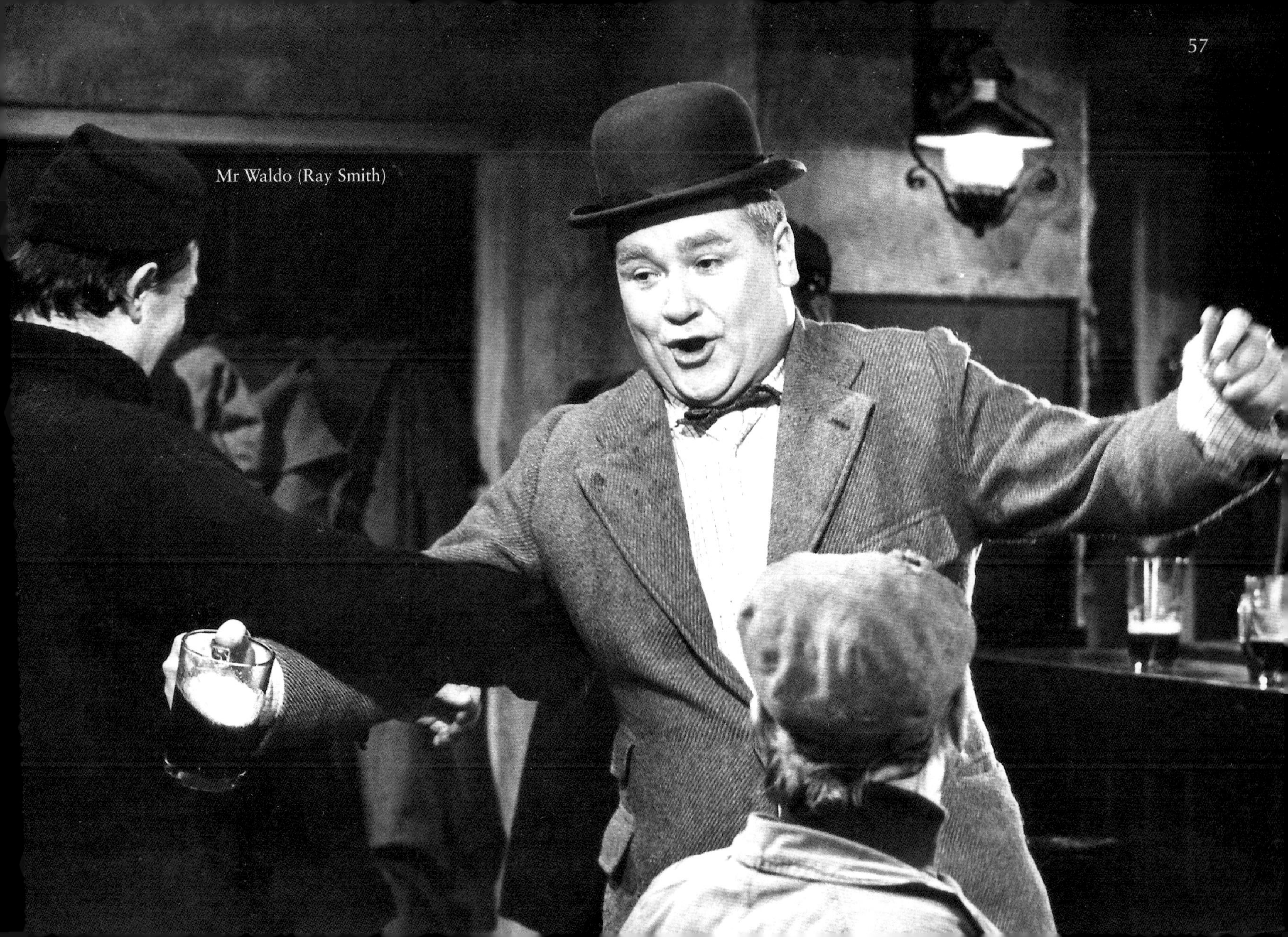

Mr Waldo (Ray Smith)

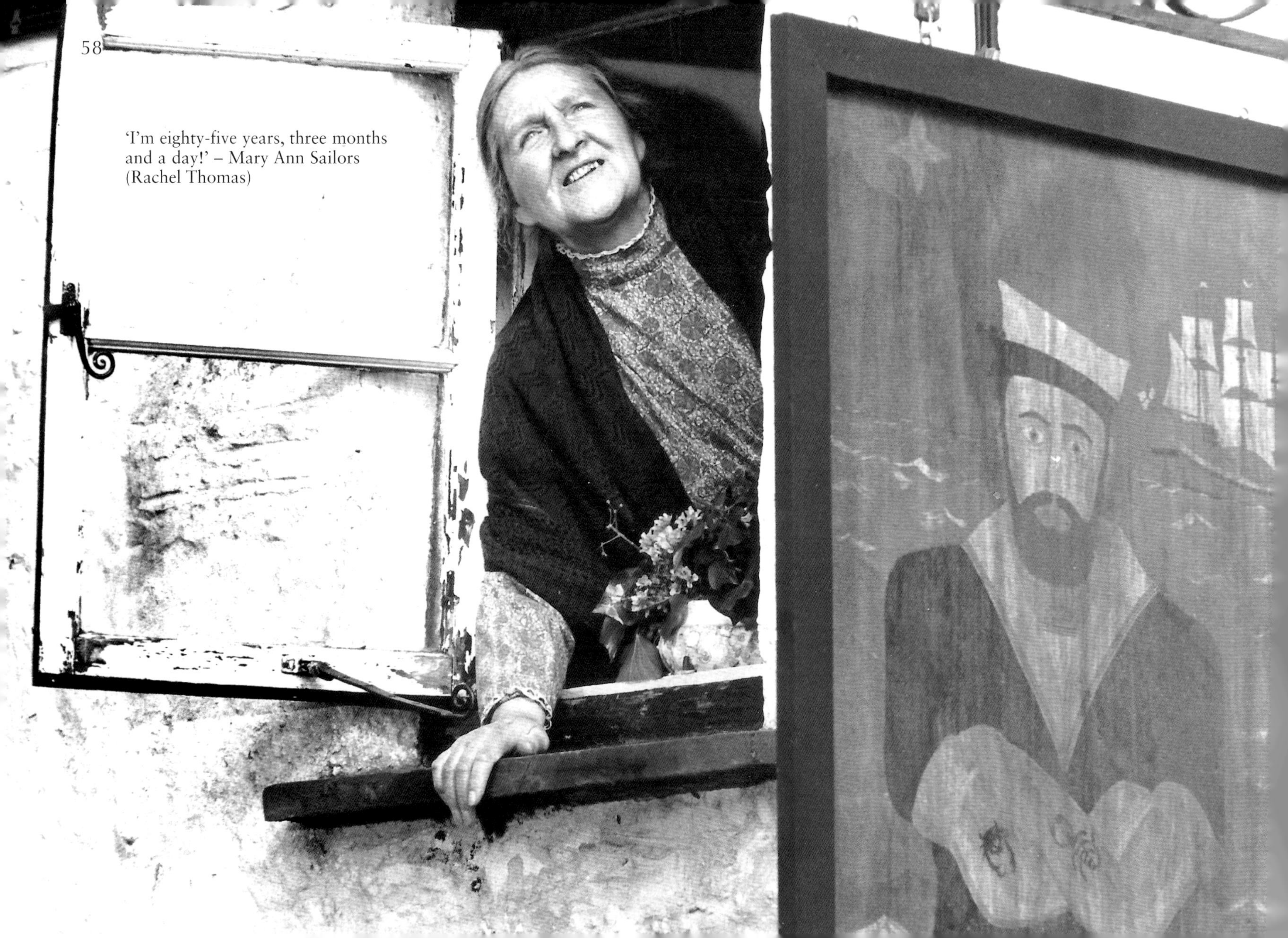

‘I’m eighty-five years, three months and a day!’ – Mary Ann Sailors (Rachel Thomas)

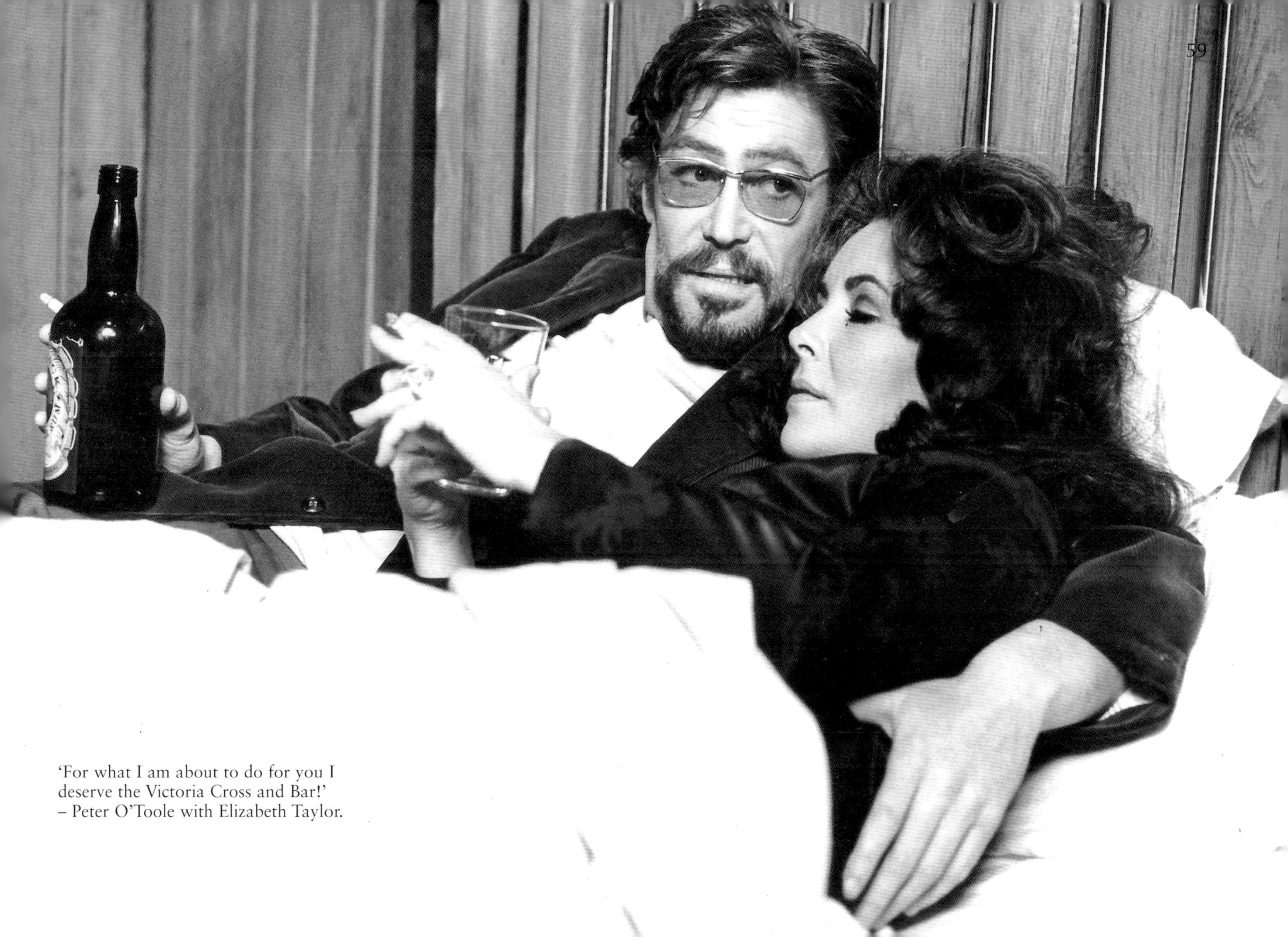

'For what I am about to do for you I deserve the Victoria Cross and Bar!' – Peter O'Toole with Elizabeth Taylor.

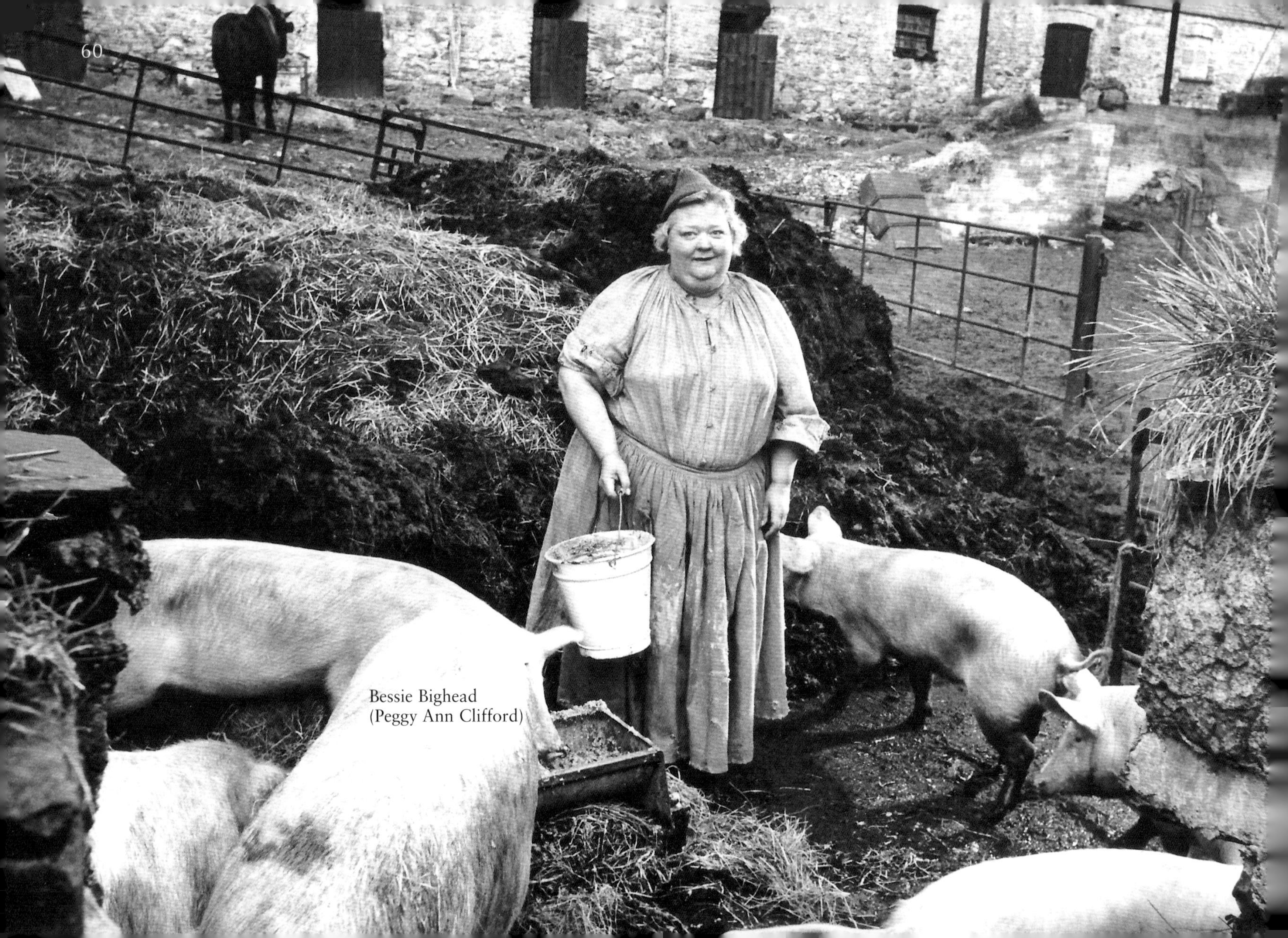

Bessie Bighead
(Peggy Ann Clifford)

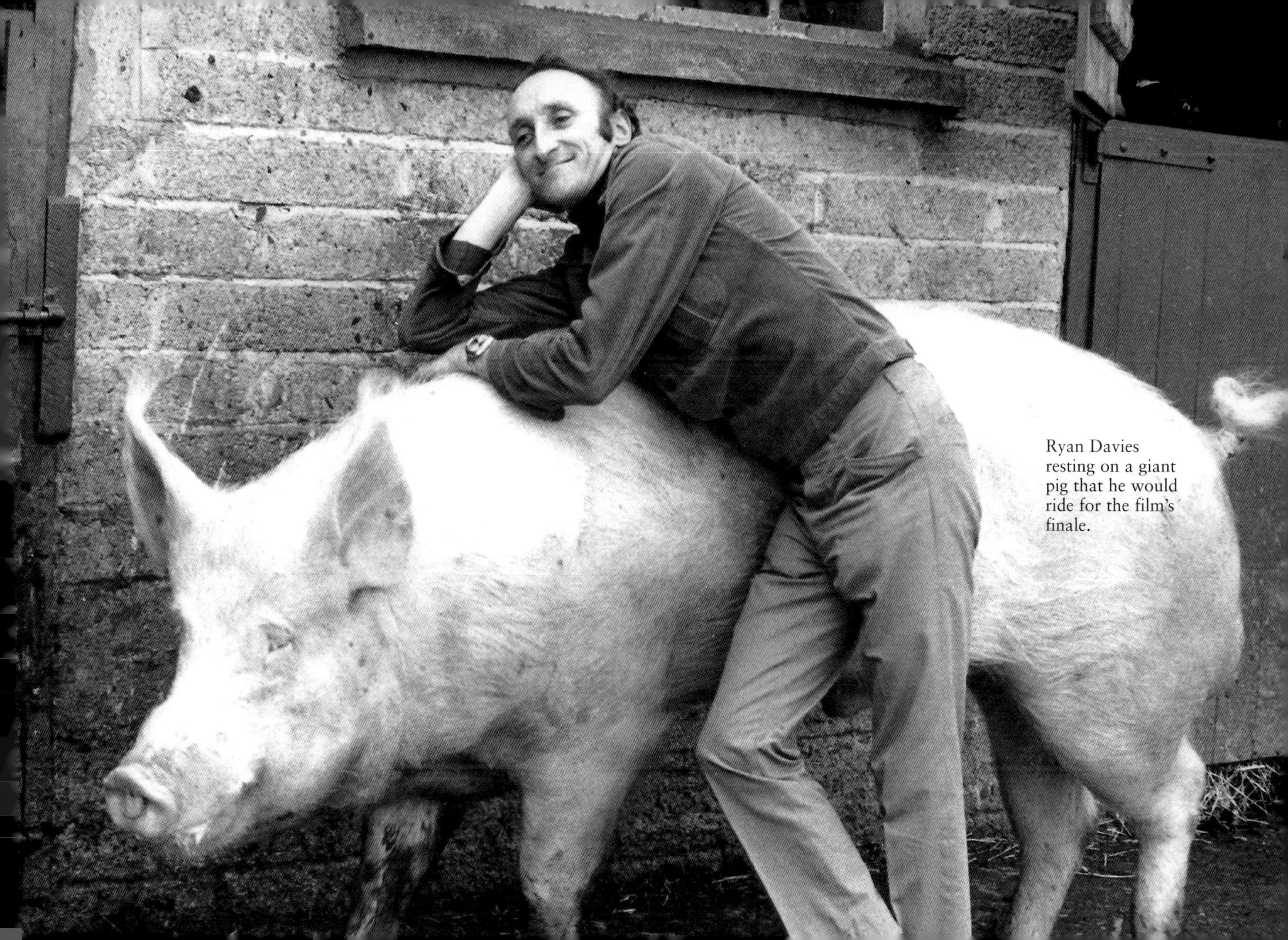

Ryan Davies resting on a giant pig that he would ride for the film's finale.

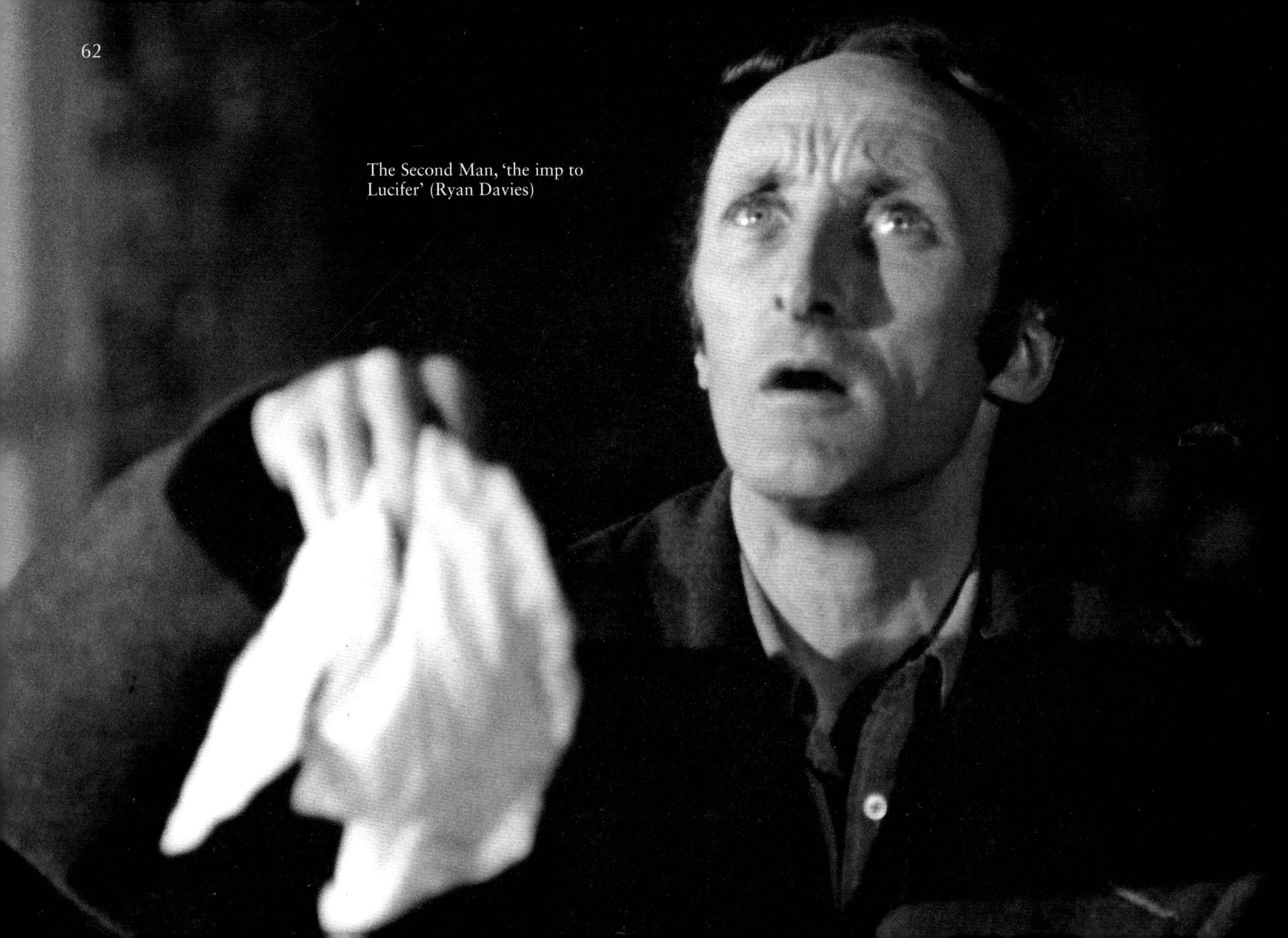

The Second Man, 'the imp to Lucifer' (Ryan Davies)

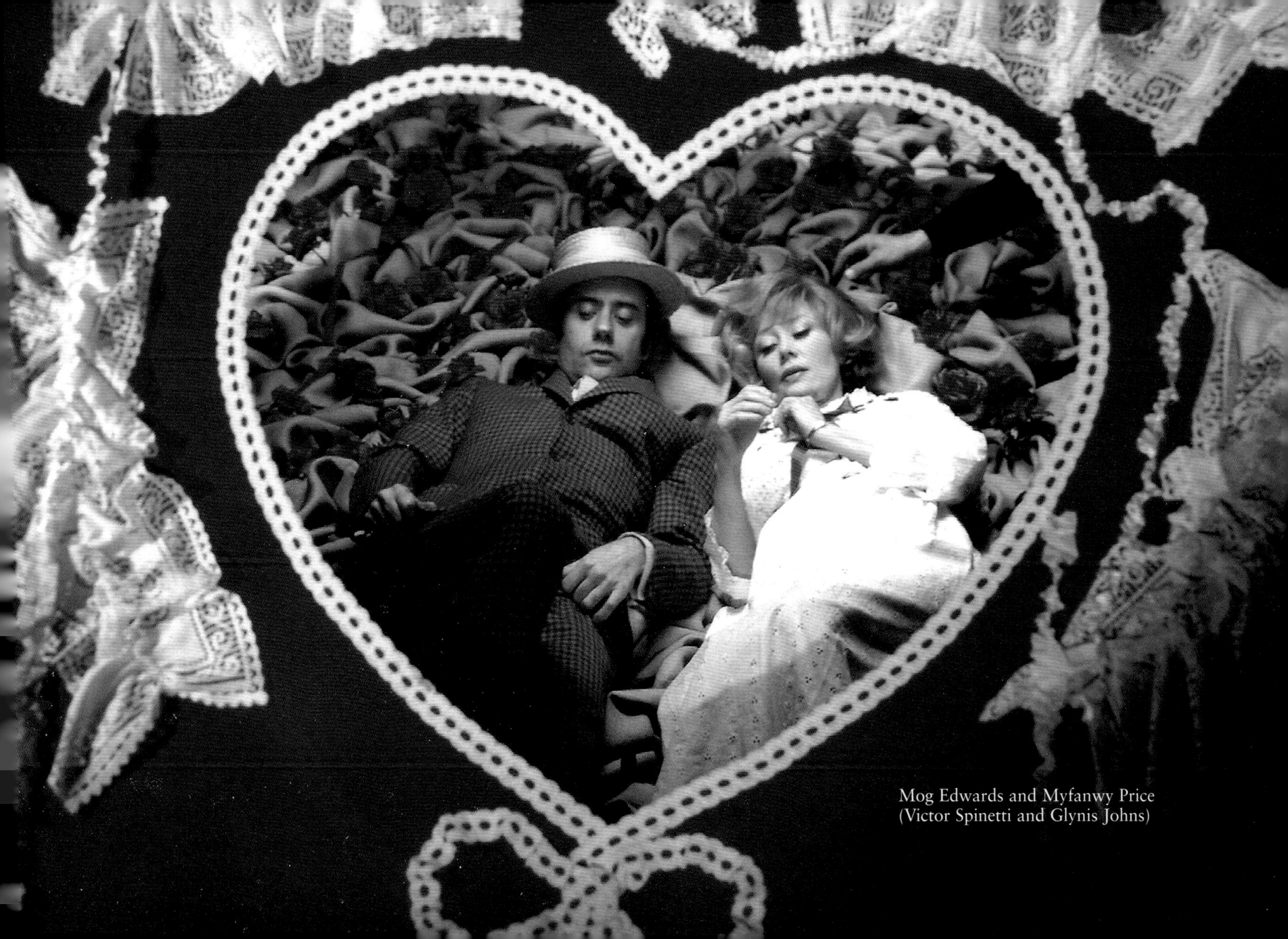

Mog Edwards and Myfanwy Price
(Victor Spinetti and Glynis Johns)

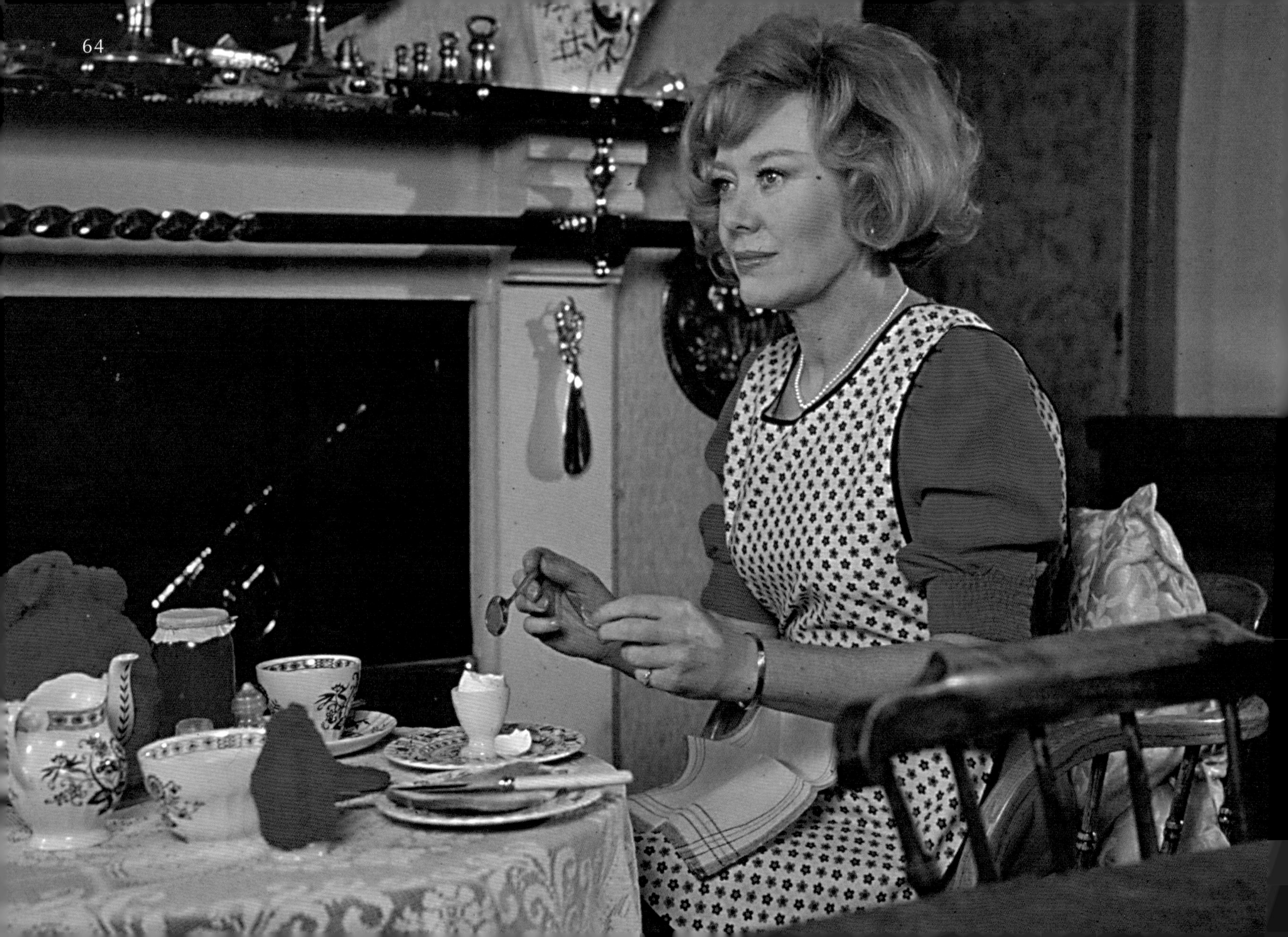

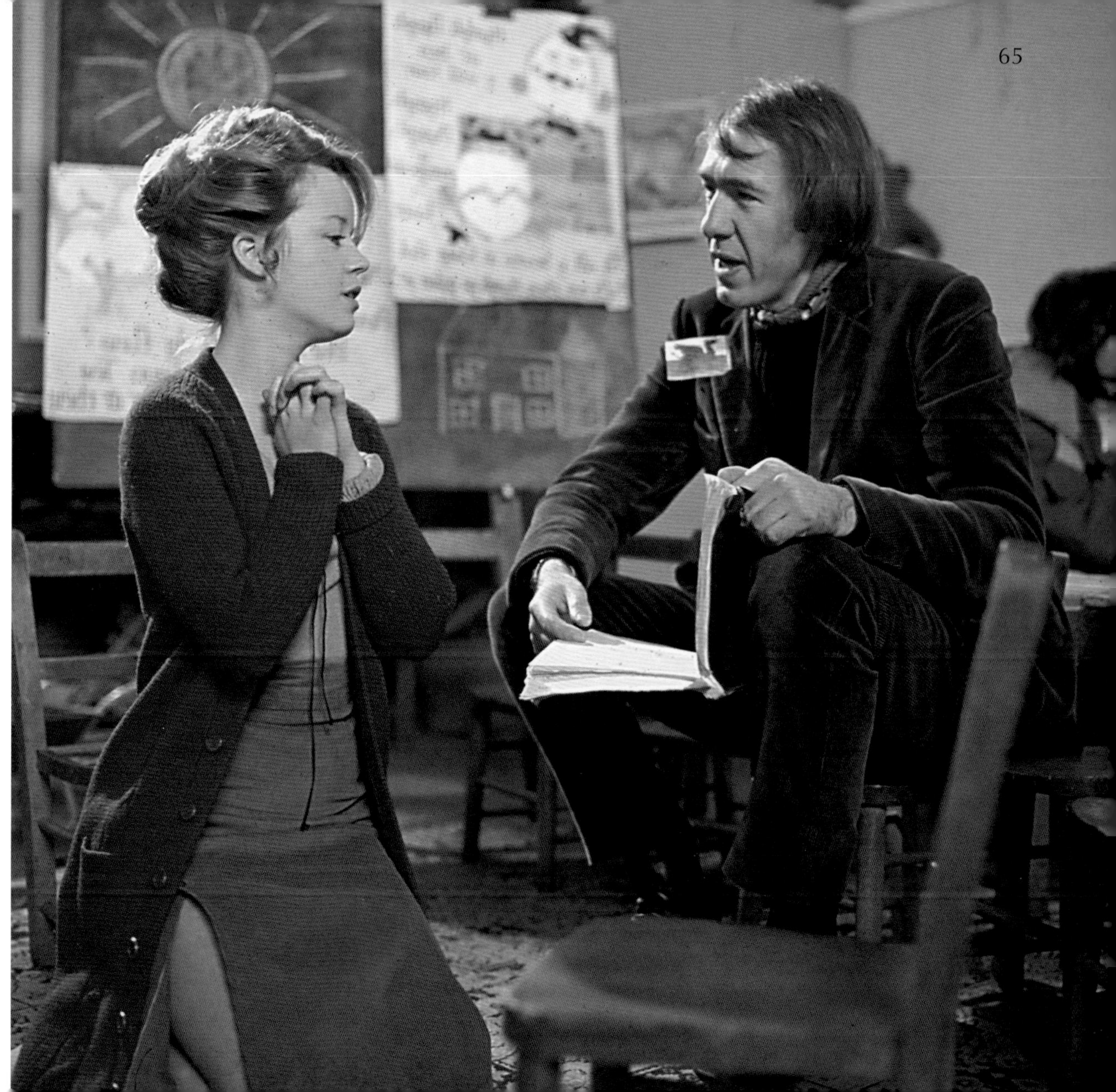

'Glynis Johns came to my door in Soho. She came up the stairs – I'd never seen her before – and said, "May I have a part in your film, Mr Sinclair?" I said, "Any part you like. I've been in love with you since I was eighteen." Once it was being made there wasn't a notable Welsh actor who didn't have to be in it. They'd never made a major Welsh film before. It's that first film. It was *Under Milk Wood*. And it was Dylan Thomas. I did have a marvellous casting director called Miriam Brickman and I did go down to Cardiff. I spent two days casting there. None of these people had been heard of. Many of them became great later, like David Jason who plays Nogood Boyo. It was David's first film.'

– Andrew Sinclair

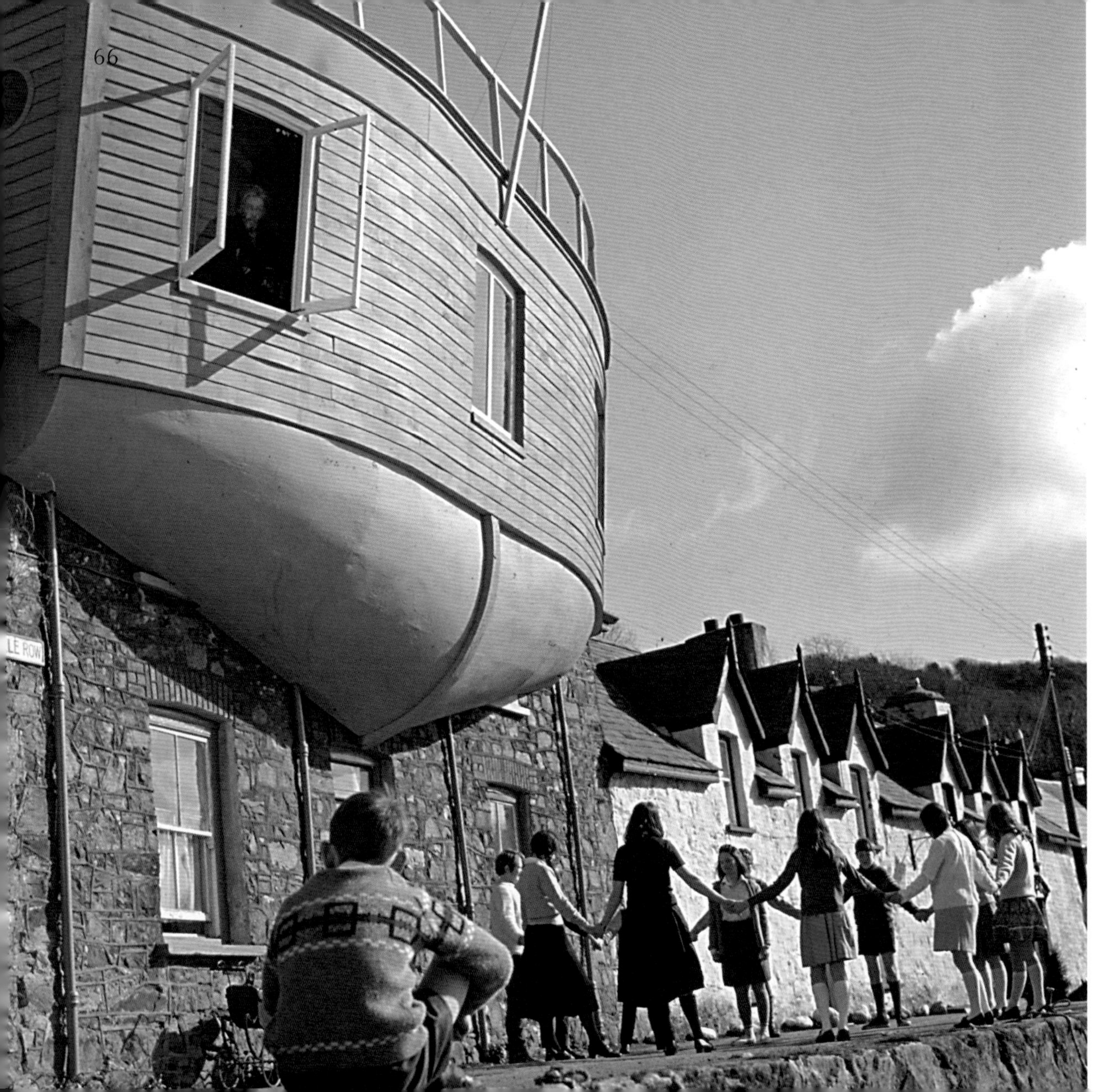

Captain Cat's cottage, Schooner House, was built as a shell that fitted over the exterior of a real home in Lower Fishguard. The children were recruited locally. Many continue to live in the town today. Andrew Sinclair has said, 'The best thing about *Under Milk Wood* was the children. They were local Fishguard children, absolutely marvellous, and all the Welsh are the best actors in all the world.' Sinclair shot extensively in Fishguard and its environs, accurately replicating Llareggub in the spirit and style of Thomas' play. *Under Milk Wood* used houses all along the Quayside as well as The Ship Inn and older buildings along the Musland. The Revd Eli Jenkins' Bethseda was recreated in the harbour village of Solva, using the Baptist chapel at Felin Ganol. Locals became used to seeing Richard Burton's Rolls-Royce and Peter O'Toole's Daimler negotiating the narrow streets. Burton and O'Toole stayed in the Fishguard Bay Hotel in Goodwick. Elizabeth Taylor never came to Wales. Despite Richard Burton being overheard on the telephone exhorting Taylor to come – 'Get your fat arse down to Pembrokeshire!' – all of her scenes were shot in London over two packed days.

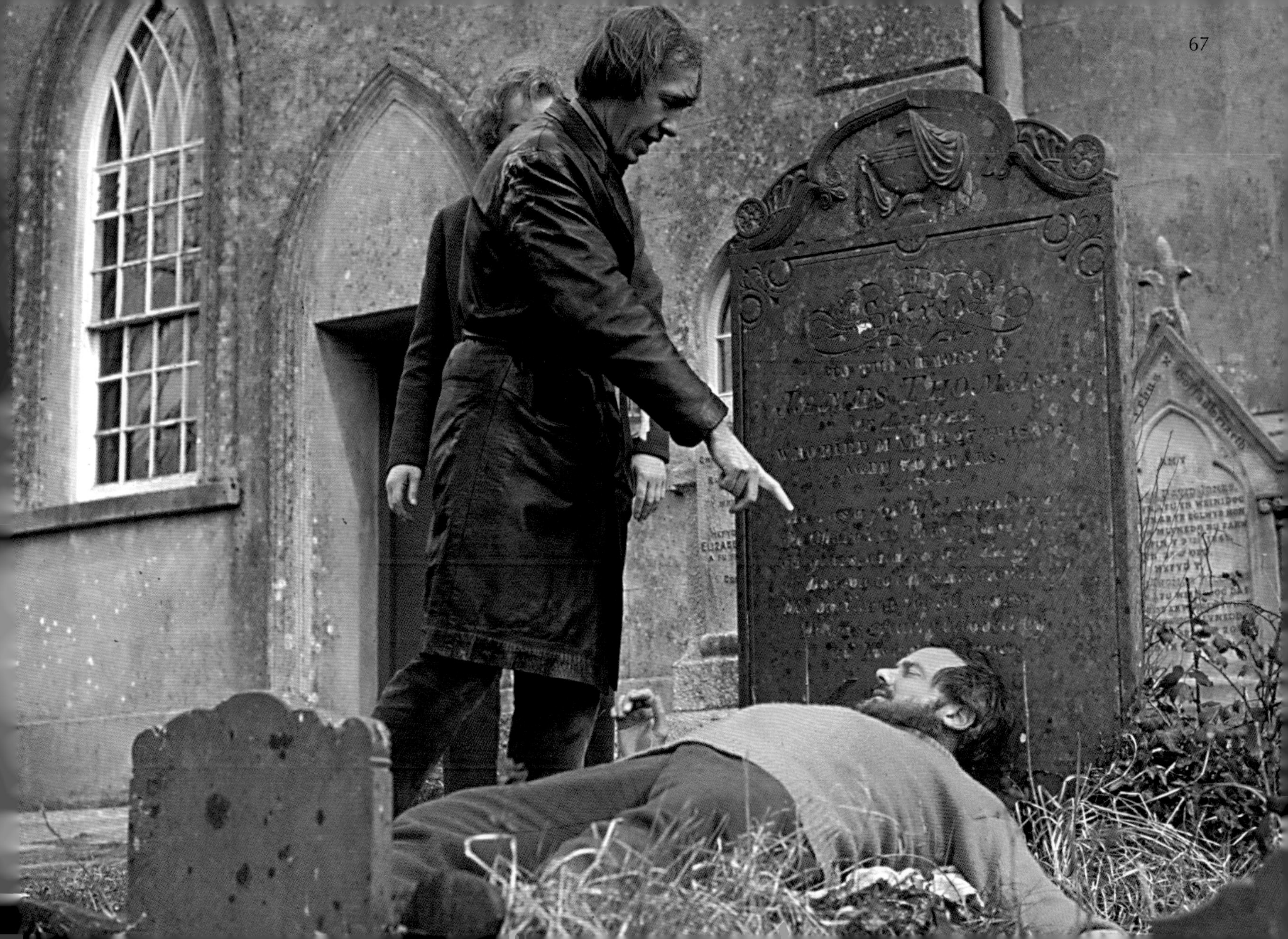

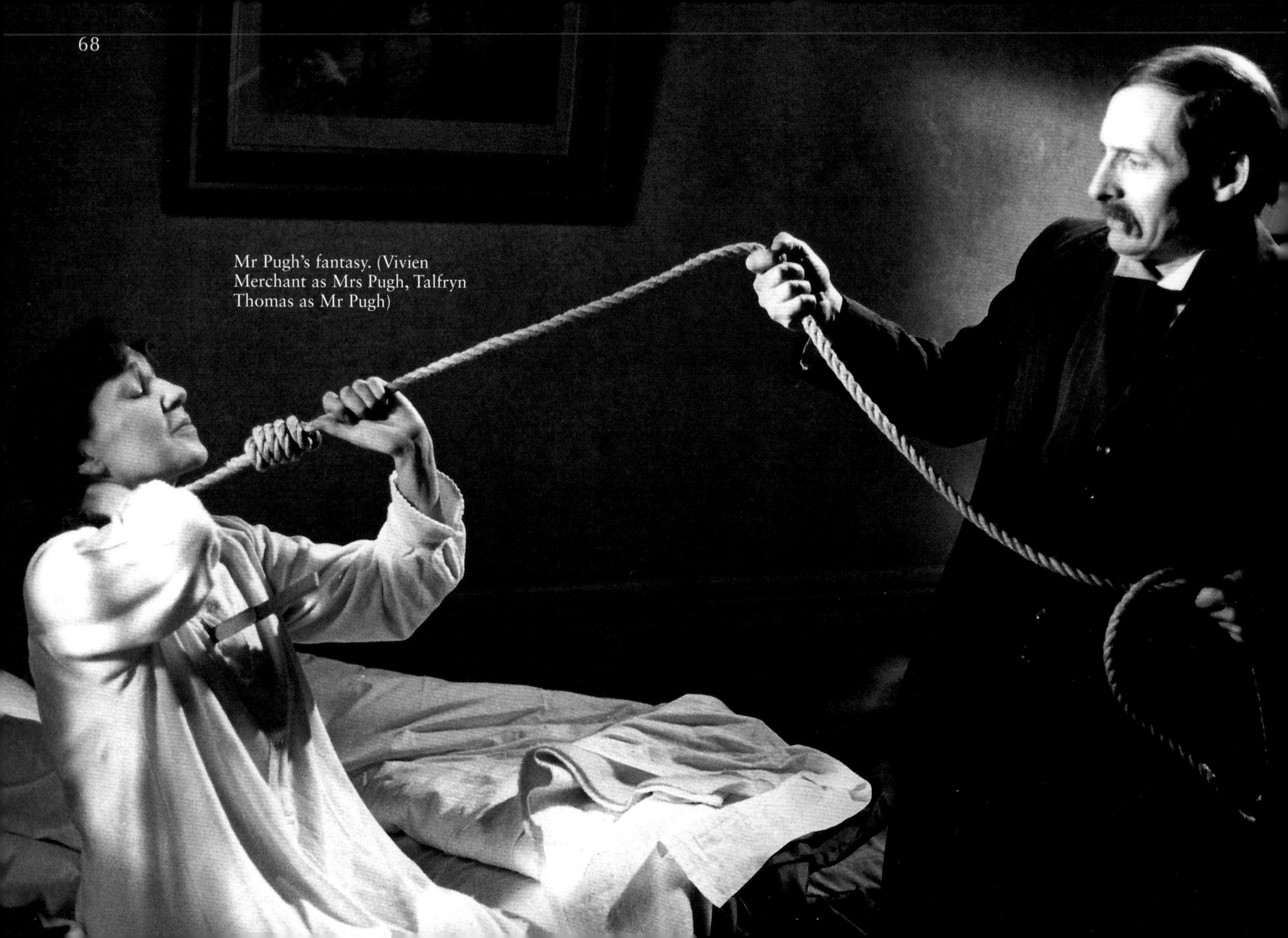

Mr Pugh's fantasy. (Vivien Merchant as Mrs Pugh, Talfryn Thomas as Mr Pugh)

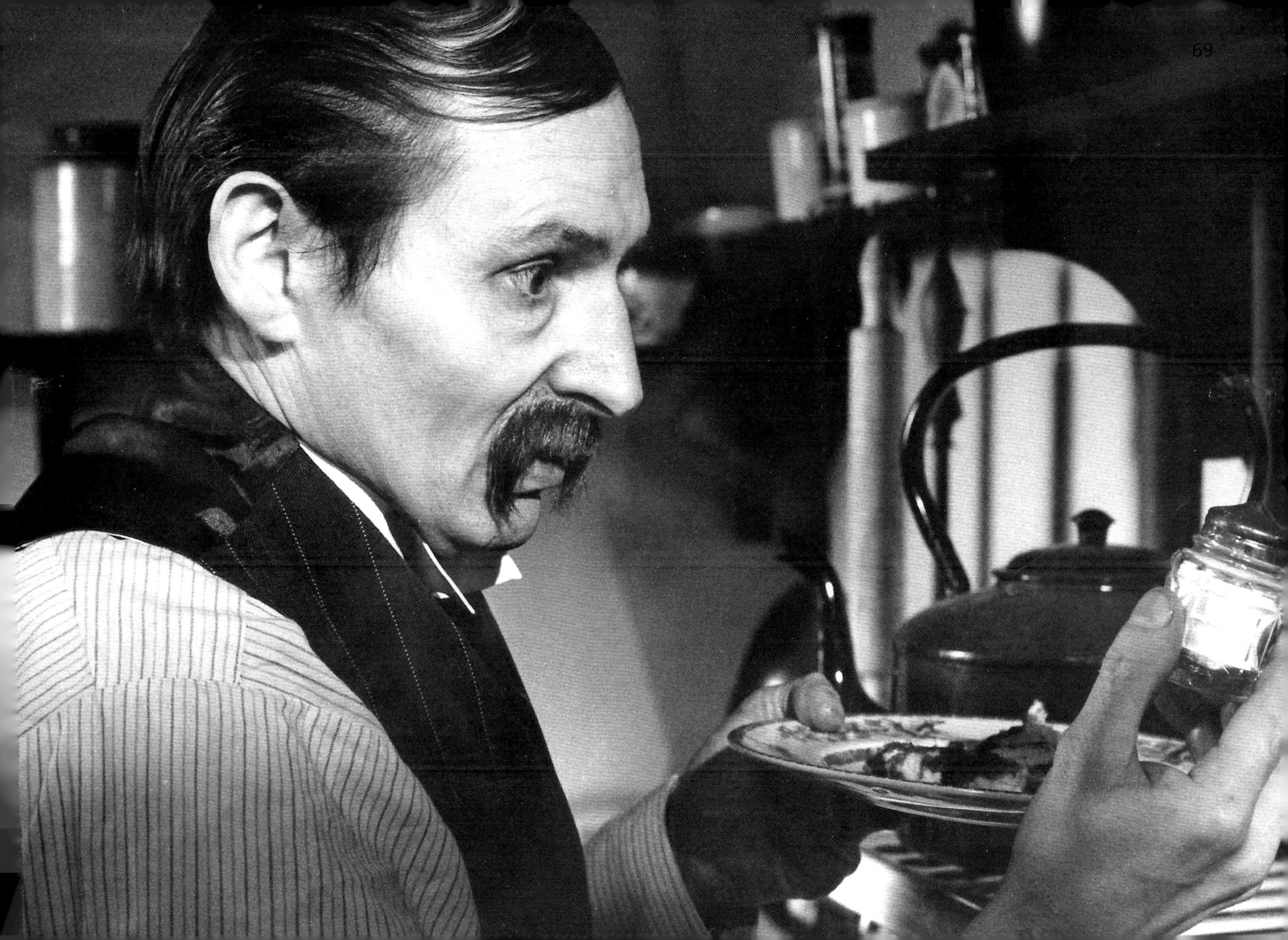

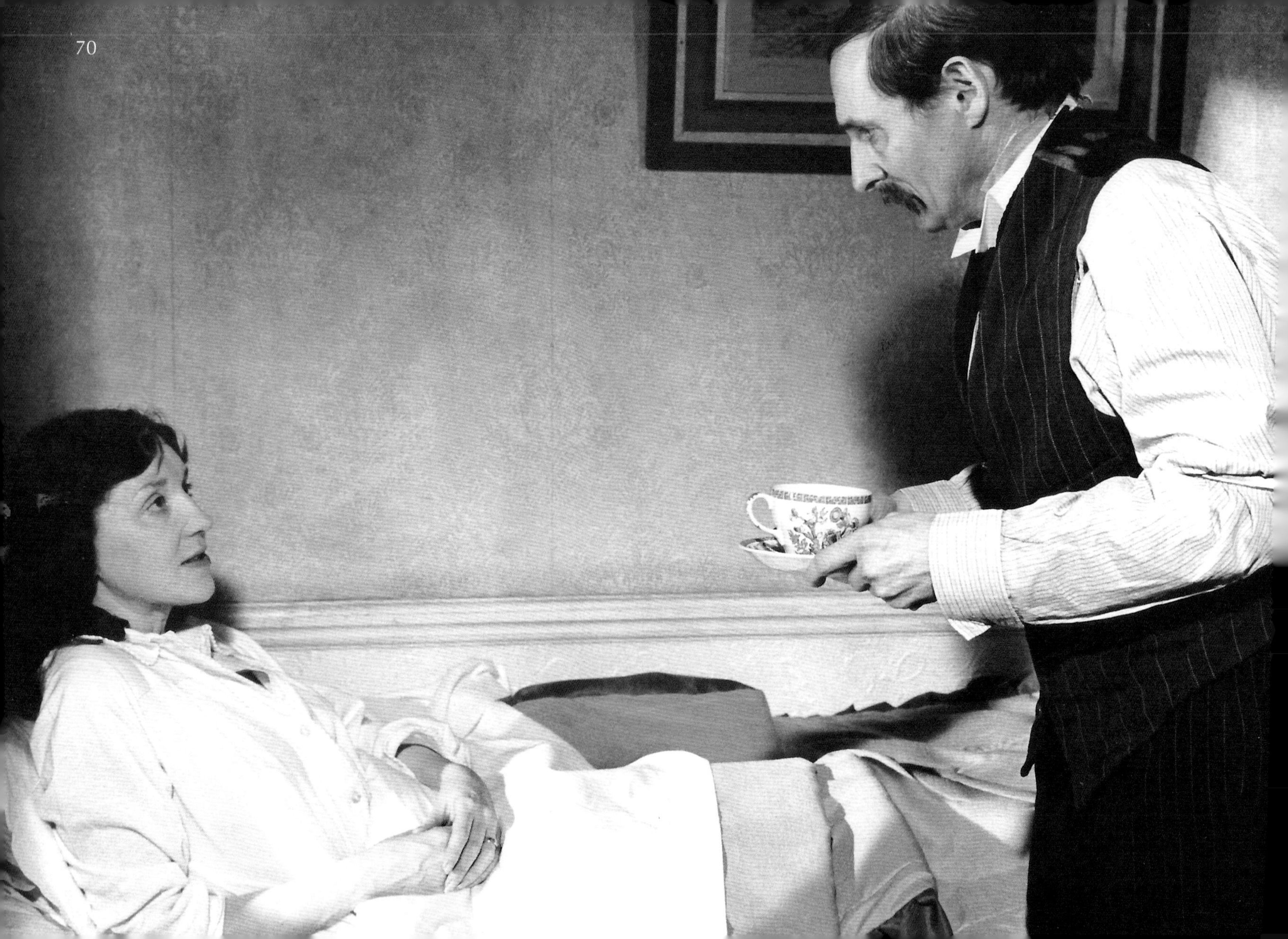

Left:
'Here's your arsenic, dear,
And your weedkiller biscuit.
I've throttled your parakeet.
I've spat in the vases.
I've put cheese in the mouseholes.
Here's your... nice tea, dear.'

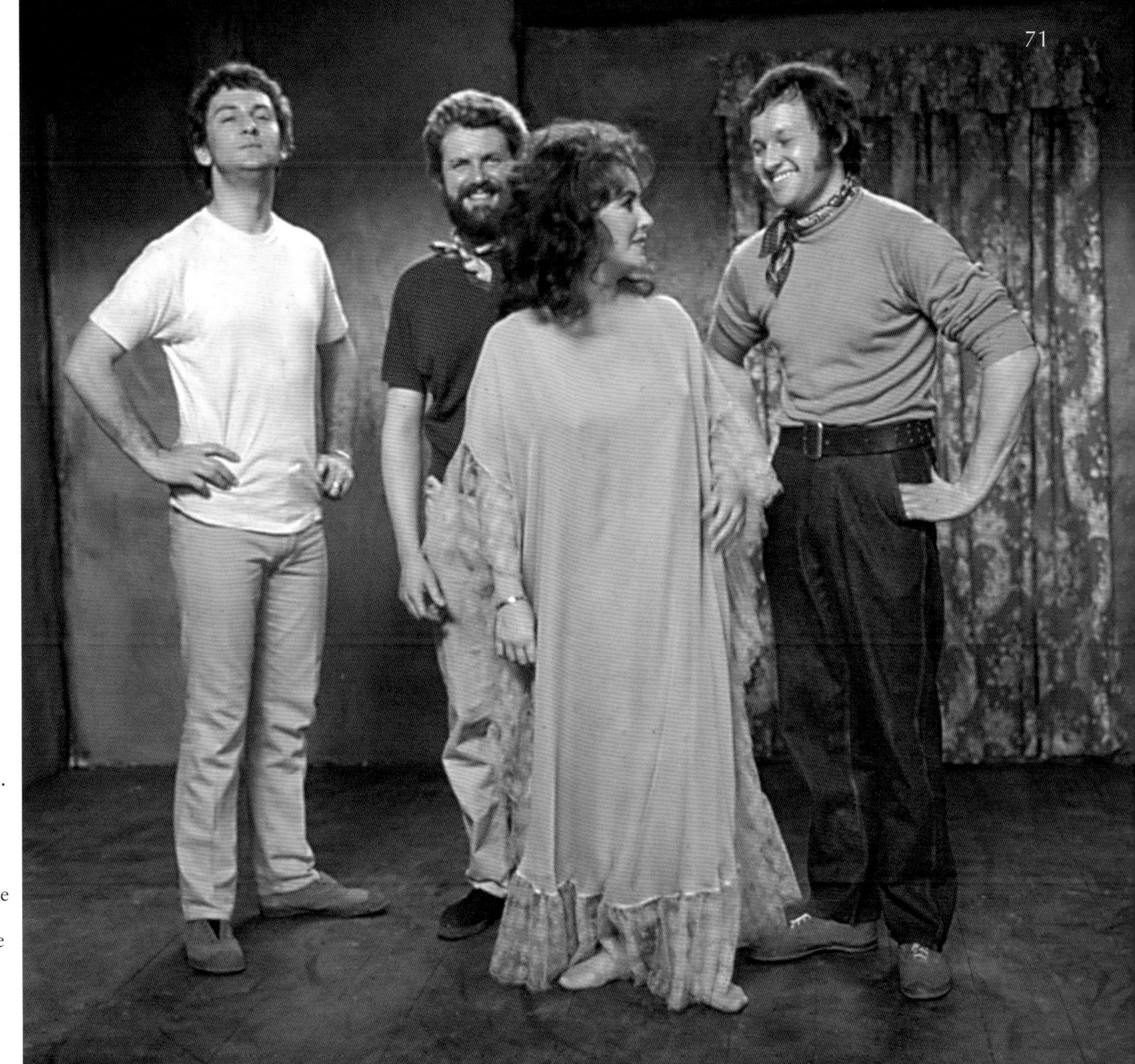

Right: Elizabeth Taylor as Rosie Probert, rehearsing with the drowned dead. She is wearing one of the haute couture nightdresses that cost half of the film's meagre costume budget.

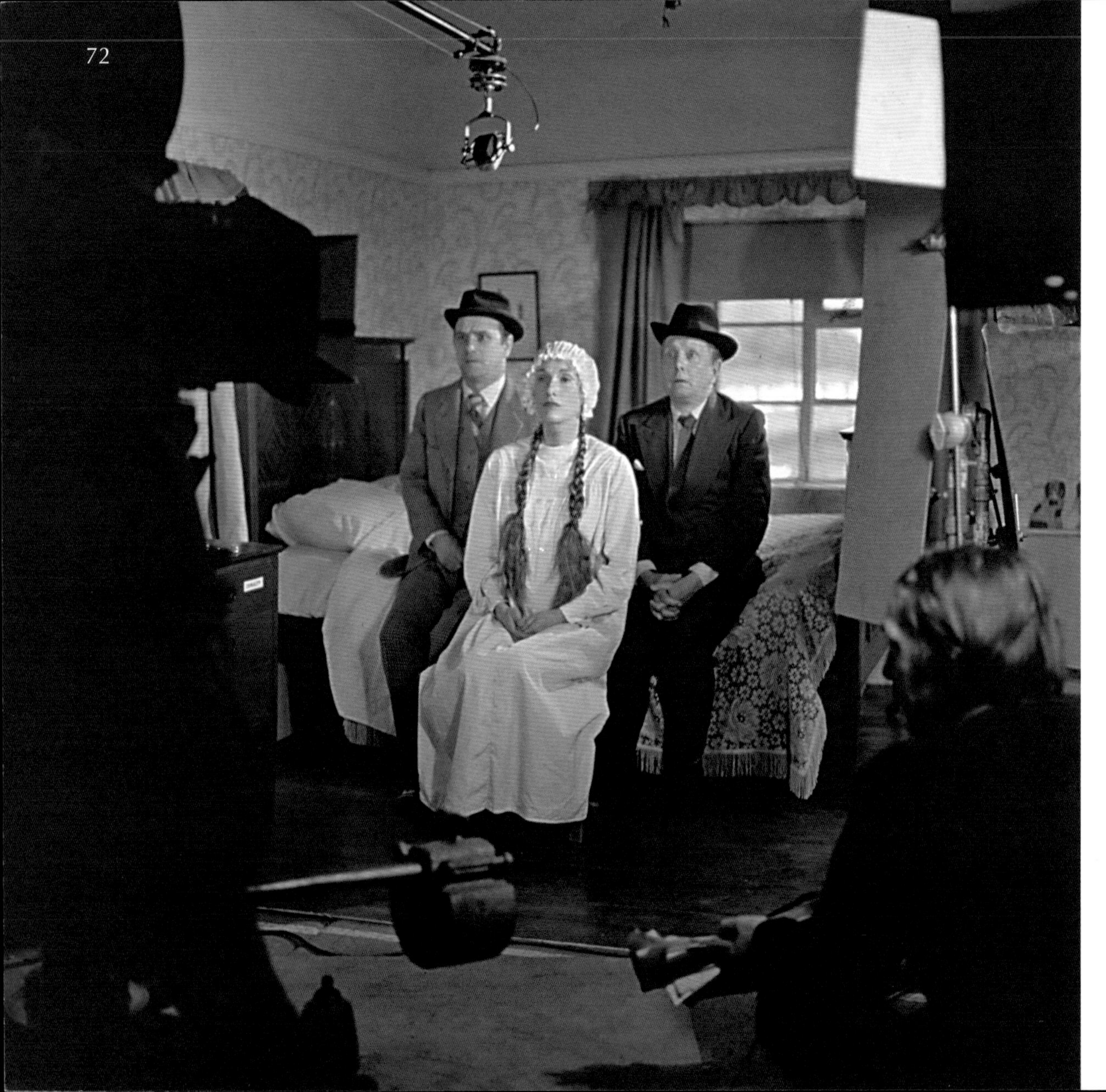

Left: Rehearsing Siân Phillips (as Mrs Ogmore-Pritchard) with Dillwyn Owen (as Mr Ogmore) and Richard Davies (as Mr Pritchard). Phillips, then married to Peter O'Toole, was one of the film's three guest stars. (The others were Glynis Johns and Vivien Merchant). She worked on the film for just one day.

Right: Davydd Havard as Lord Cut Glass. Havard had appeared in Richard Burton's film debut, *The Last Days of Dolwyn*, in 1948 and later joined Stanley Baker in *Zulu*.

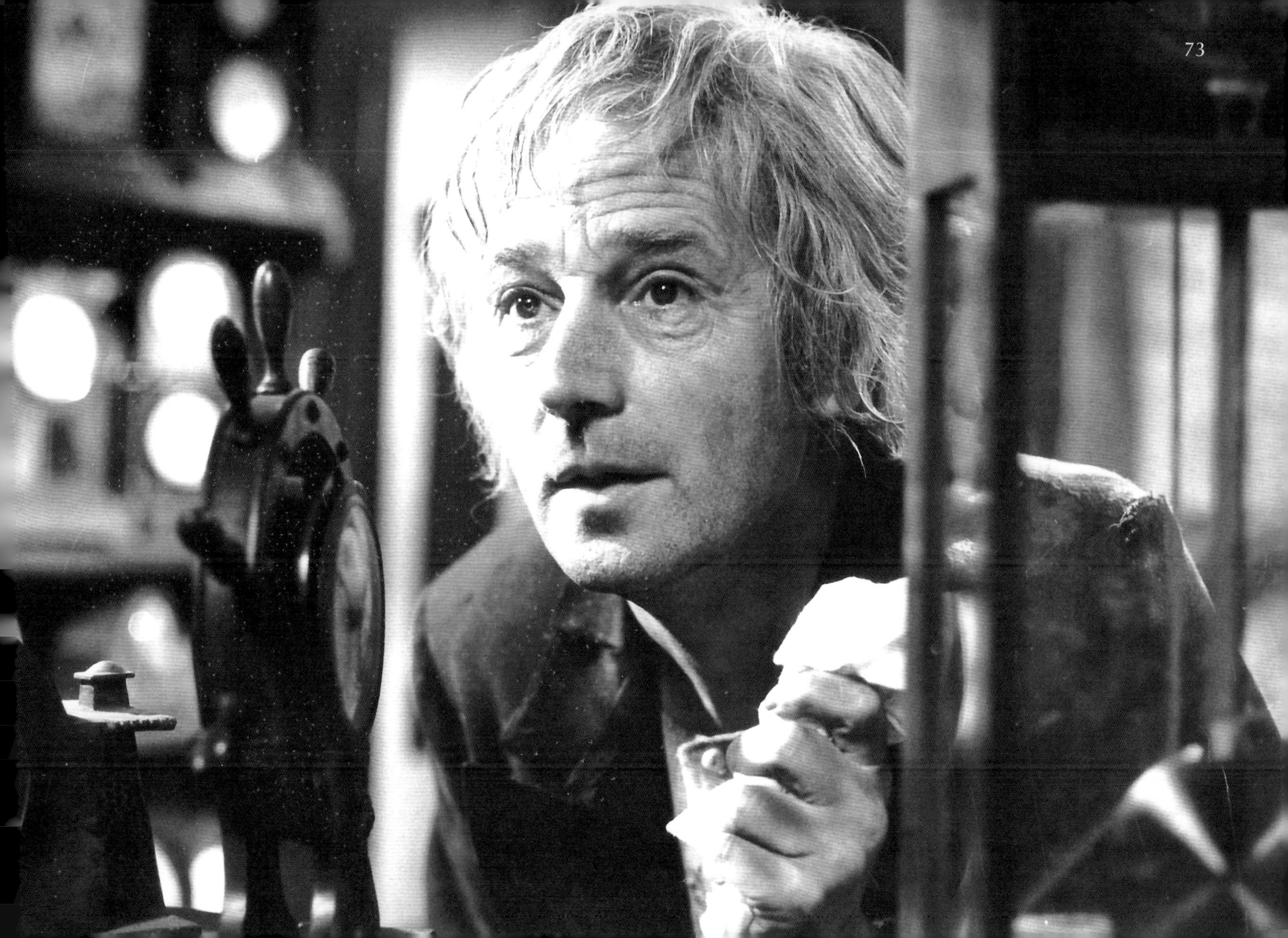

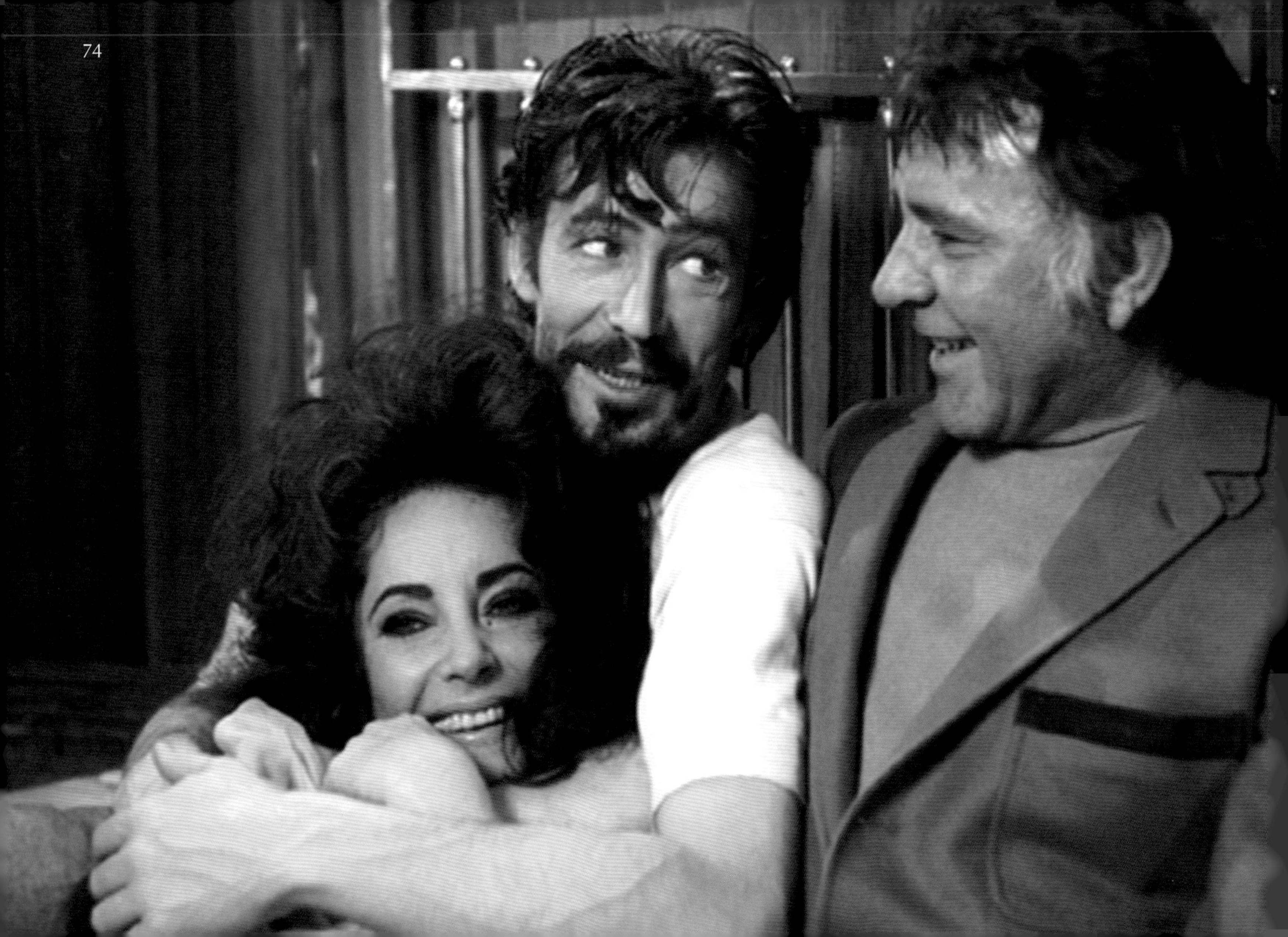

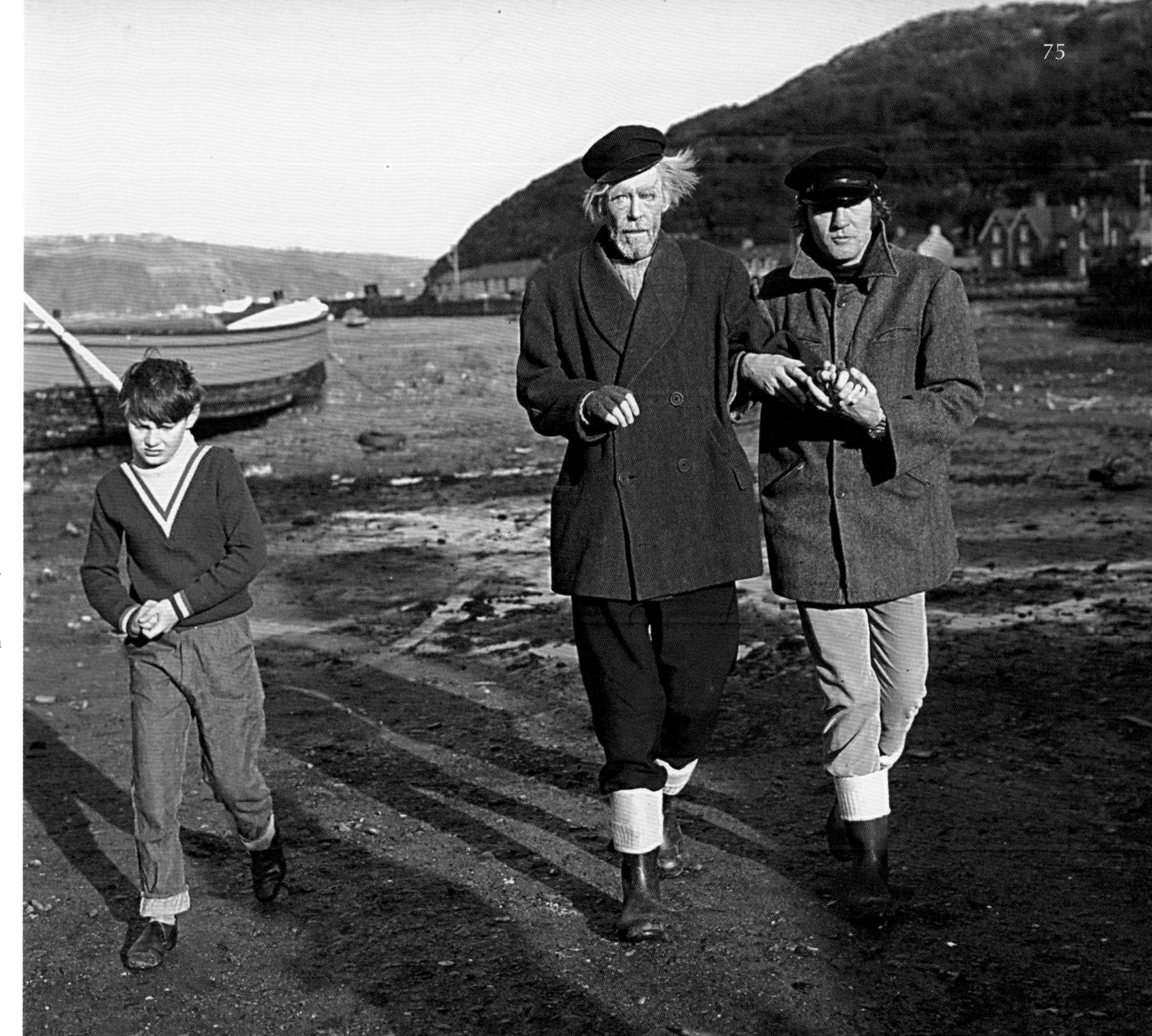

Left: A unique shot of the three stars of *Under Milk Wood* taken at Lee Studios in London. Richard Burton and Peter O'Toole shot their scenes at different times and never worked together on location in Fishguard. All Taylor's scenes were shot in the studio.

Right: Peter O'Toole as the old Captain Cat. Wearing huge contact lenses that covered his eyes made him genuinely blind. Andrew Sinclair was acutely concerned that O'Toole would lose his sight permanently.

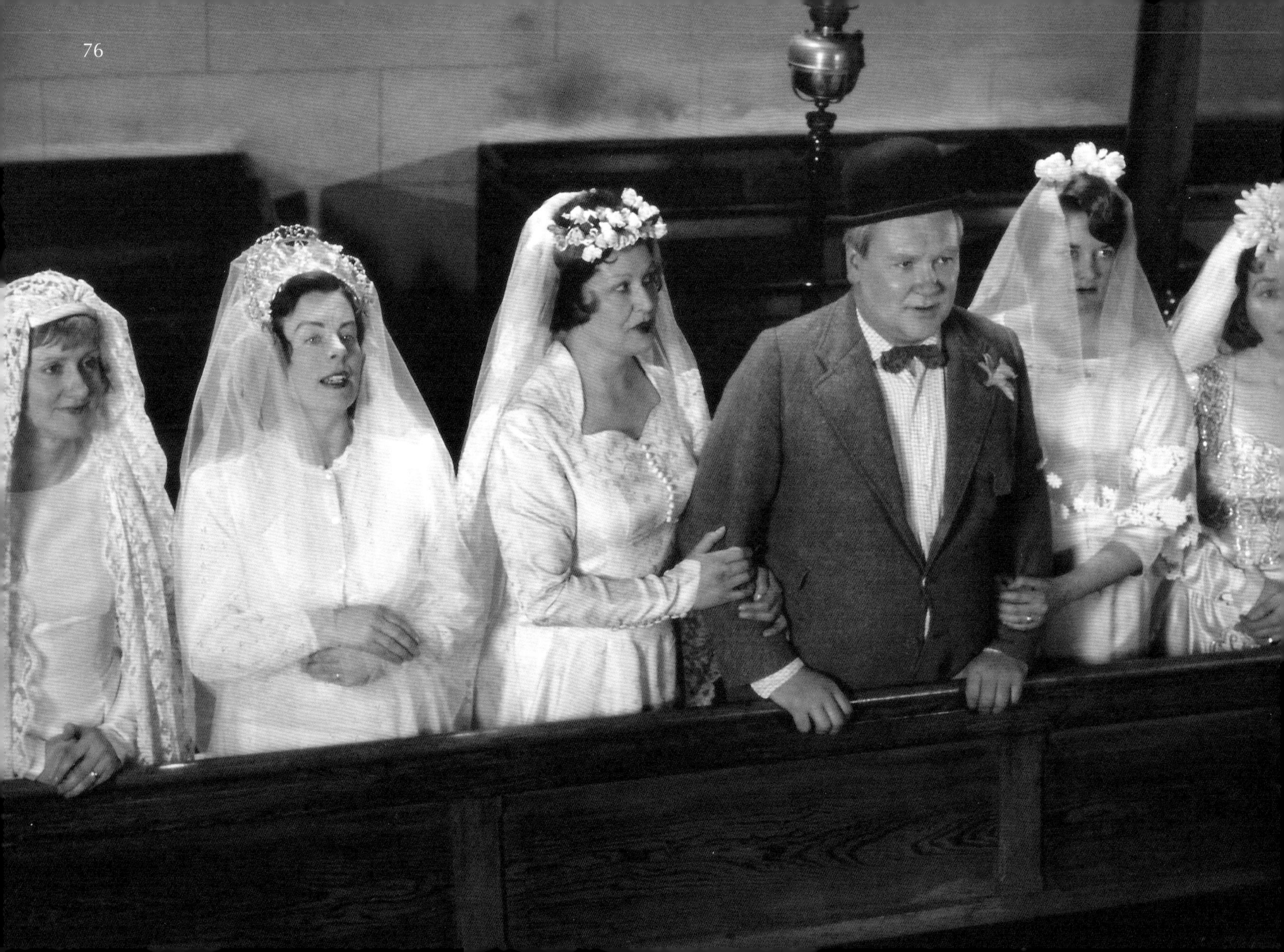

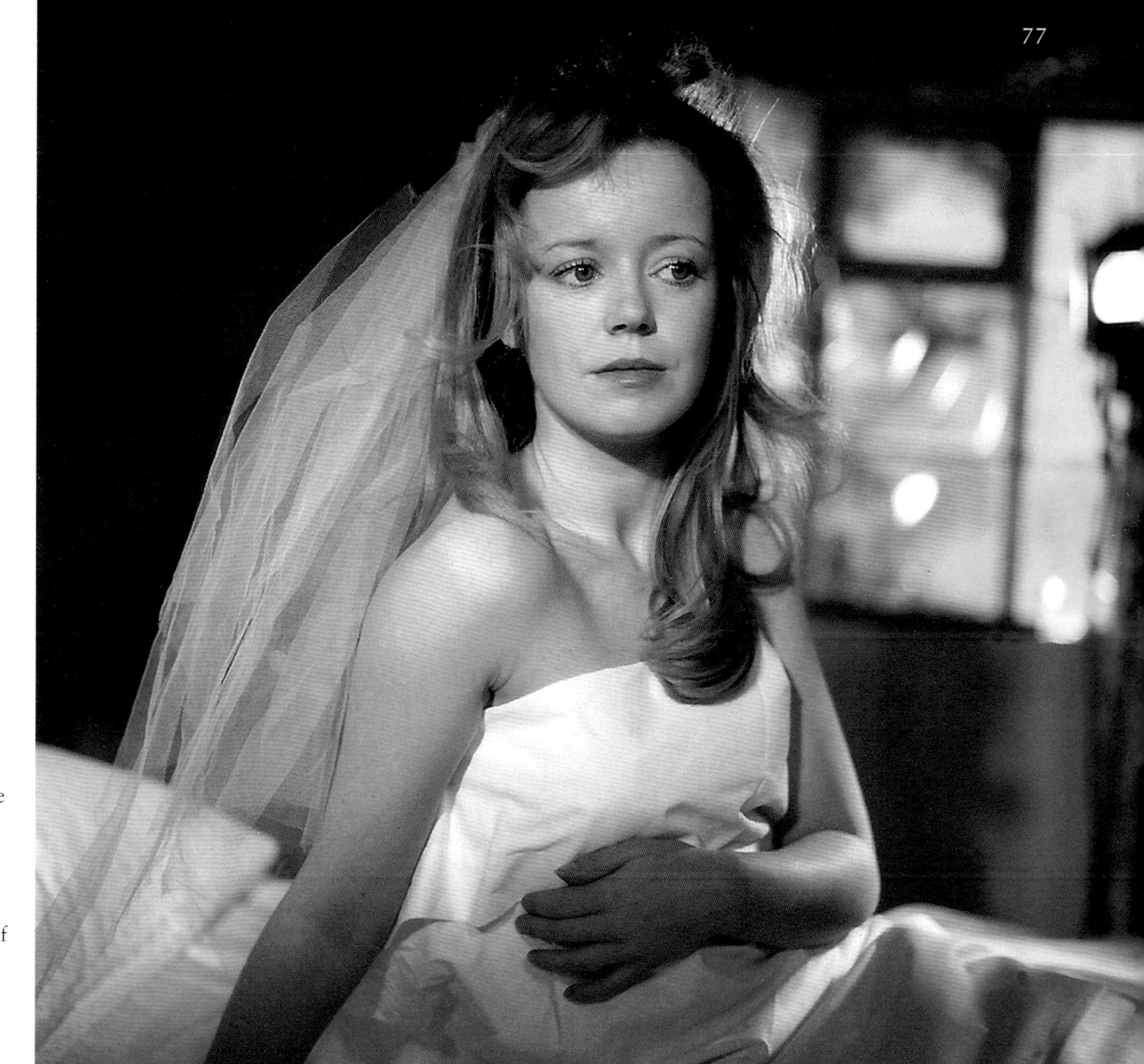

Left: Mr Waldo and brides Andree Gaydon, Eira Griffiths, Margaret Courtenay, Rhoda Lewis and Pamela Miles.

Right: Gossamer Beynon (Angharad Rees), dreaming deep of her wedding.

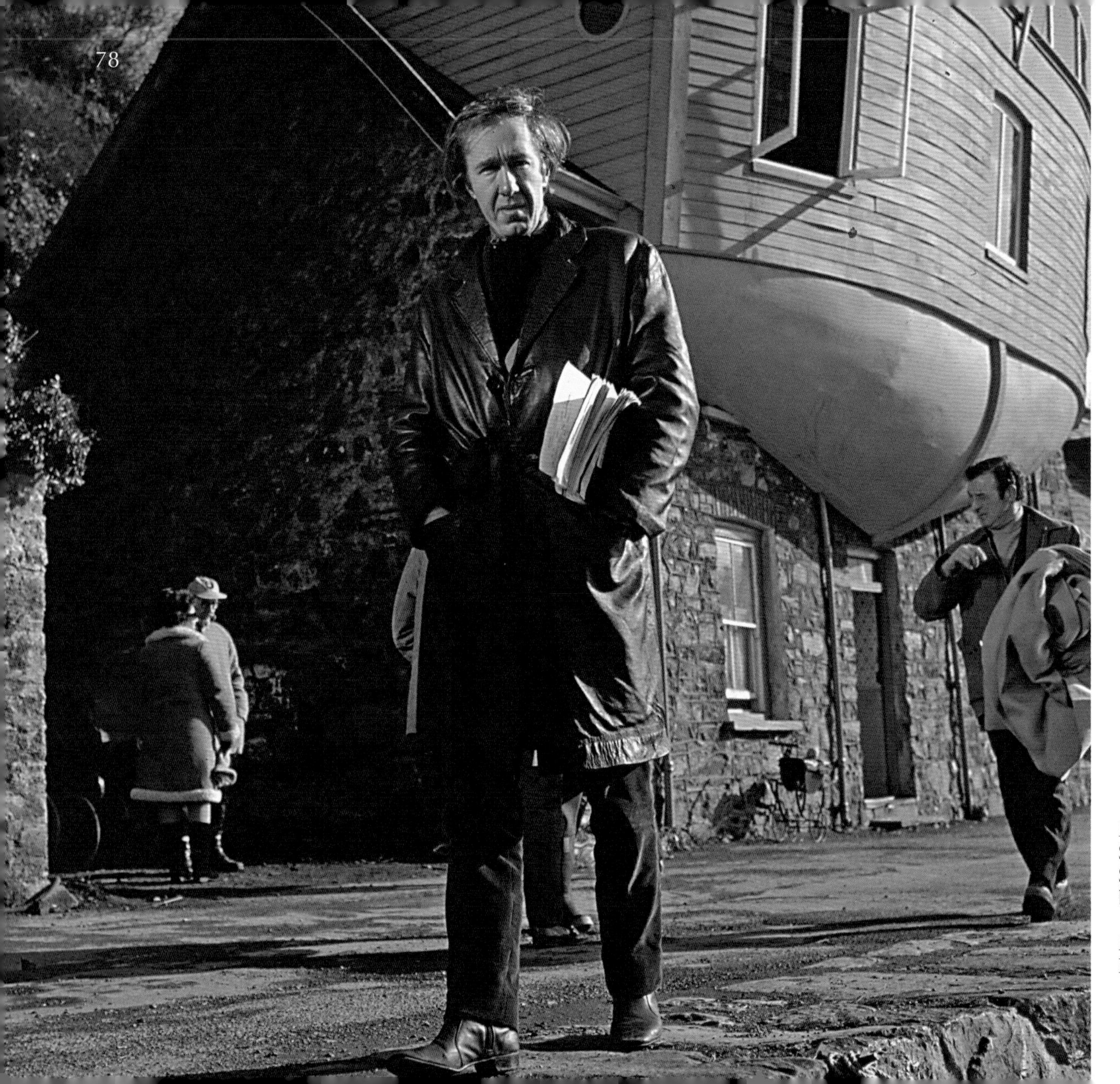

Left: Writer/director Andrew Sinclair on location in Fishguard. Schooner House in the background.

Right: Victor Spinetti as Mog Edwards outside his emporium.

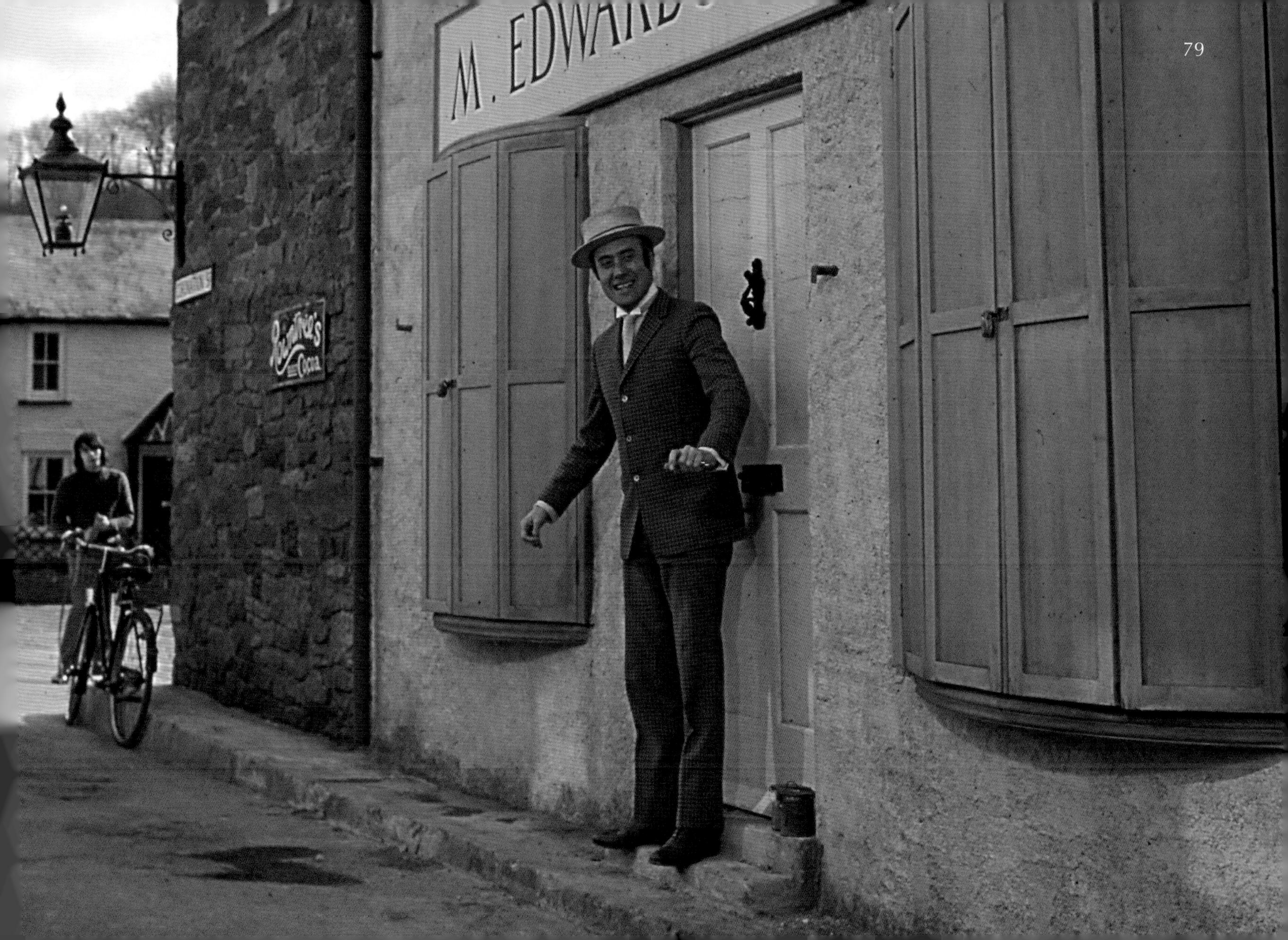
M. EDWARD
Rowntree's
Cocoa

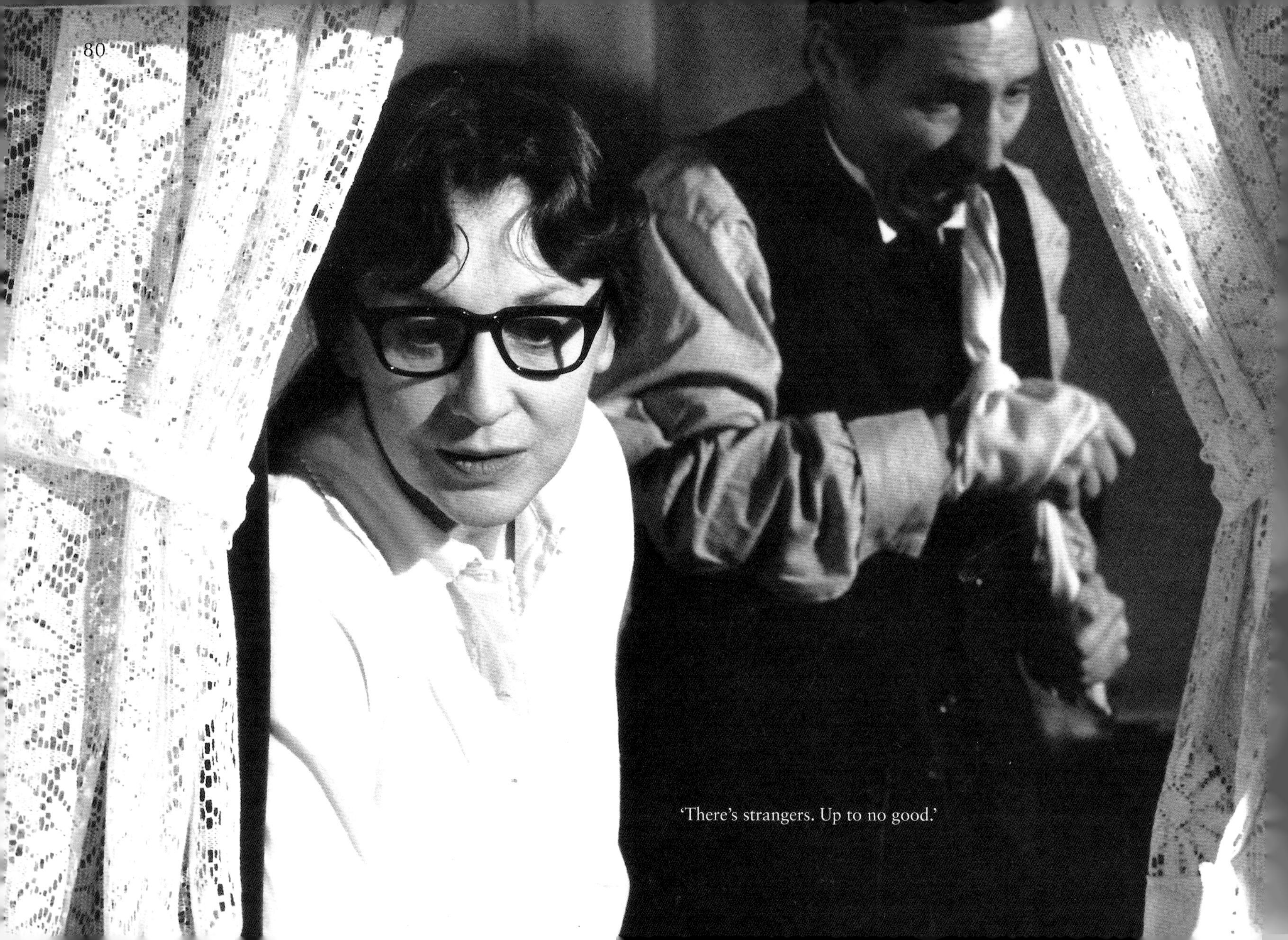

'There's strangers. Up to no good.'

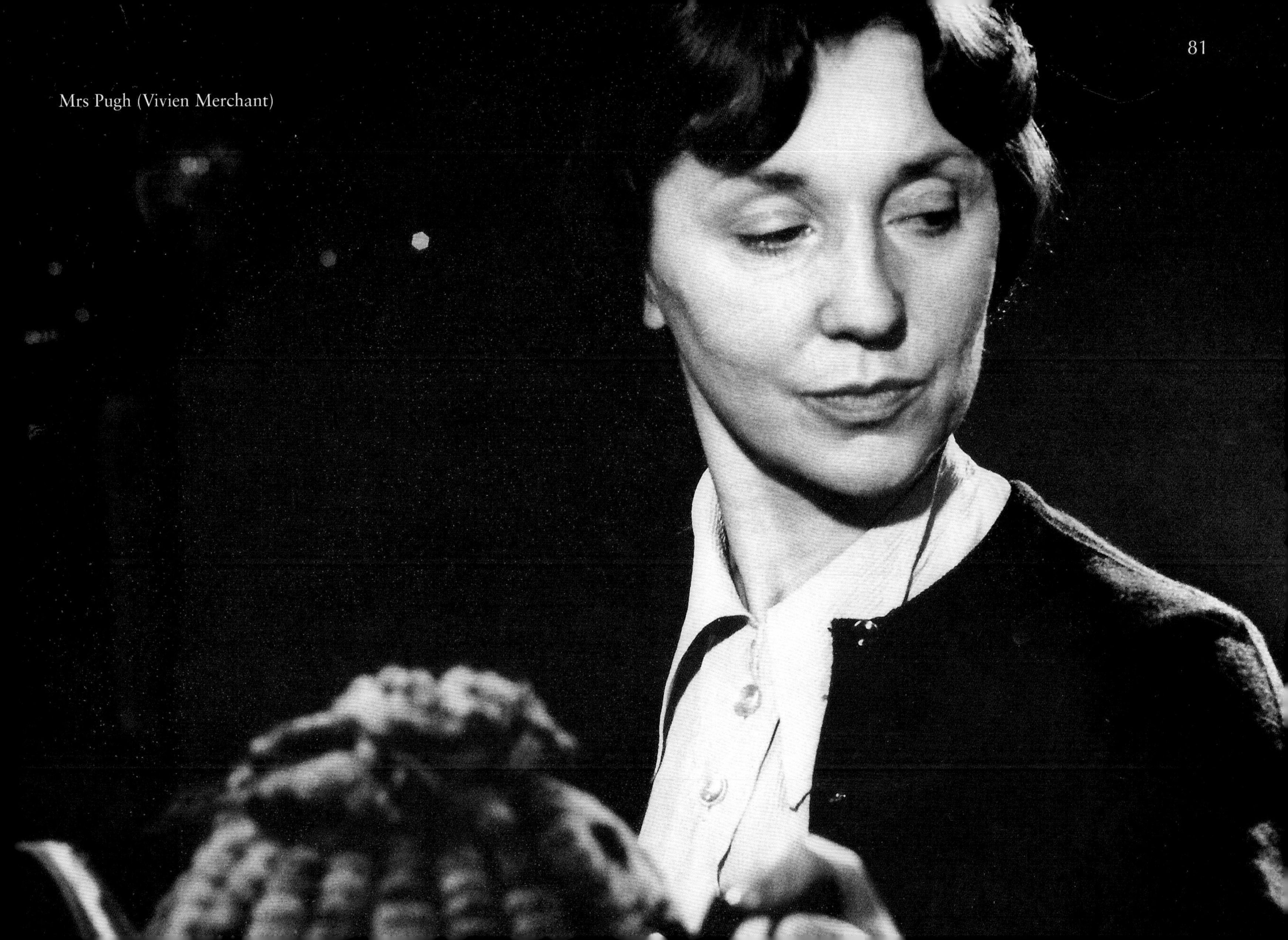

Mrs Pugh (Vivien Merchant)

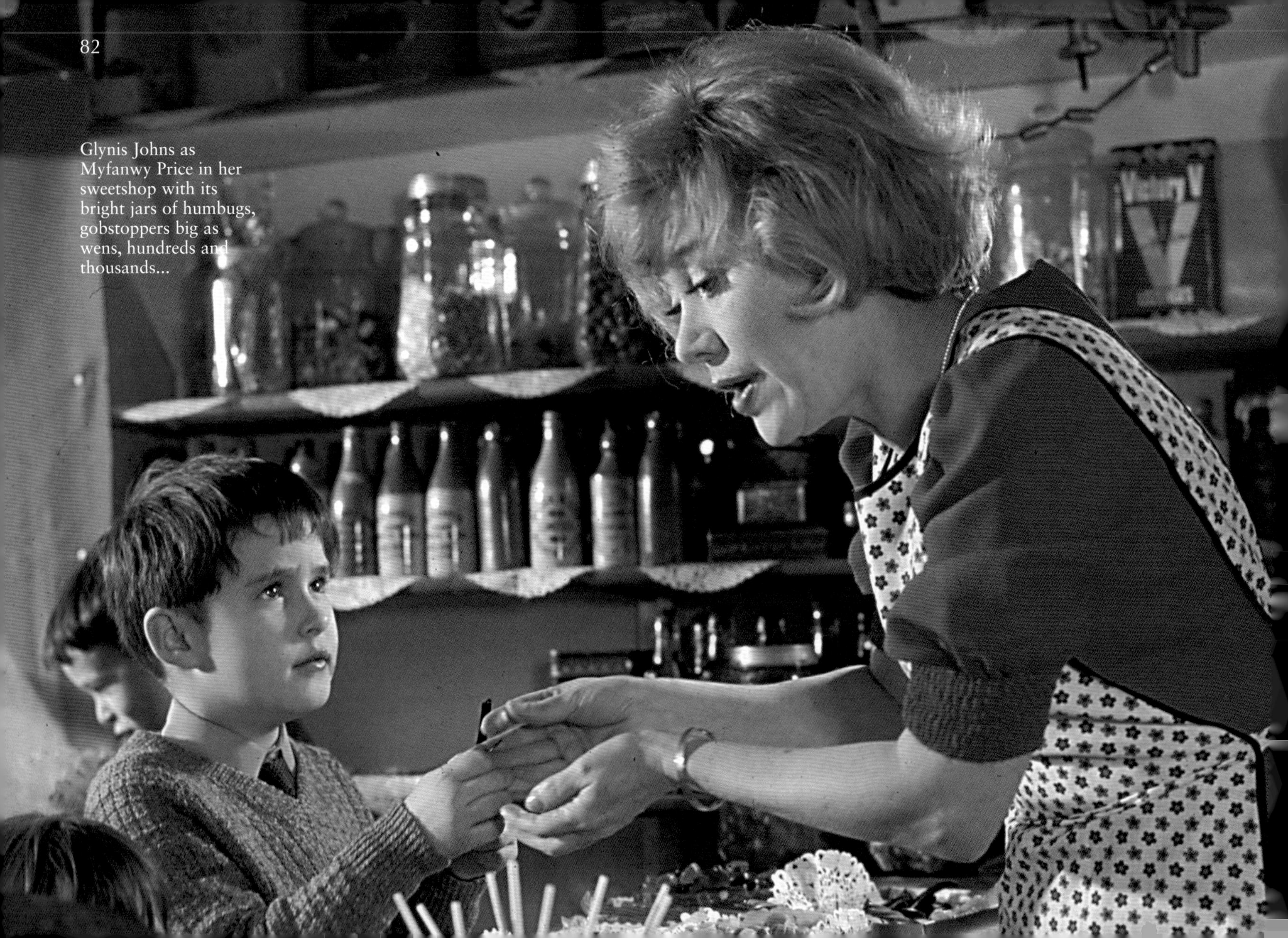

Glynis Johns as Myfanwy Price in her sweetshop with its bright jars of humbugs, gobstoppers big as wens, hundreds and thousands...

End credits.

1st Man RICHARD BURTON
2nd Man RYAN DAVIES
Dai Bread DUDLEY JONES
Dancing Williams SHANE SHELTON
Tom Fred PAUL GRIST
Rosie Probert ELIZABETH TAYLOR
Jonah Jarvis BRYN JONES
Alfred Pomeroy Jones JOHN RAINER
Curly Bevan BRYN WILLIAMS
Myfanwy Price GLYNIS JOHNS
Mog Edwards VICTOR SPINETTI
Jack Black JOHN REES
Evans the Death MARK JONES
Mr. Waldo RAY SMITH

Lower Fishguard and the harbour today.

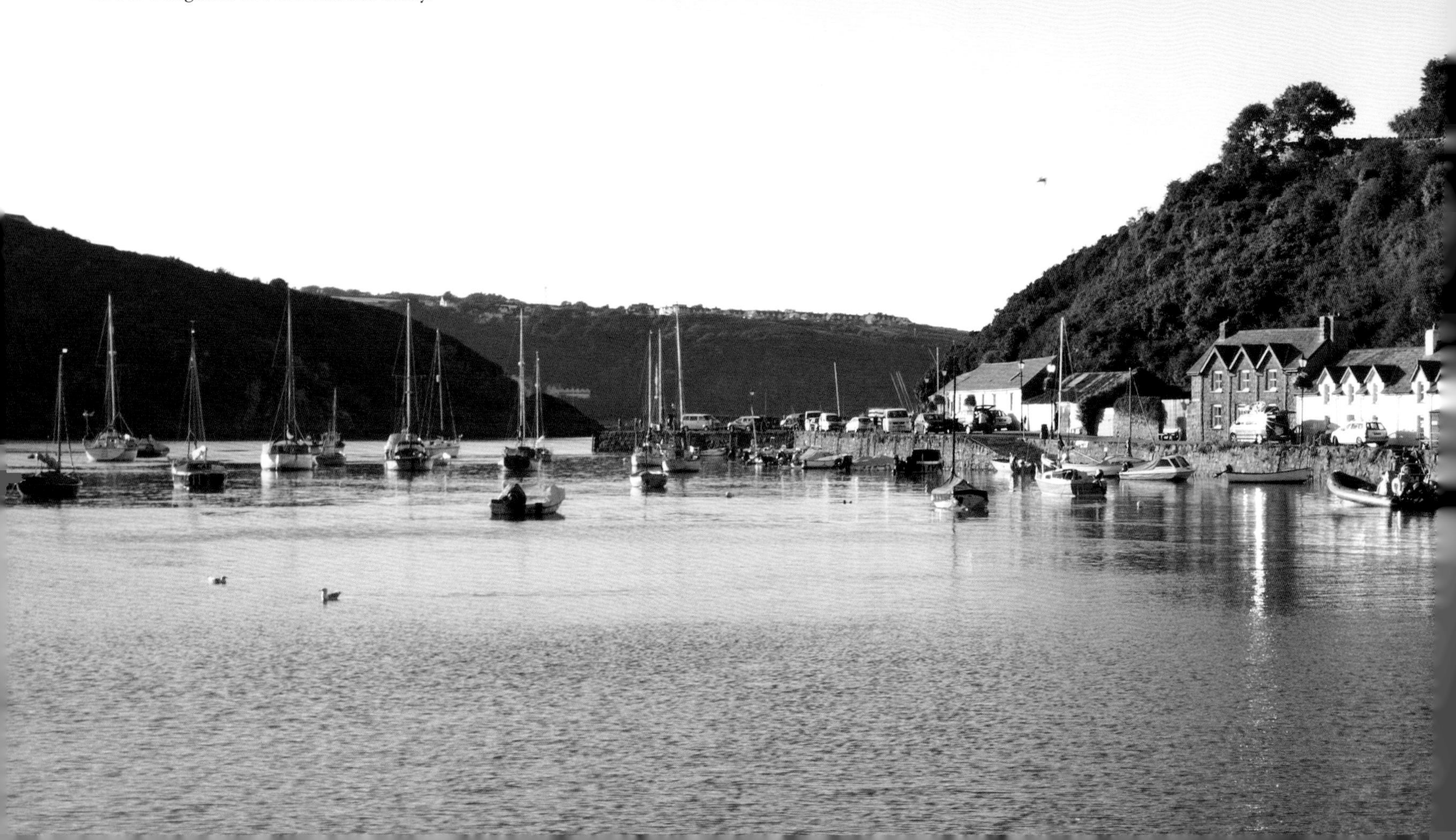

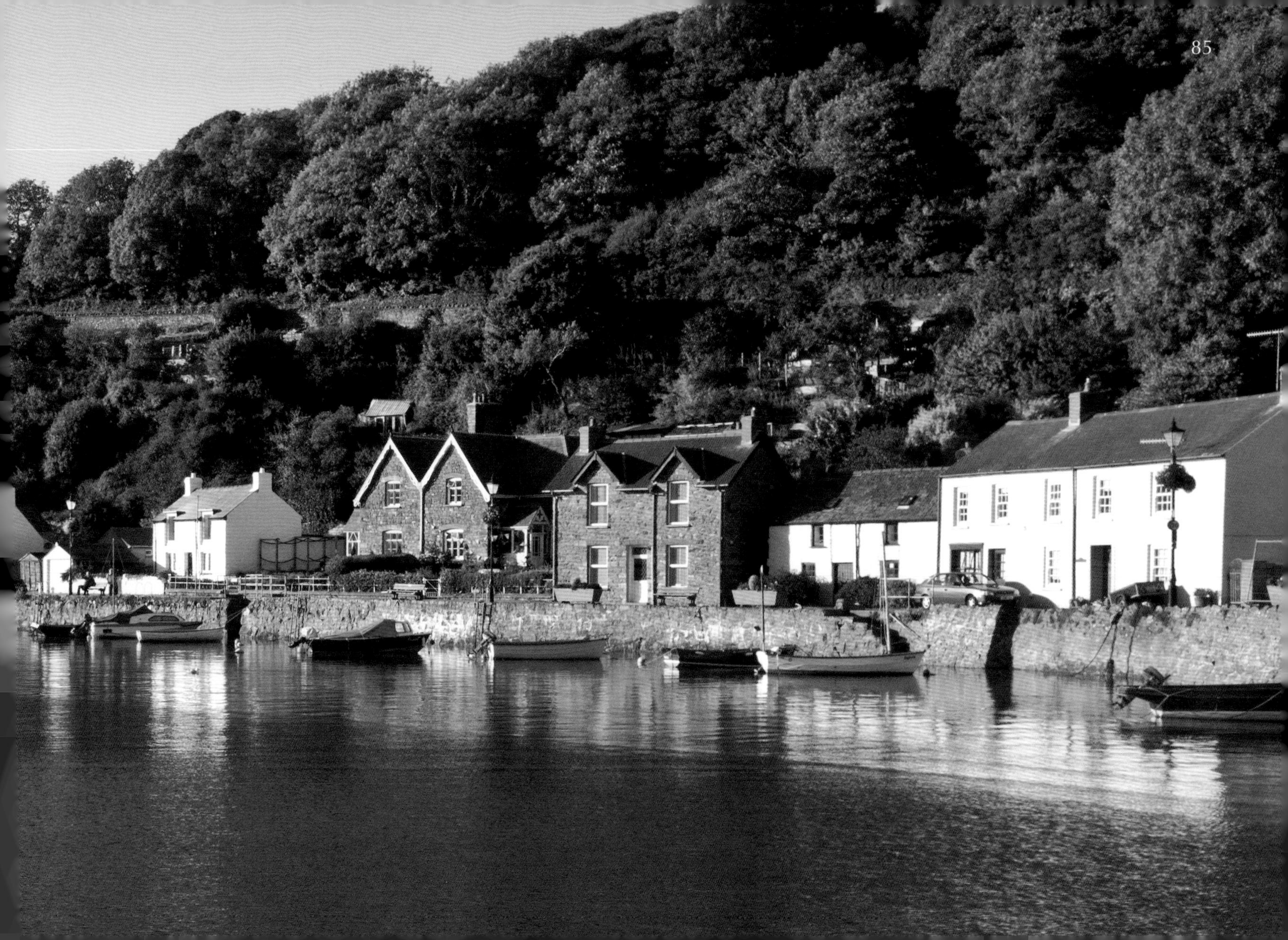

THE WELSH PREMIERE PERFORMANCE OF

'UNDER MILK WOOD' AA

AT THE ODEON CARDIFF

ON SUNDAY 6th FEBRUARY

DOORS OPEN 7.30

COMPLETE PERFORMANCE COMMENCES 8.00 p.m.

SEAT	ROW
12	F

JULES BUCK & HUGH FRENCH
PRESENT
AN ANDREW SINCLAIR FILM

RICHARD BURTON · ELIZABETH TAYLOR
PETER O'TOOLE

in

DYLAN THOMAS'

UNDER MILK WOOD

AA

SCREENPLAY & DIRECTION ANDREW SINCLAIR

GUEST STARS IN ALPHABETICAL ORDER
GLYNIS JOHNS · VIVIEN MERCHANT
SIAN PHILLIPS

EXECUTIVE PRODUCERS
HUGH FRENCH · JULES BUCK

MUSIC COMPOSED BY BRIAN GASCOIGNE · ASSOCIATE PRODUCER JOHN COMFORT

A TIMON FILMS PRODUCTION

COLOUR BY TECHNICOLOR

RELEASED THROUGH
RANK FILM DISTRIBUTORS LTD.

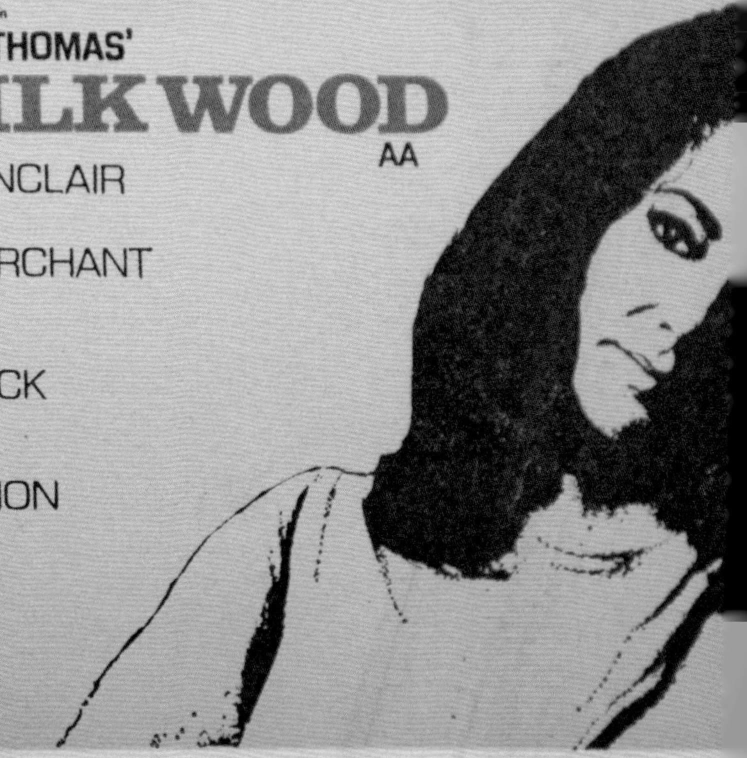

THE PREMIERE PERFORMANCE OF

'UNDER MILK WOOD' AA

AT THE ODEON CARDIFF
ON SUNDAY 6th FEBRUARY
DOORS OPEN 7.30 PERFORMANCE COMMENCES 8.00 p.m.

BLACK TIE
WOULD YOU PLEASE REGARD

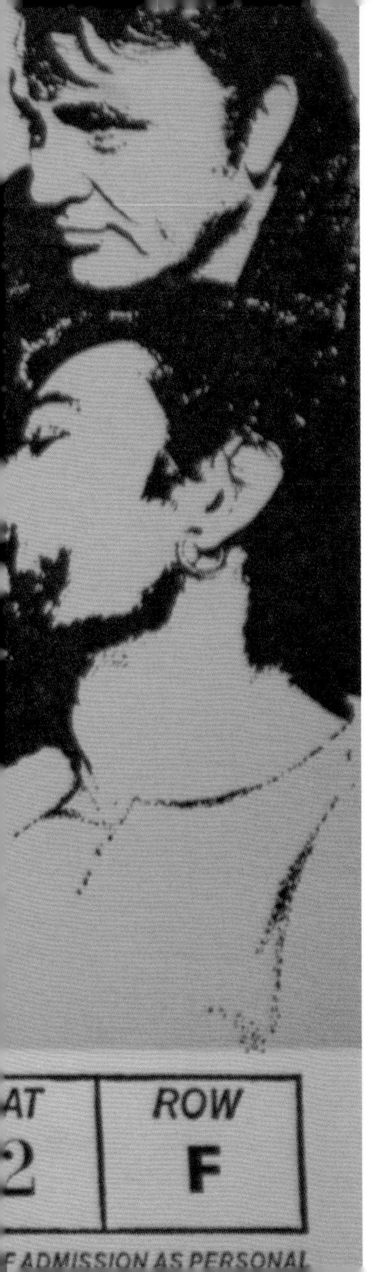

Under Milk Wood was selected in 1971 to open the Venice Film Festival. In a crusade against elitism no Golden Lion was awarded that year. The president of the Festival, Réné Clair, told Andrew Sinclair 'I wish I had made your film.' 'M'sieu,' replied Sinclair, 'I could not have made it without watching all your films.' The UK premiere took place at the Odeon, Cardiff, on Sunday 6 February 1972. Over the years the film, which is notable for being the only picture to combine the stellar talents of Burton, Taylor and O'Toole, has acquired a reputation among aficionados as a cult movie. This is what the critics said:

> 'The film, beautifully photographed and spoken, casts the brooding spell of Thomas' verse in its reconstruction of the sea-wide village and the daily round of its inhabitants.'
>
> – *The Intl Herald-Tribune*

> '*Under Milk Wood* got a great popular ovation. It soaks in beauty from its Fishguard landscape. Its verse is spoken with the freshness that the cast might get from their first drink of the day.'
>
> – Alexander Walker, *Evening Standard*

Dead, Dead, Dead

Last Days in Laugharne

'From where you are, you can hear their dreams.'
– First Voice, *Under Milk Wood*

Laugharne had been a part of Dylan's life since 1936, when he met Caitlin Macnamara and the artist Augustus John at the Castle, the Georgian house of author Richard Hughes, which bordered the ruins of the old fortifications at Laugharne. They met again in the summer of 1937 in Cornwall, married in Penzance, lived off the generosity of friends and neighbours and finally moved to Laugharne following a book deal that temporarily cured his penury.

Laugharne was Dylan's haven. Whether he lived in Sea View or, for the last four years of his tragically truncated life, at the Boathouse, it was his bolthole – a coastal oasis of family and thoughtful industry overlooking the Taf estuary and its deadly sands.

He moved there courtesy of the largesse of Margaret Taylor, a benefactor and patroness who first bought the Thomases a cottage in South Leigh, Oxfordshire. Later she sold it and bought the Boathouse – 'a sea-shaken house on a breakneck of rocks' – with a separate outbuilding for Dylan to work in. It has been variously described as a shack, a tool-shed study and a writing shed.

The roots of what was to become *Under Milk Wood* lay in Laugharne. As early as 1935, following a trip to Laugharne, he wrote a story called *The Orchards* in which he mentioned the Black Book of Llareggub. Later Richard Hughes recalled in a BBC broadcast that Dylan had spoken of composing a play about well-known Laugharne characters.

During the war Dylan wrote *Quite Early One Morning*, which included tales of a town not quite awake and a narrator who 'walked through the streets like a stranger come out of the sea'. The concept evolved into something he called *The Village of the Mad* in which the community of Llareggub was put on trial for insanity. Later it evolved further into 'an impression for voices, an entertainment out of the darkness of the town I live in'.

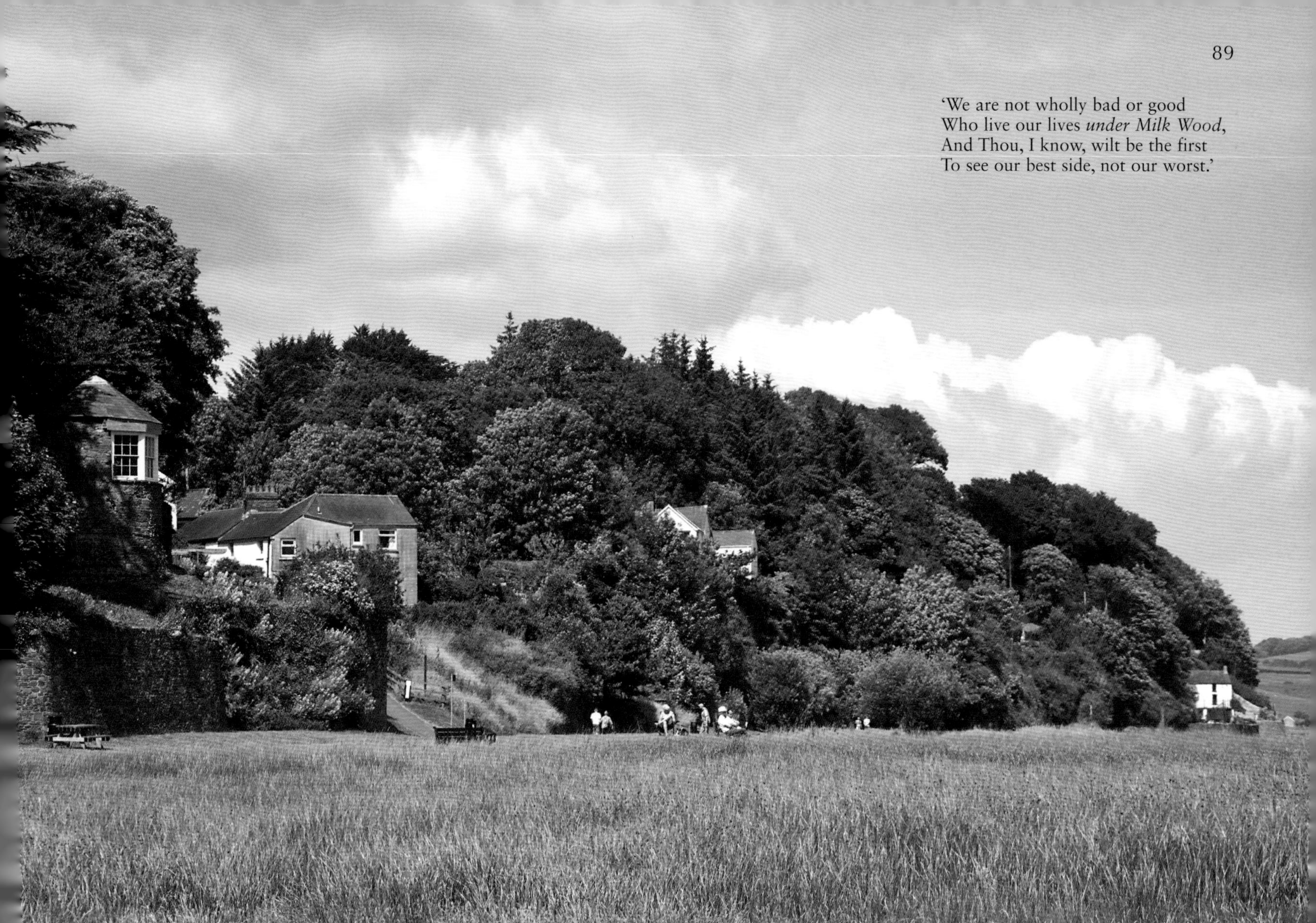

'We are not wholly bad or good
Who live our lives *under Milk Wood*,
And Thou, I know, wilt be the first
To see our best side, not our worst.'

In 1952, he produced *Llareggub, a Piece for Radio Perhaps*, an unfinished script that appeared in Countess Caetani's *Botteghe Obscure*. Dylan claimed he had not the finances to complete it. To make money he must venture out. To London. To America.

In the midst of his American trips he appeared to tarry with the notion of his own death. He drank with fury – 'bottle-scarred', Andrew Sinclair called him. In Brown's Hotel, the hostelry that for years afterwards carried a photograph of Dylan and Caitlin on its wall, he suffered a blackout and collapsed at the bar. He was unconscious for two minutes.

In America he found himself trapped on an exhausting treadmill of poetry readings, hovering between exhilaration and collapse. What was to become *Under Milk Wood* was still unfinished. Dylan lamented that he 'made money, and it went'. He returned to Laugharne with none.

Penniless, he was back in America in April 1953. Six weeks, fifteen readings and an opportunity to complete, fine tune and perform his 'looney maybe-play', which was now called *Under Milk Wood*. He engaged five actors who, with himself, played fifty-five parts. 'Love the words,' he implored them.

Under Milk Wood premiered on 14 May at Kaufmann Auditorium, but it was a close-run thing. Dylan was still revising it an hour before curtain. At its conclusion the cast accepted fifteen curtain calls. Then it was back home to Wales, to Laugharne, to Caitlin and the children.

He made his fourth trip to America in October, arriving in New York on the 19th. He was subdued, ill in body and spirit, said one observer, and he was drinking with abandon. On 4 November he binged on booze at the White Horse Tavern in Greenwich Village, later claiming, 'I've had eighteen straight whiskies. I think that's the record!' He was sick throughout the day of 4 November and, when he slipped into a coma, he was rushed to hospital. He never awoke and died at noon on 9 November.

Dylan Thomas was brought home to Laugharne and buried in St Martin's churchyard on 24 November 1953. Now, as then, a simple white wooden cross marks the spot where he lies.

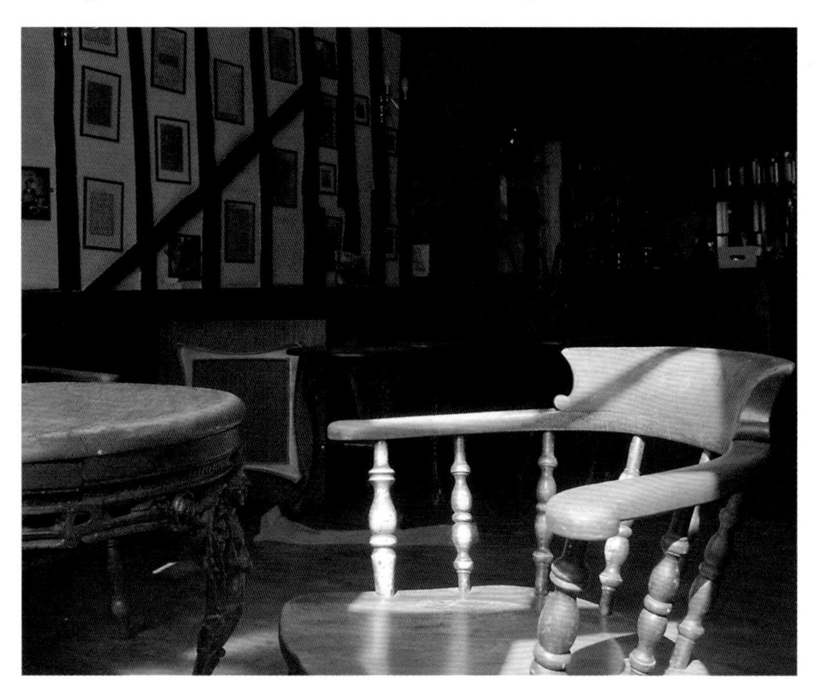

Above and right: Brown's Hotel, the social hub of Laugharne and the favourite watering hole of Dylan Thomas, who famously left the bar's 'phone number as his own.

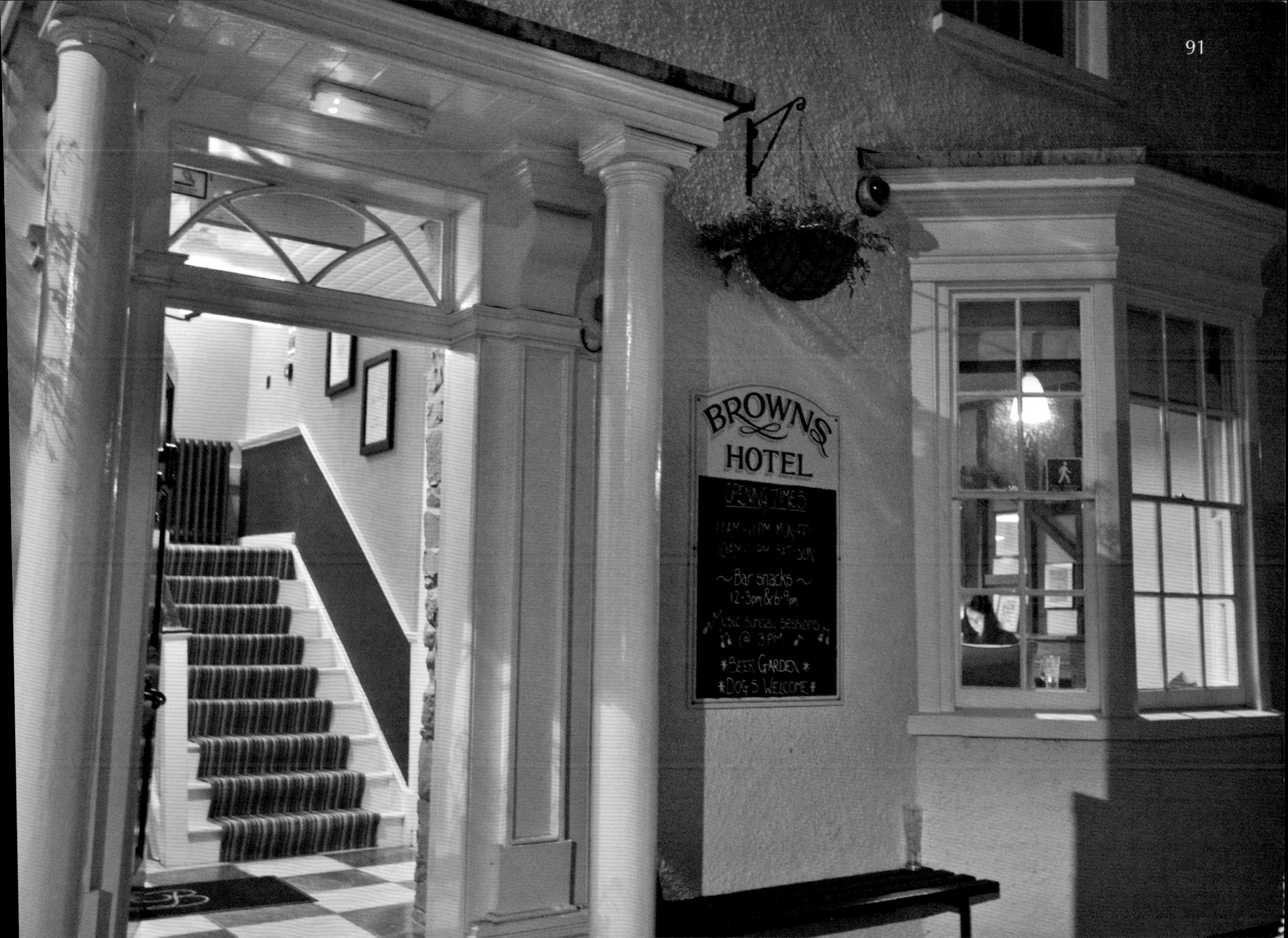
BROWNS
HOTEL
OPENING TIMES
11AM - 11PM MON-FRI
~ Bar snacks ~
12-3pm & 6-9pm
Music sunday sessions
@ 3PM
* BEER GARDEN *
* DOGS WELCOME *

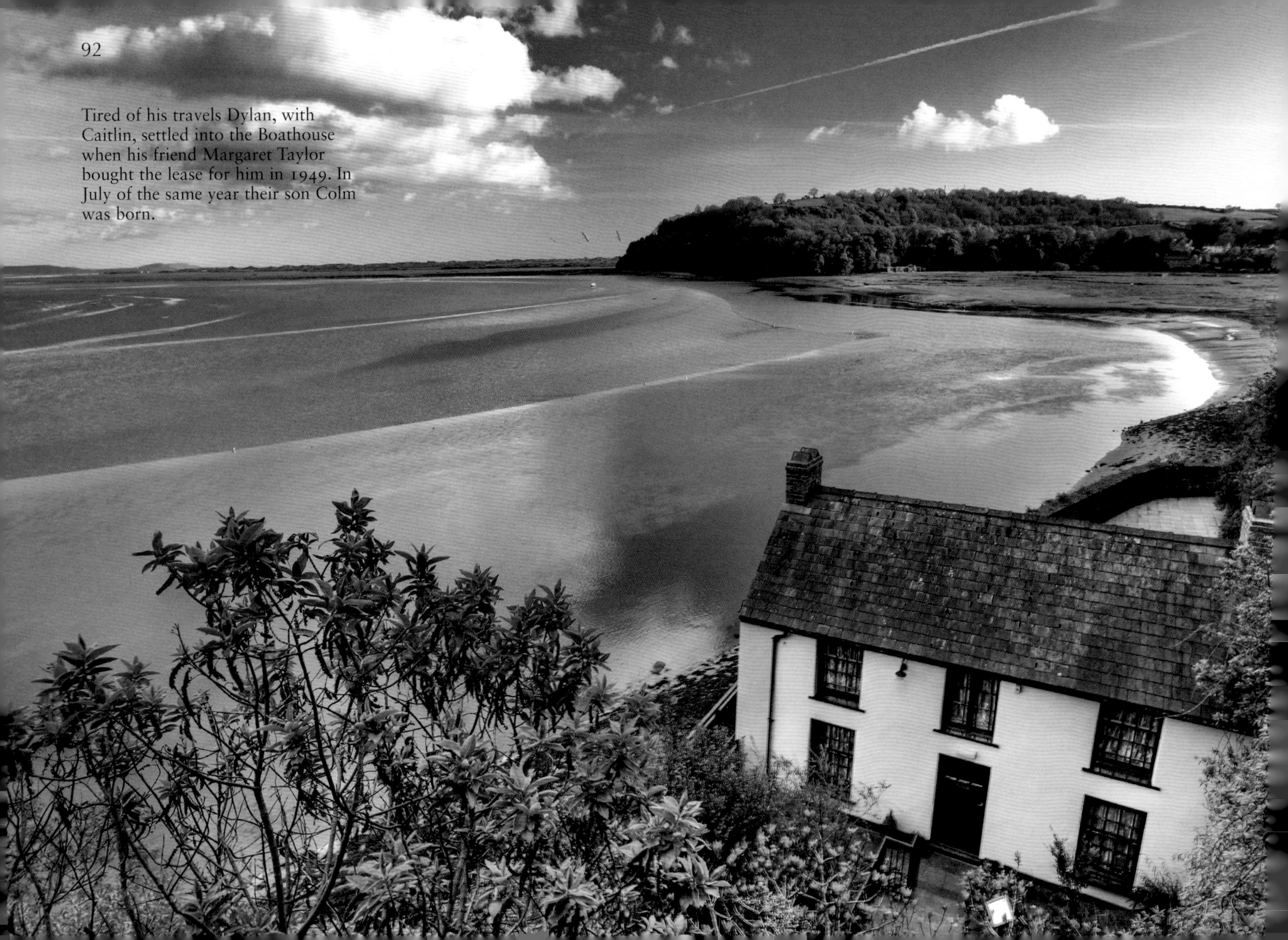

Tired of his travels Dylan, with Caitlin, settled into the Boathouse when his friend Margaret Taylor bought the lease for him in 1949. In July of the same year their son Colm was born.

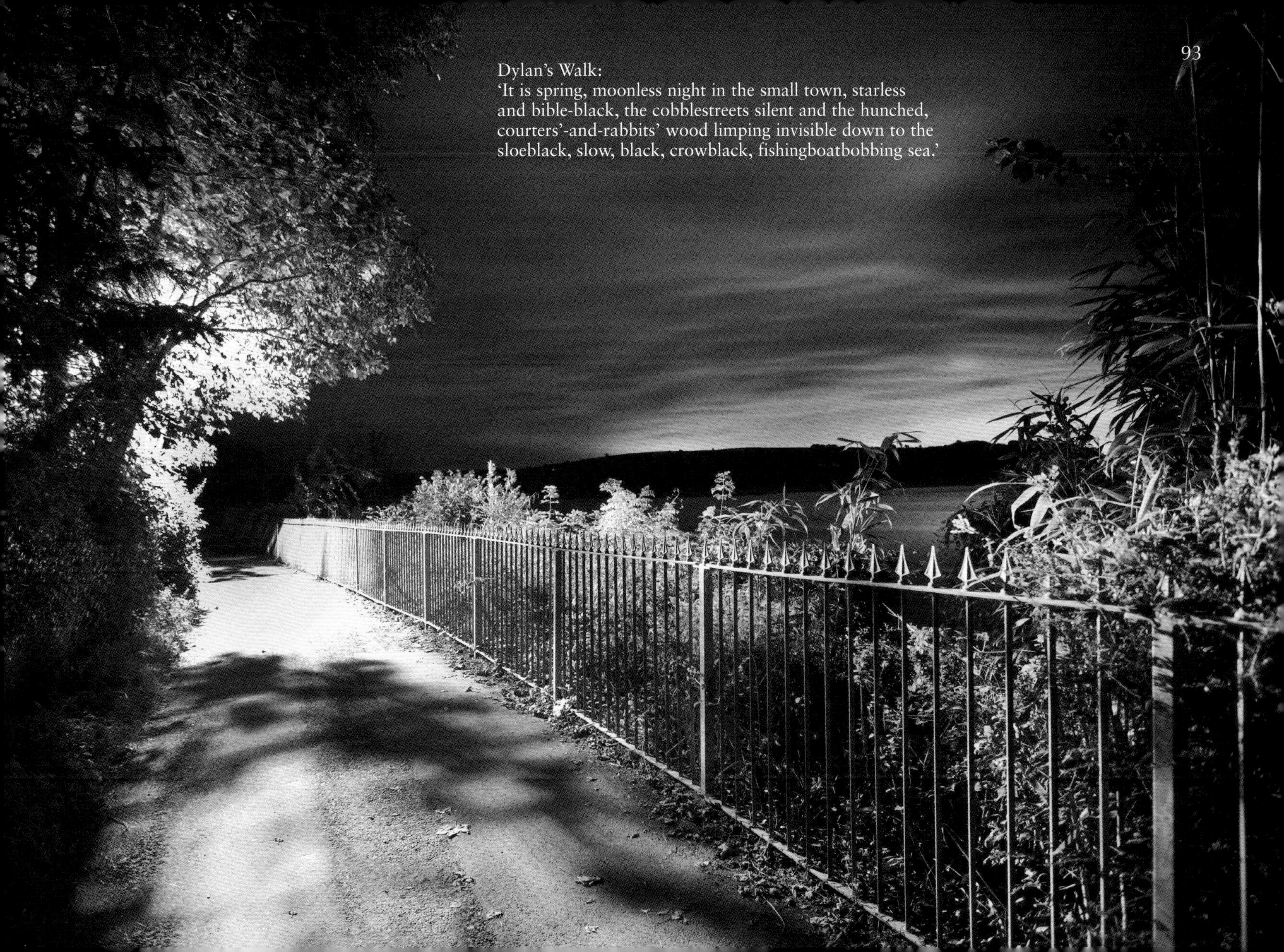

Dylan's Walk:
'It is spring, moonless night in the small town, starless and bible-black, the cobblestreets silent and the hunched, courters'-and-rabbits' wood limping invisible down to the sloeblack, slow, black, crowblack, fishingboatbobbing sea.'

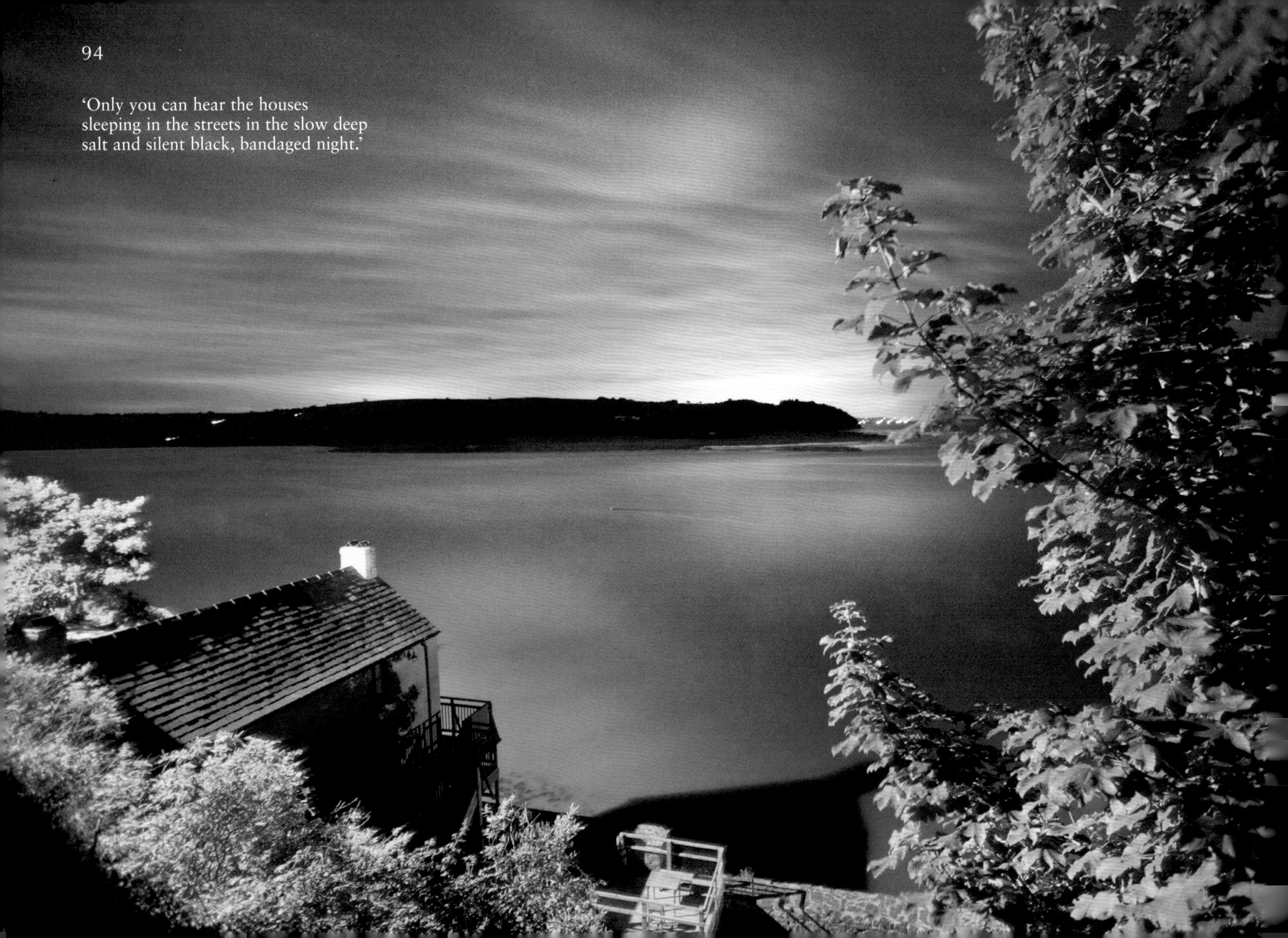

'Only you can hear the houses
sleeping in the streets in the slow deep
salt and silent black, bandaged night.'

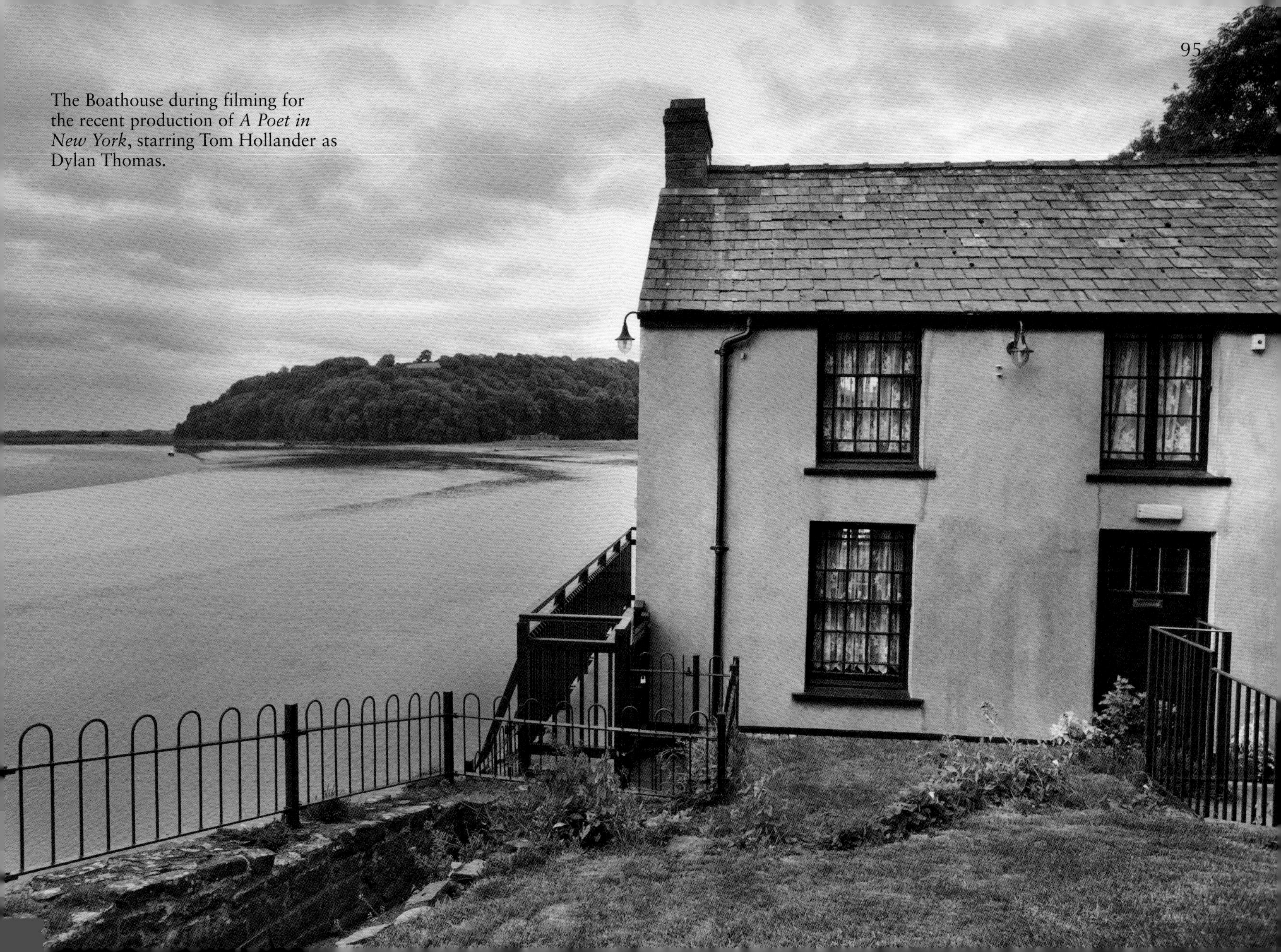

The Boathouse during filming for the recent production of *A Poet in New York*, starring Tom Hollander as Dylan Thomas.

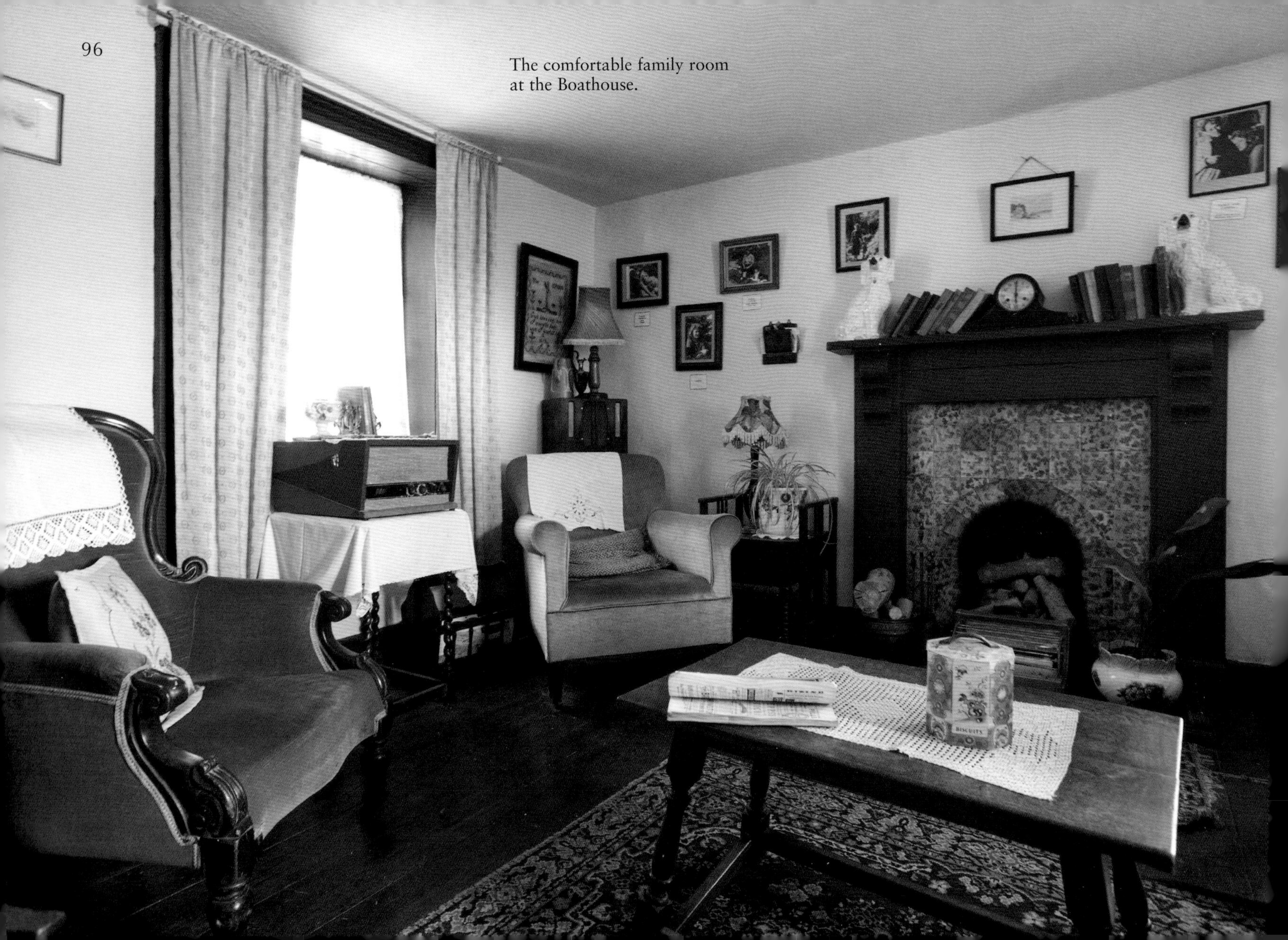

The comfortable family room at the Boathouse.

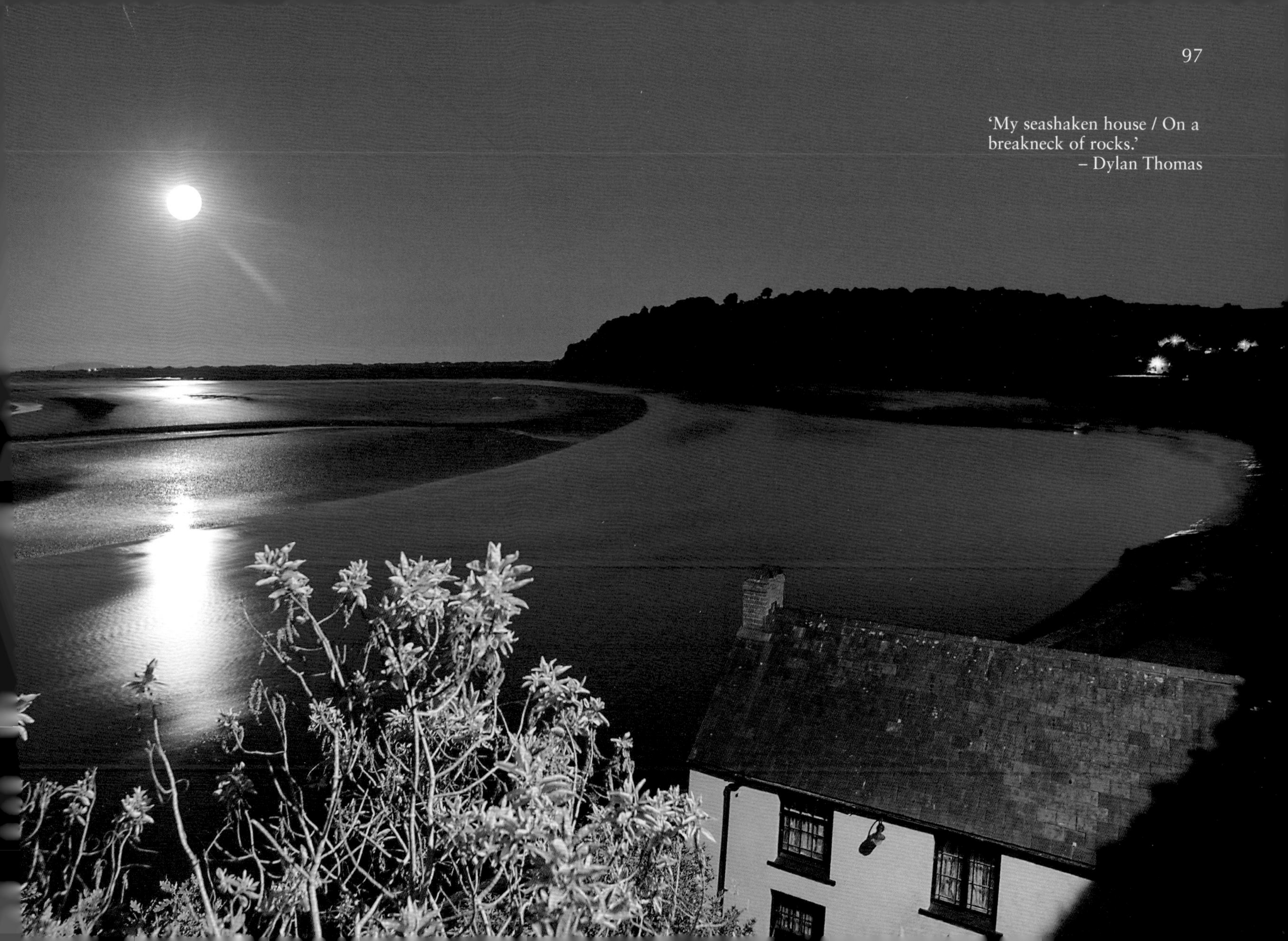

'My seashaken house / On a breakneck of rocks.'
– Dylan Thomas

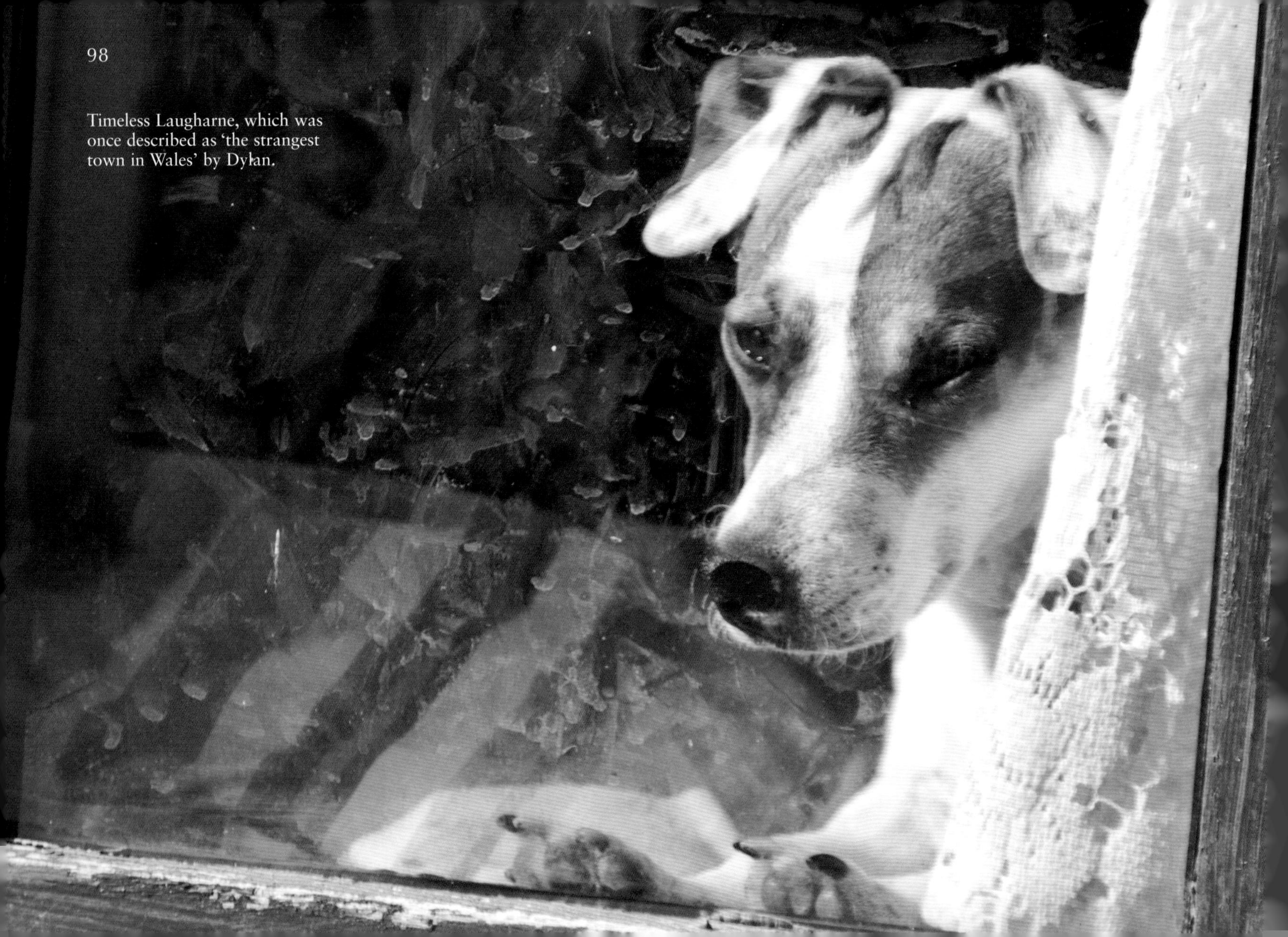

Timeless Laugharne, which was once described as 'the strangest town in Wales' by Dylan.

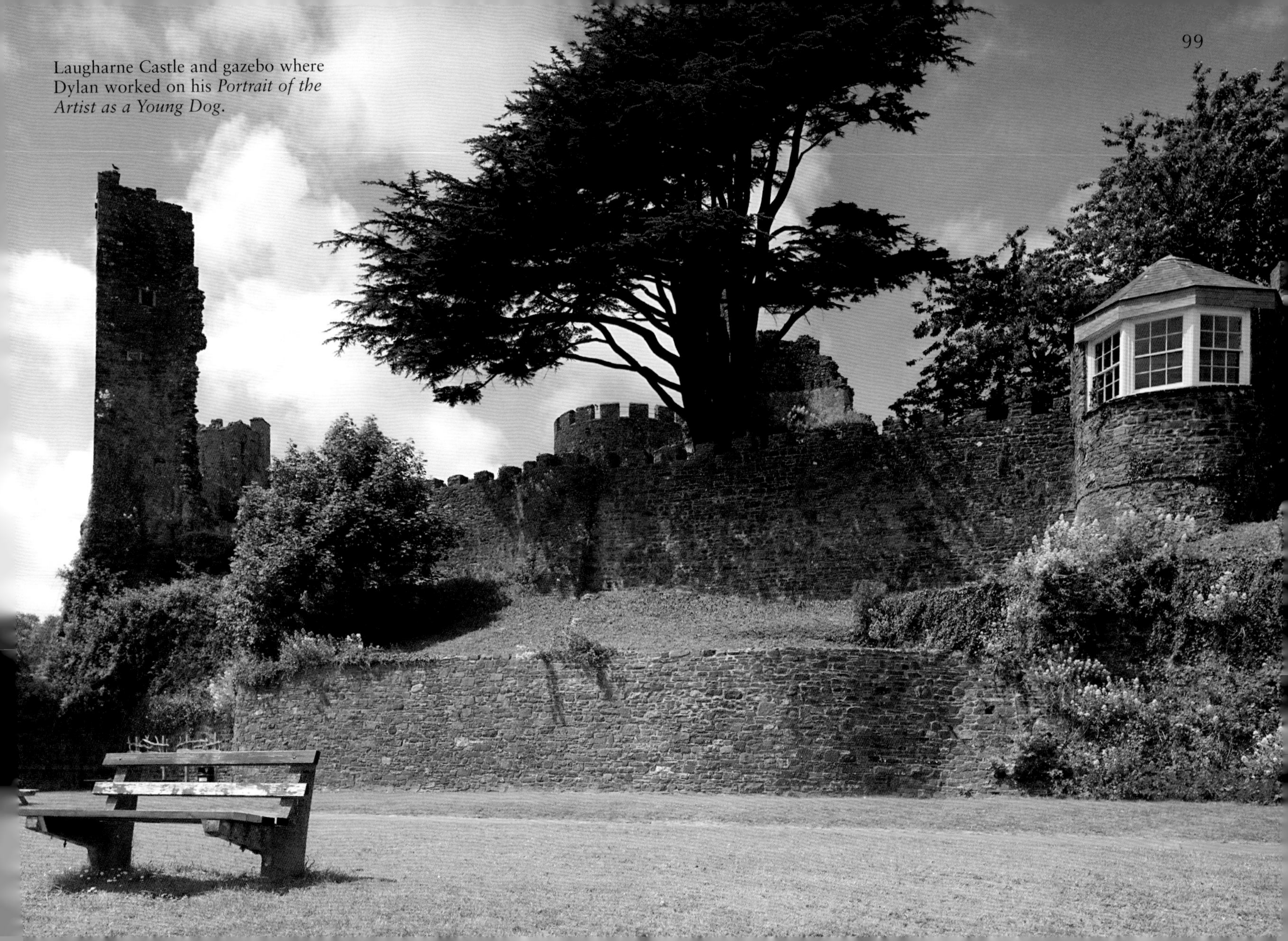

Laugharne Castle and gazebo where Dylan worked on his *Portrait of the Artist as a Young Dog*.

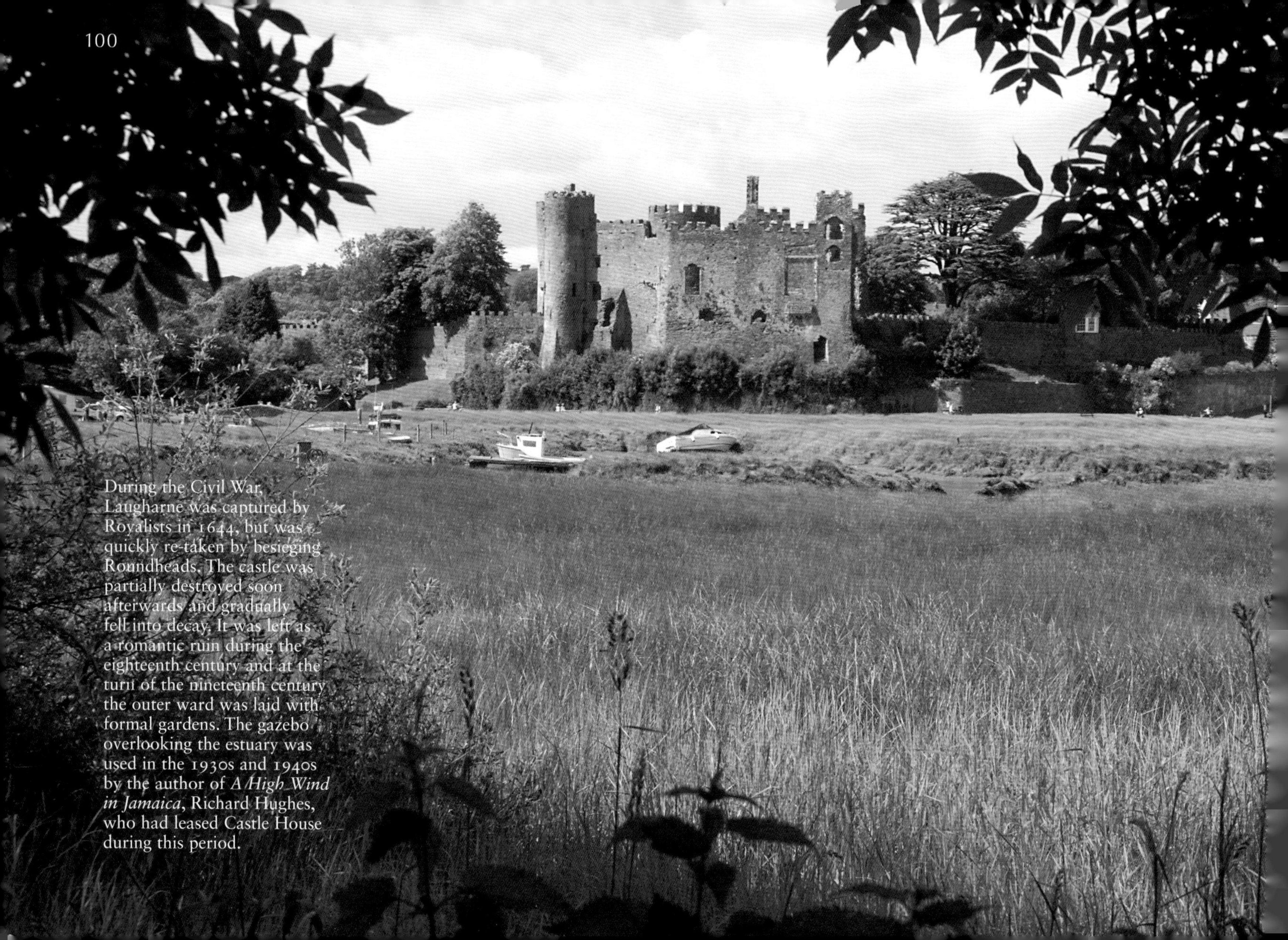

During the Civil War, Laugharne was captured by Royalists in 1644, but was quickly re-taken by besieging Roundheads. The castle was partially destroyed soon afterwards and gradually fell into decay. It was left as a romantic ruin during the eighteenth century and at the turn of the nineteenth century the outer ward was laid with formal gardens. The gazebo overlooking the estuary was used in the 1930s and 1940s by the author of *A High Wind in Jamaica*, Richard Hughes, who had leased Castle House during this period.

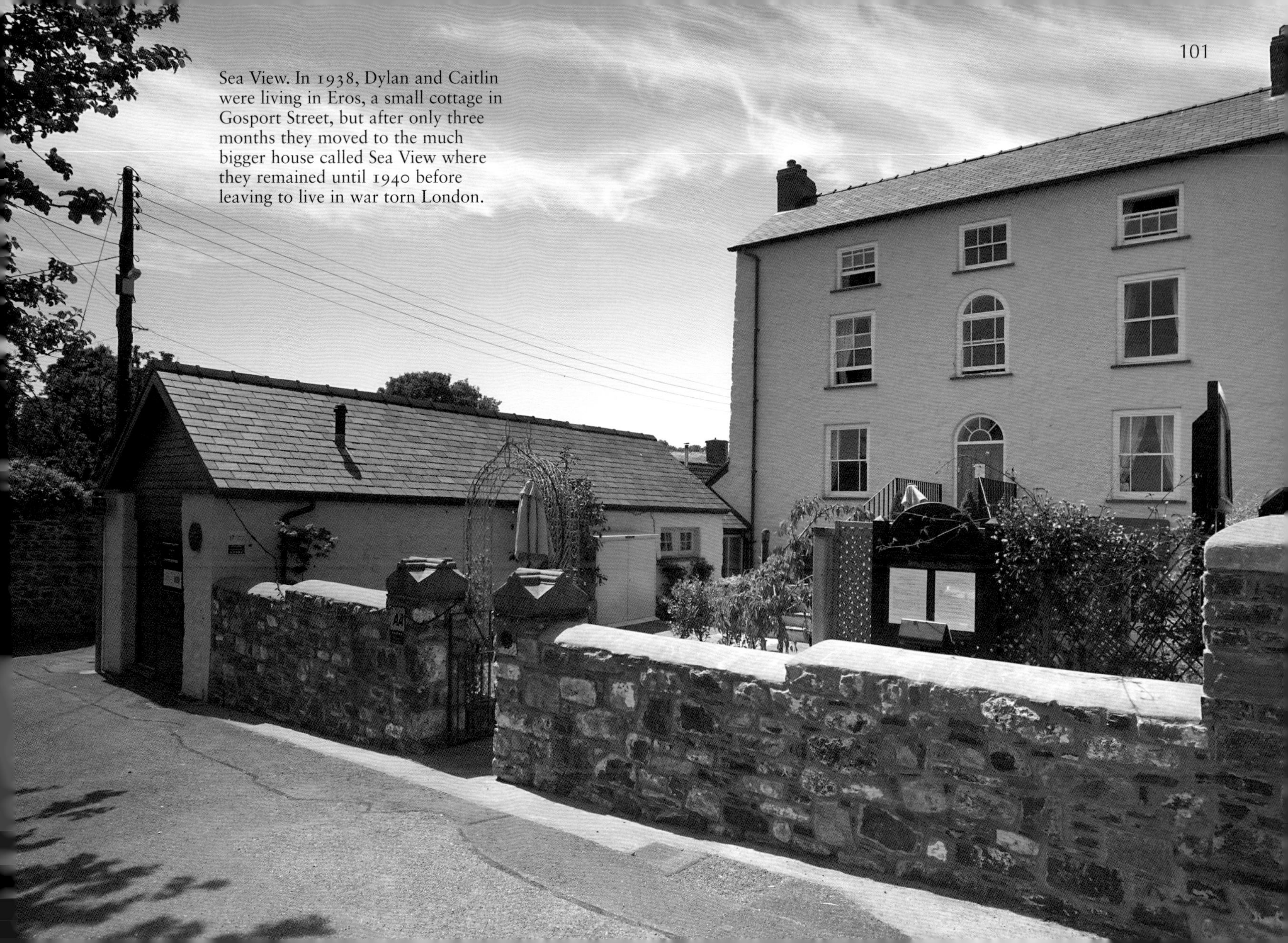

Sea View. In 1938, Dylan and Caitlin were living in Eros, a small cottage in Gosport Street, but after only three months they moved to the much bigger house called Sea View where they remained until 1940 before leaving to live in war torn London.

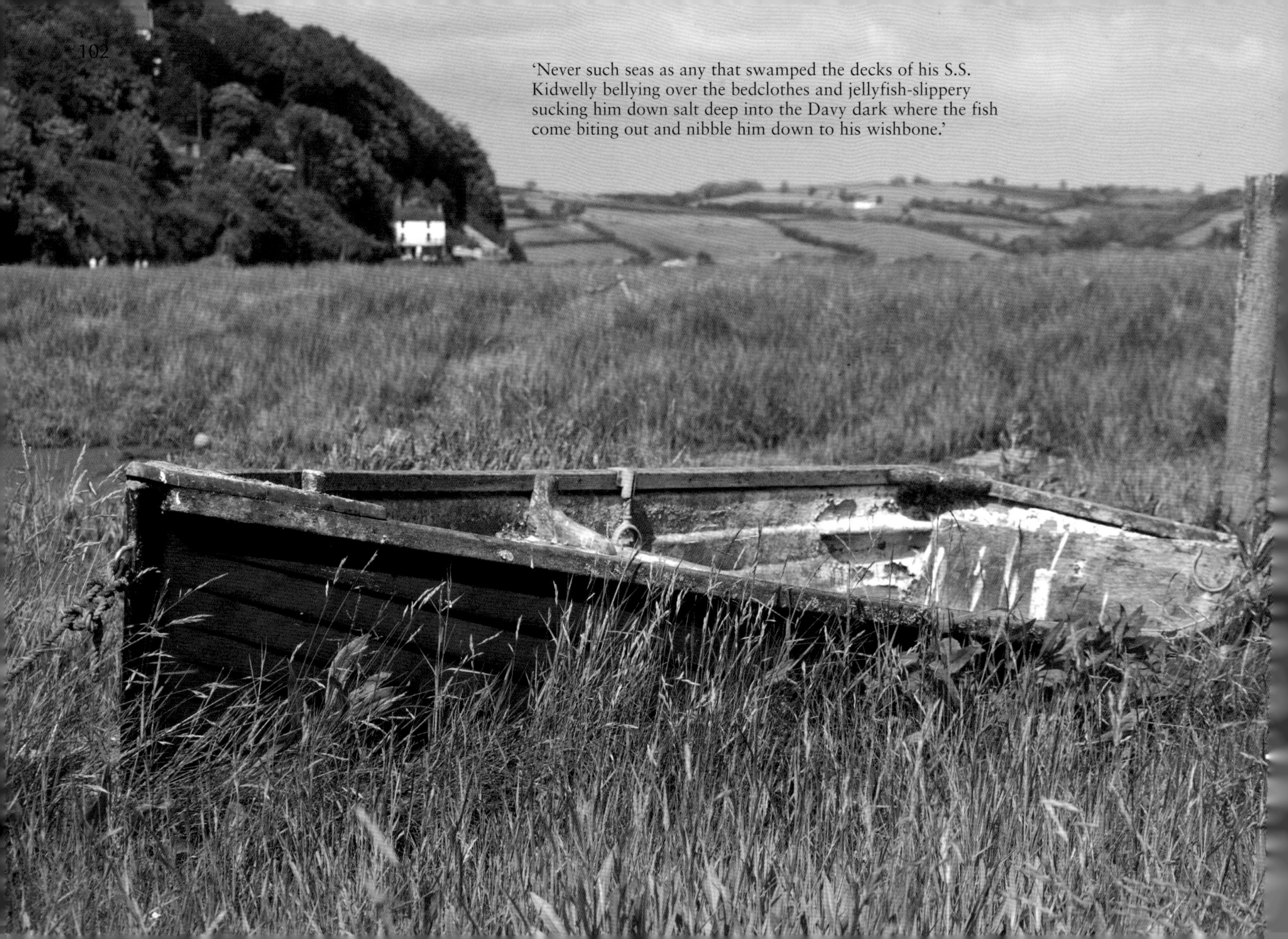

'Never such seas as any that swamped the decks of his S.S. Kidwelly bellying over the bedclothes and jellyfish-slippery sucking him down salt deep into the Davy dark where the fish come biting out and nibble him down to his wishbone.'

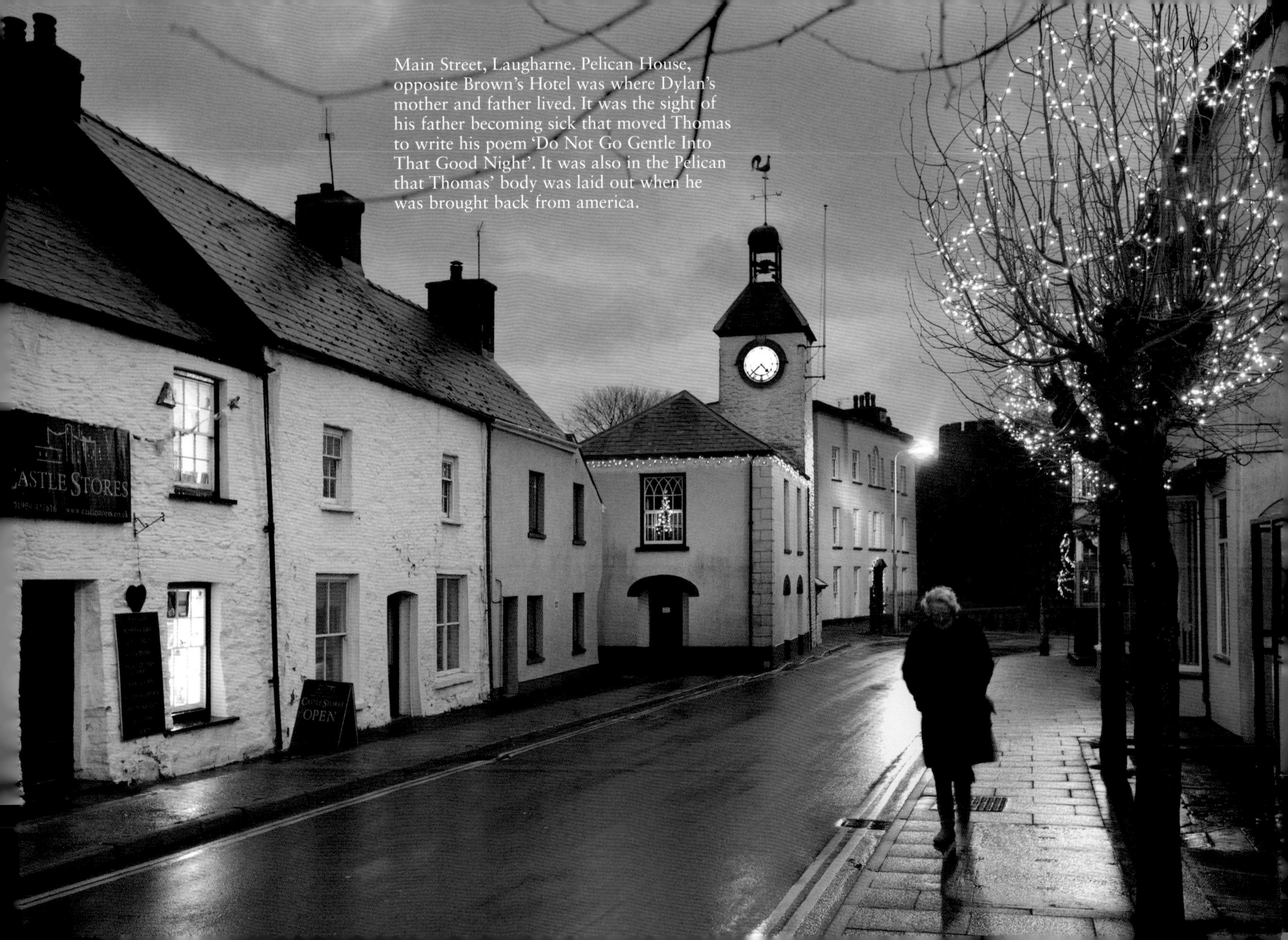

Main Street, Laugharne. Pelican House, opposite Brown's Hotel was where Dylan's mother and father lived. It was the sight of his father becoming sick that moved Thomas to write his poem 'Do Not Go Gentle Into That Good Night'. It was also in the Pelican that Thomas' body was laid out when he was brought back from america.

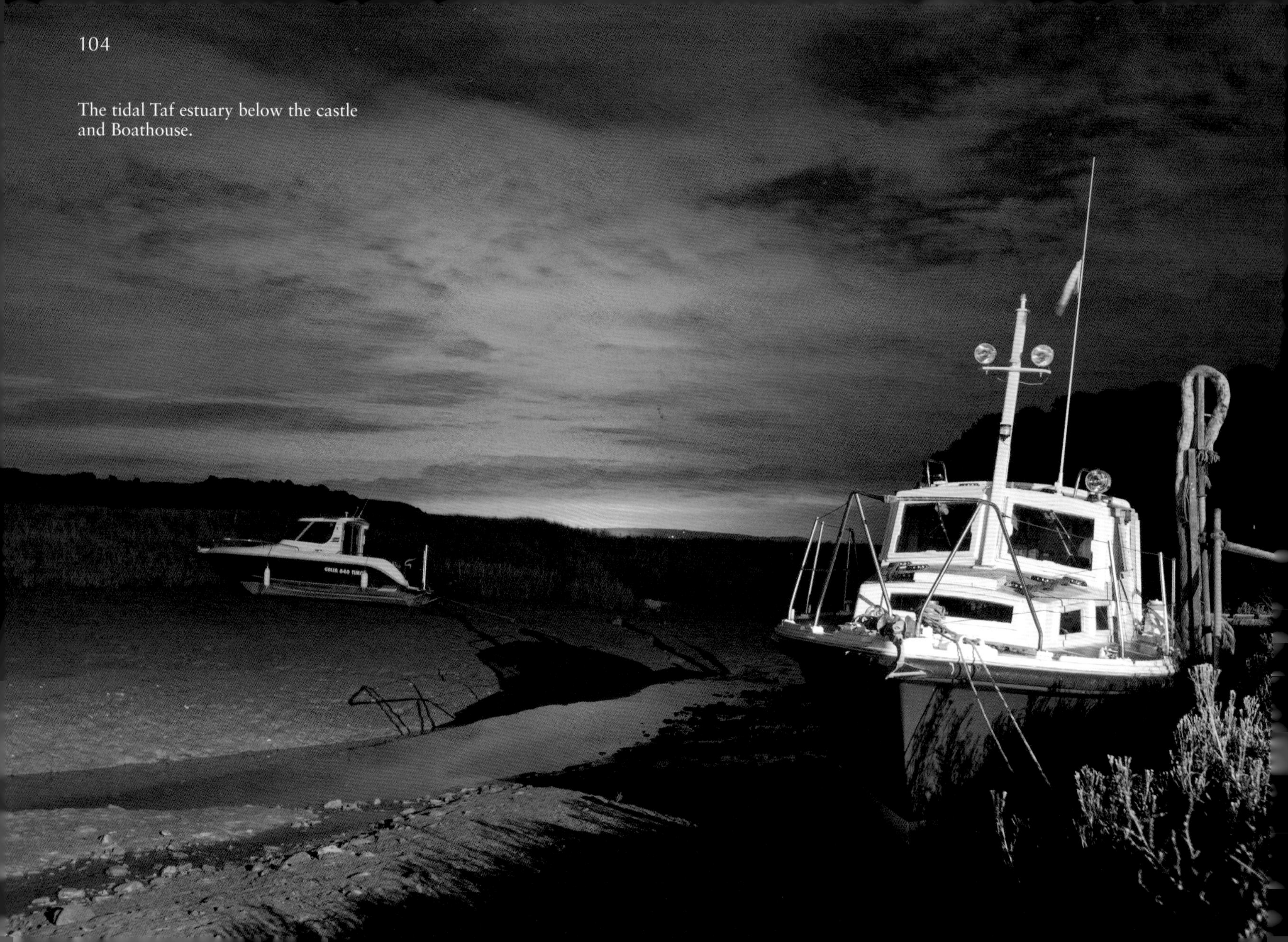

The tidal Taf estuary below the castle and Boathouse.

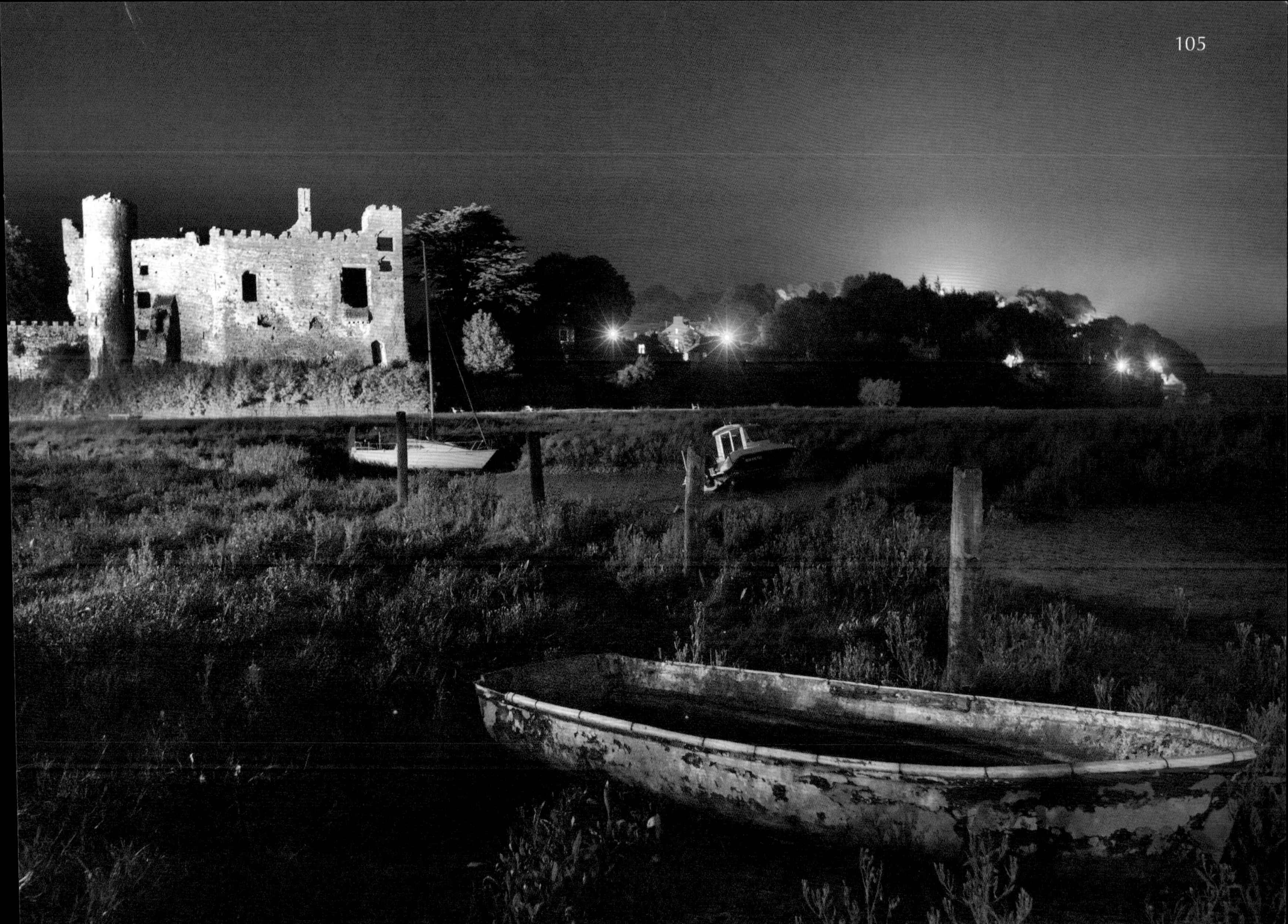

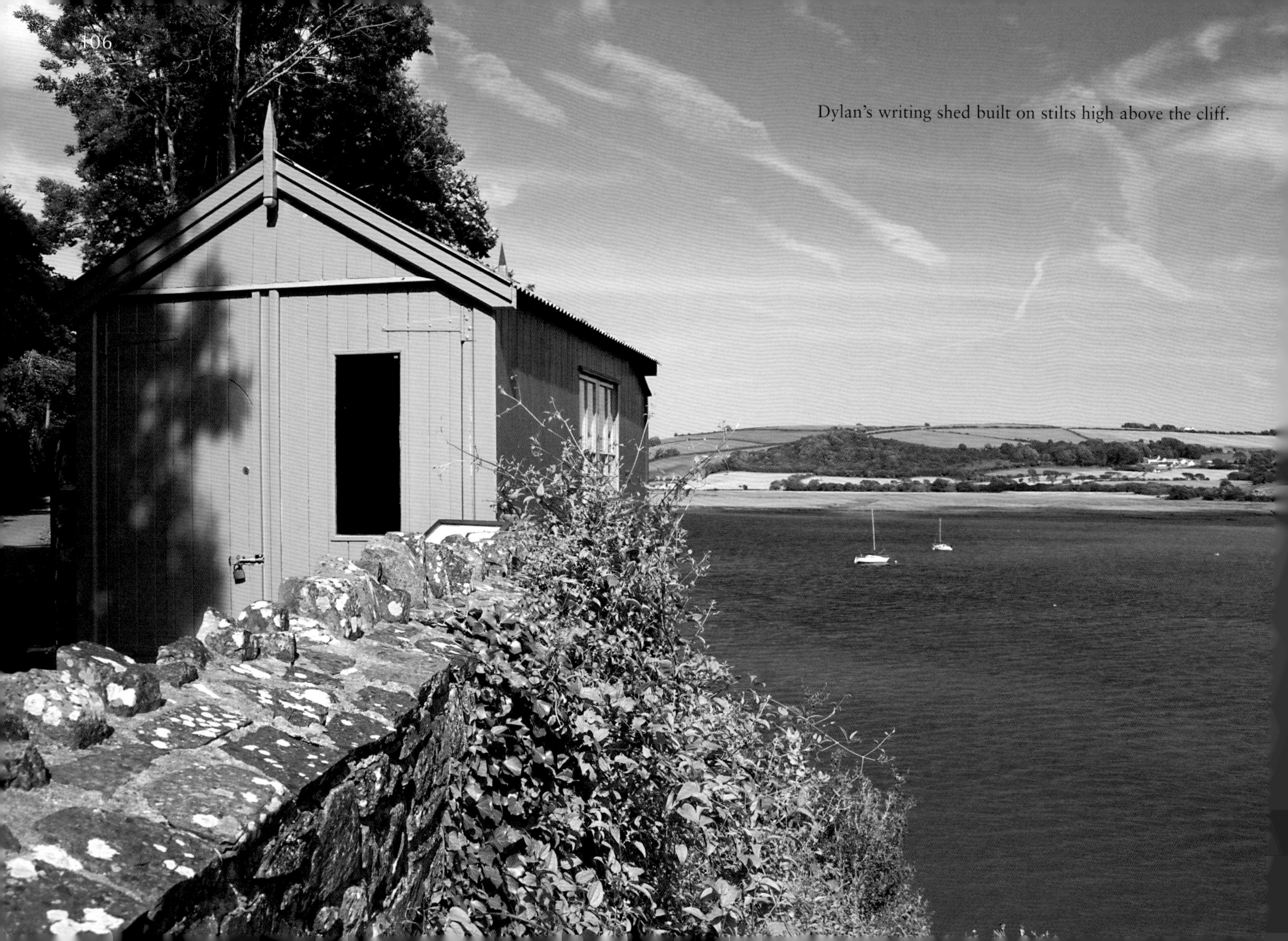

Dylan's writing shed built on stilts high above the cliff.

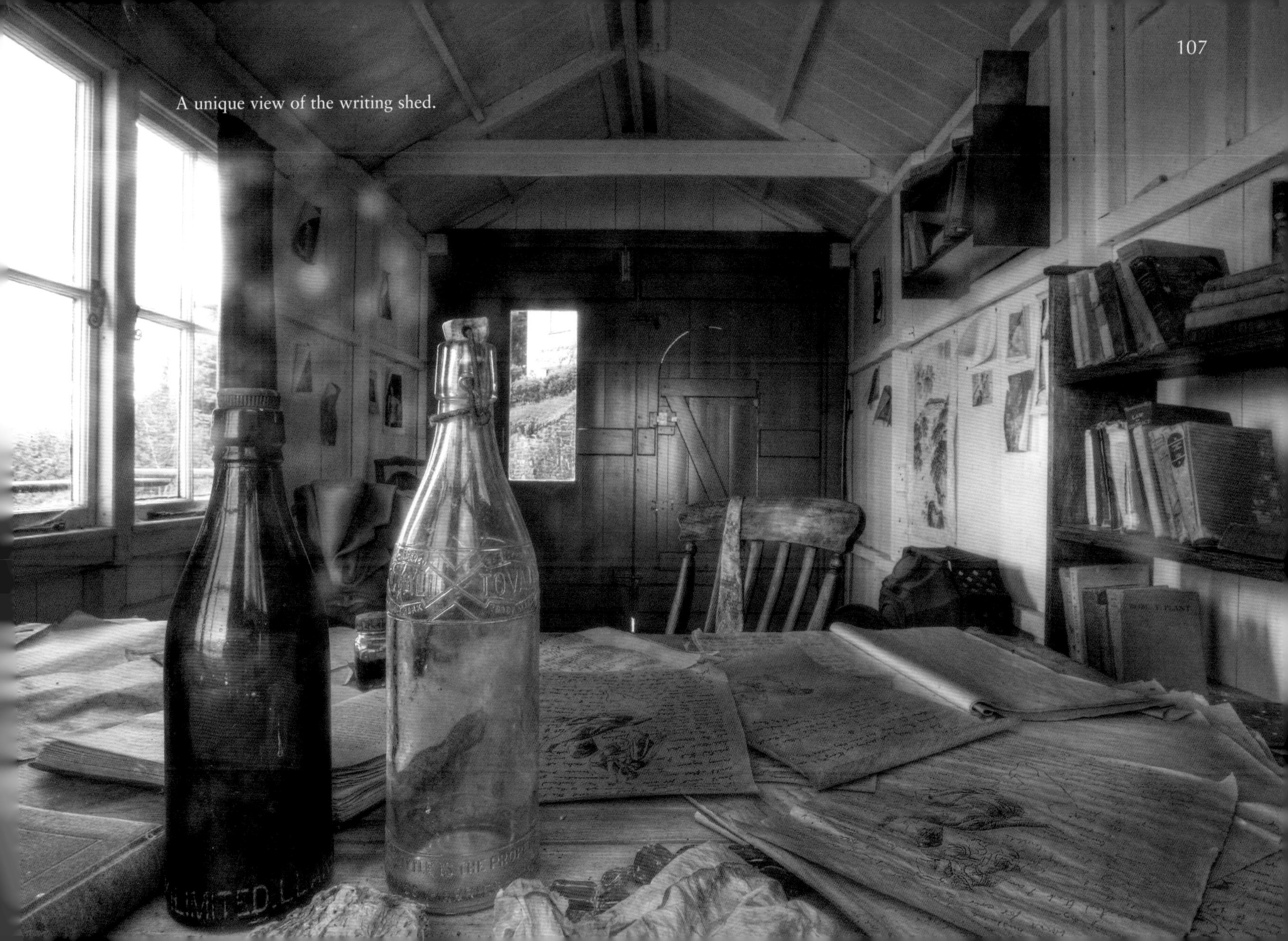

A unique view of the writing shed.

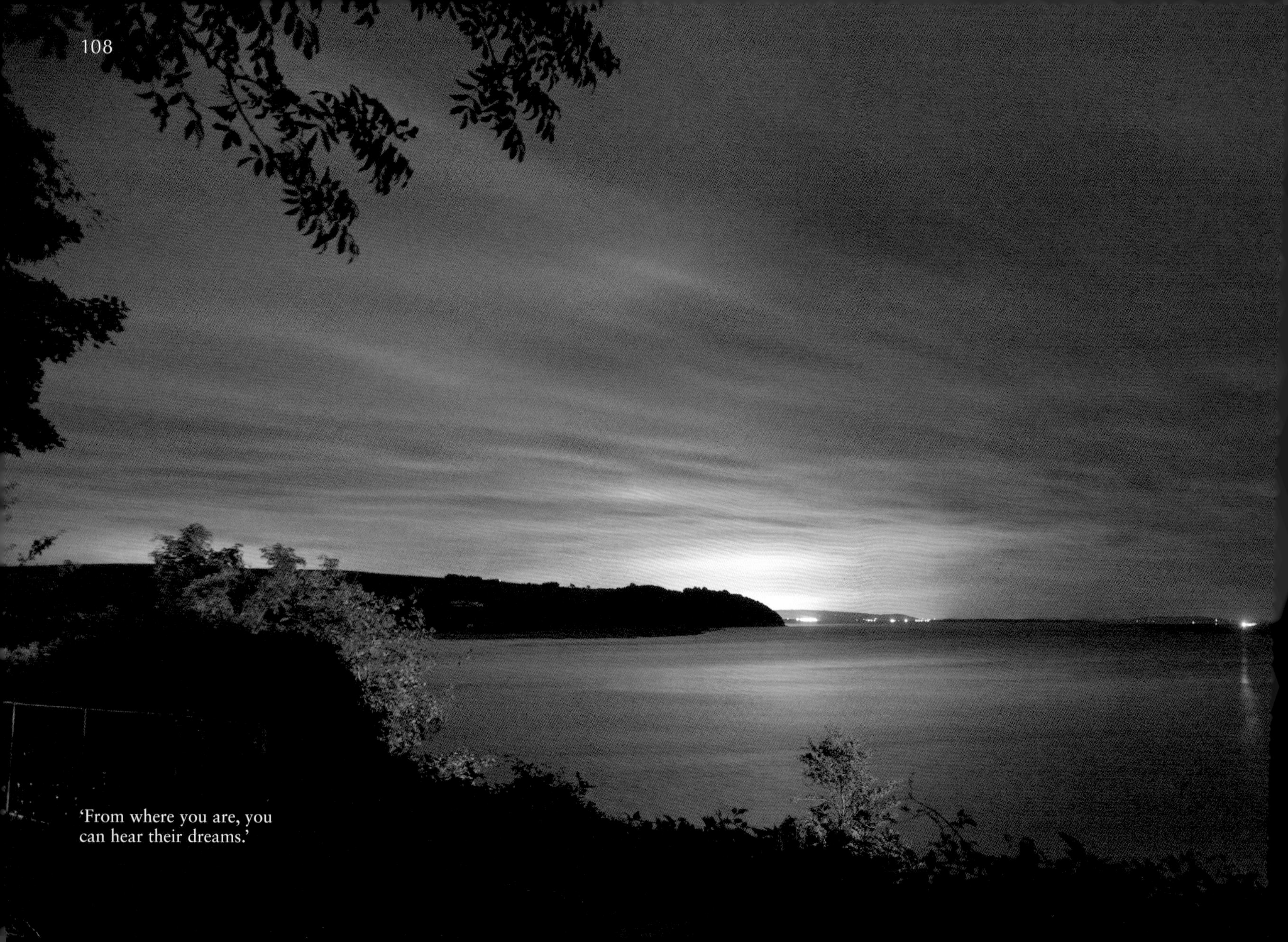

'From where you are, you
can hear their dreams.'

Right: In 1913 the harbour wall was built to the front of the Boathouse to bring coal into the town. In recent years this has been filled in.

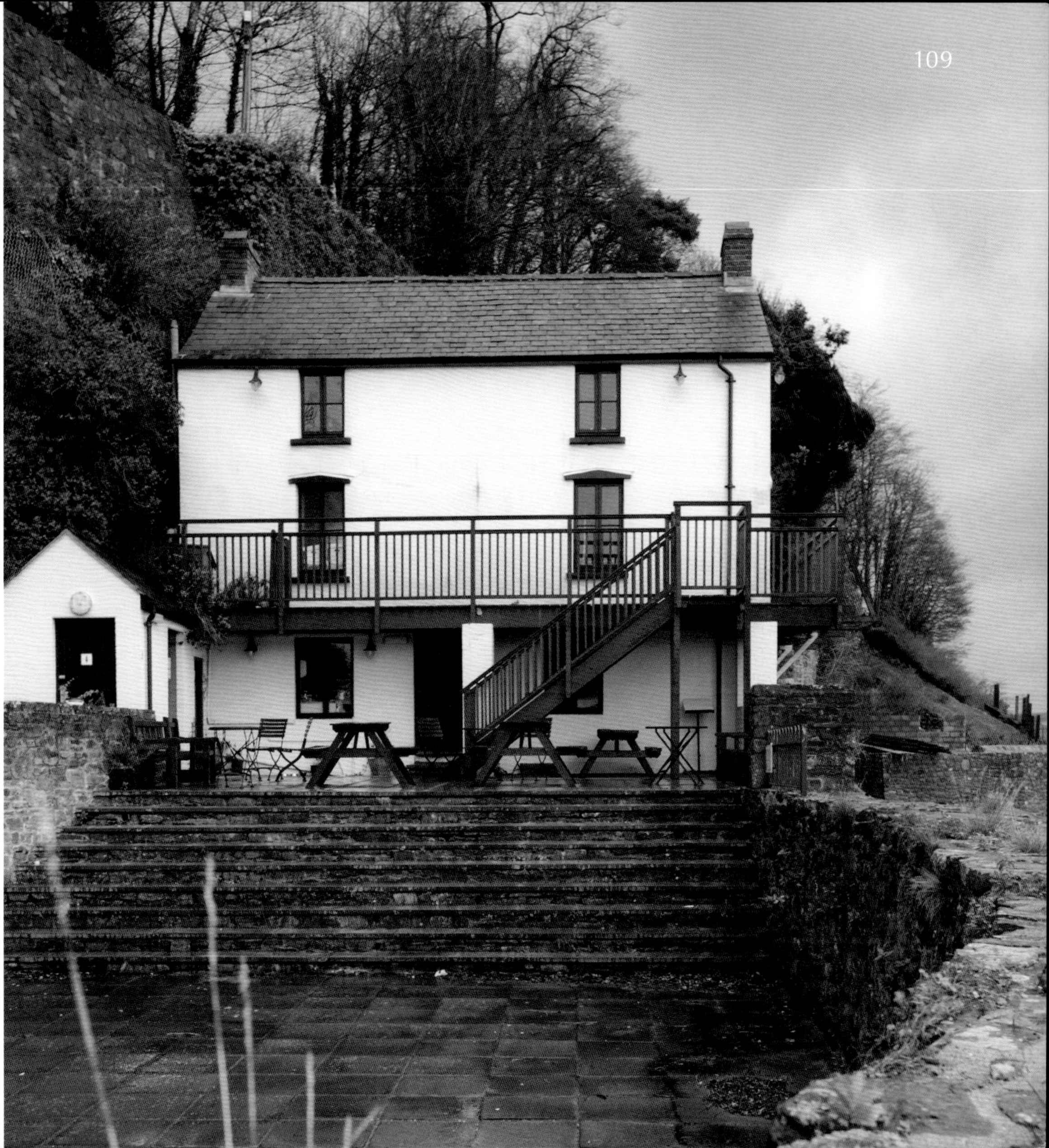

Dylan's first poem written at the Boathouse was 'Over Sir John's Hill'. The poem is Thomas' interpretation of the view from his window over Sir John's Hill and the Towy estuary.

'Now on Sir John's hill. The heron,
ankling the scaly
Lowlands of the waves,
Makes all the music; and I who hear
the tune of the slow,
Wear-willow river, grave,
Before the lunge of the night, the
notes on this time-shaken
Stone for the sake of the souls of the
slain birds sailing.'

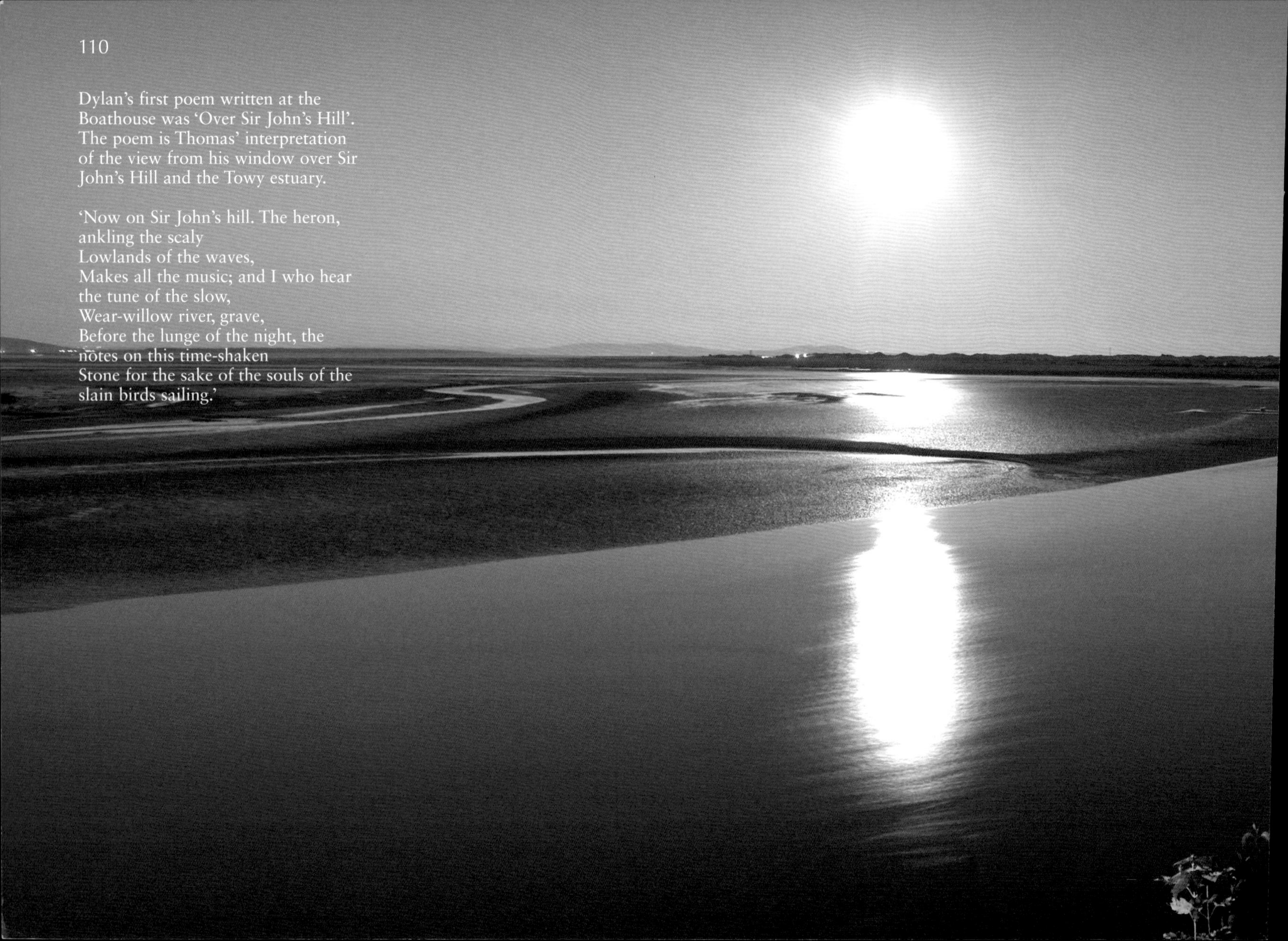

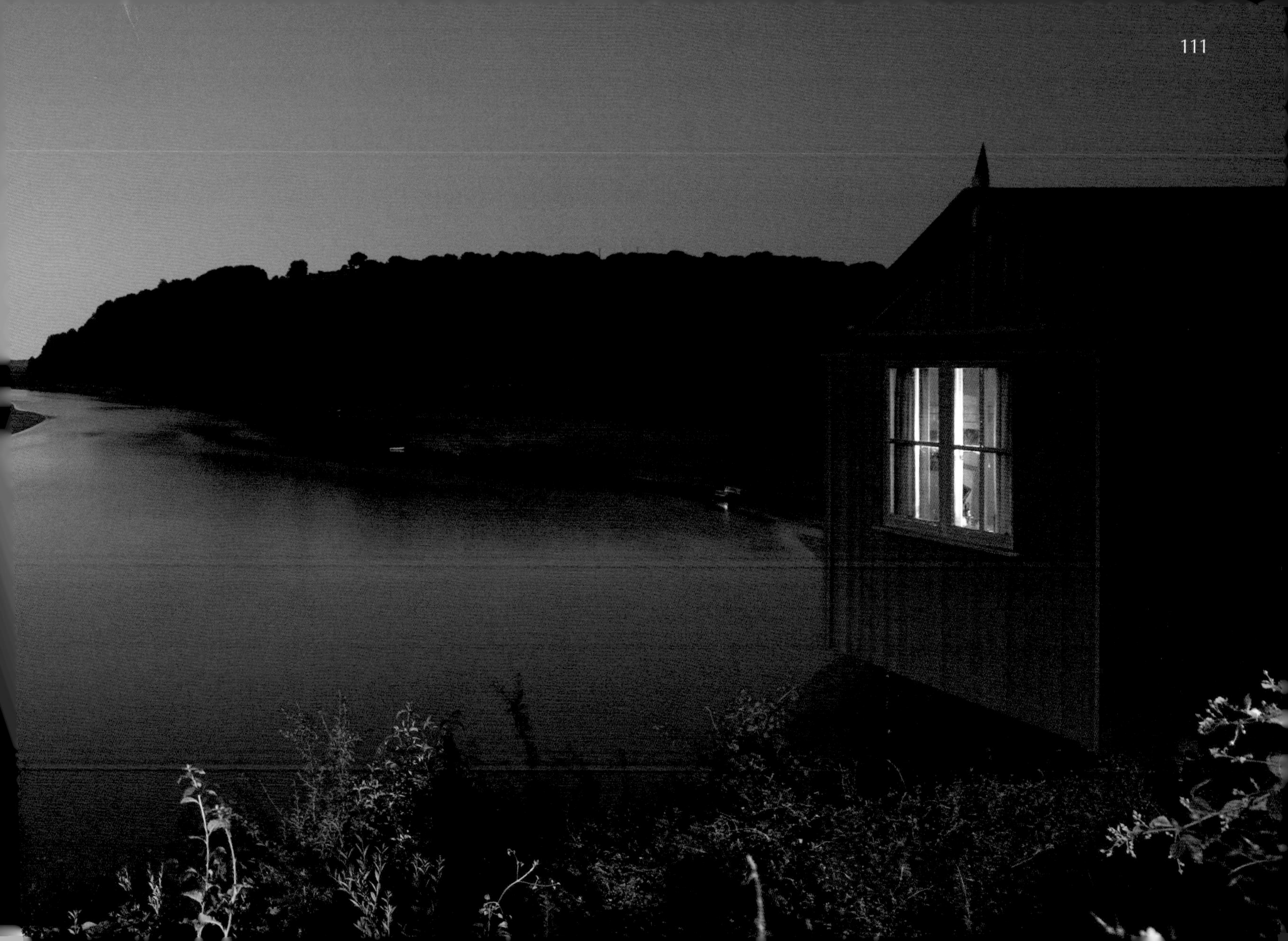

In Conversation

Andrew Sinclair and Sally Burton

On 6 August 1984, Channel 4 screened Andrew Sinclair's 1972 film adaptation of Dylan Thomas' 'play for voices' *Under Milk Wood* as a tribute to Richard Burton, who had died suddenly the day before. Accompanying it was a short documentary, *Making Milkwood*, which had been produced twelve years earlier for Welsh television. It was fitting that this quirky, unusual film should be drawn from the vaults to represent Burton's presence on screen. Nineteen years later, I made the acquaintance of Andrew Sinclair and have since interviewed him many times. This unique interview – the only pairing of Andrew Sinclair and Sally Burton, the actor's widow – was conducted in March 2003. It is reproduced here for the first time.

– Tony Earnshaw

Tony Earnshaw: Caitlin Thomas said, 'You have picked the plums and touched the living quick of the Dylan situation with penetrating insight. What baffles me is from whence first did your passion and your understanding of your subject come?' I'd like to ask you the same question.

Andrew Sinclair: He was the adolescent, romantic dream of our generation. At that time there was nobody else like him around. He seemed to be a sort of Rimbaud figure. And he was extraordinary. The dozen great poems he wrote really were our own incantations. I personally got involved [with him when] I wrote a novel when at Cambridge called *My Friend Judas*. My influences were his: the King James Bible, Dylan Thomas and J. D. Salinger's *The Catcher in the Rye*. We all seemed to have this sort of sweeping prose along with James Joyce. Later on when I got back to Cambridge as a don the Dylan Thomas Estate came to me and said, 'We want to do a stage version of *Adventures in the Skin Trade*.' Dylan was dead by this time but he had co-operated with a man called John Davenport, who had written an extremely bad novel called *The Death of the King's Canary*. Davenport was an odd figure but he had been rich, put up with Dylan and was now extremely poor and living on boiled potatoes near Cambridge. So I went with John, and then John died so I ended by adapting it myself. I never got the second act right because the novel was unfinished. There was only the first act and I had to do the second act. I didn't get it right. I forged it as well as I could. It went on at the Hampstead Theatre, extraordinarily, and we starred an unknown actor. His wages were £20 a week and he was called David Hemmings. He was the poor man's Terence Stamp on that occasion. We put it on and I was dating somebody called Clare Peploe at the time. She came in with a tall, dark Italian gentleman, to whom I lost her, called Antonioni, and she ended by scouting locations for *Blow Up*. So David left – he was staying with me in Limehouse at the time – in a large white Rolls-Royce on 10,000 a week to play in *Blow Up* and became what he became. But he simply was the most beautiful fallen angel you've ever seen. That was the beginning of my long history of forging or adapting Dylan Thomas.

Tony Earnshaw: So you never met Thomas.
Andrew Sinclair: I never did. He was dead. That's why I had to adapt *Adventures in the Skin Trade* for the stage. Thereafter I went into films to some degree. I became a screenwriter in Hollywood. I was paid far too much money. And I used the money to buy an option on the impossible thing to make: *Under Milk Wood*. Nobody thought it could ever be made. Because there was no way of getting Richard Burton or O'Toole into the same film. But incredibly I had known O'Toole when we were both students. My first novel was going to be put on by Tony Richardson at the Royal Court as a musical. O'Toole was going to play the lead. I'd met him at Cambridge and the actual secret of making films is to know a star before they become a star. It's as simple as that. O'Toole had played Captain Cat at RADA. So the impossible happens.

Tony Earnshaw: Was it a shared Welshness that made Richard and Dylan friends or was it something far deeper than that?
Sally Burton: I think it was a great thrill for Richard to have Dylan Thomas as a friend because Richard had discovered his poetry before he knew him. It was through reading Dylan Thomas that Richard went to Philip Burton and said, 'Look, I've found this poem. I understand it and I think I can read it.' And indeed he could. So to then go to London on his big adventure and meet Dylan and to become a friend of his and to work with him – because they would go to the BBC and do Radio 4 poetry readings together – and then, of course, go to the pub. So it was a great thing for Richard, who became a Welsh hero, but in Richard's mind Dylan was the hero to him.

Tony Earnshaw: Richard didn't appear to be easily impressed by people generally. He wasn't someone who would hero worship but in this particular case he obviously did.
Sally Burton: Yes. Dylan Thomas and Louise MacNeice... these people he had infinite respect for, along with rugby players. That was where it was.

Tony Earnshaw: Did Richard speak to you about Dylan? If so, how did he remember the man?
Sally Burton: With infinite fondness. And he always loved his poetry. The poem he loved the most was 'Fern Hill'. But Richard was extraordinary because he could recite poetry and I think, Andrew, he must have said to you, 'Oh, I can do *Under Milk Wood*. I've done it so many times. I can do it.'
Andrew Sinclair: He said he'd done it a thousand times and did it perfectly with two hiccups in a cellar in Soho. That [recording

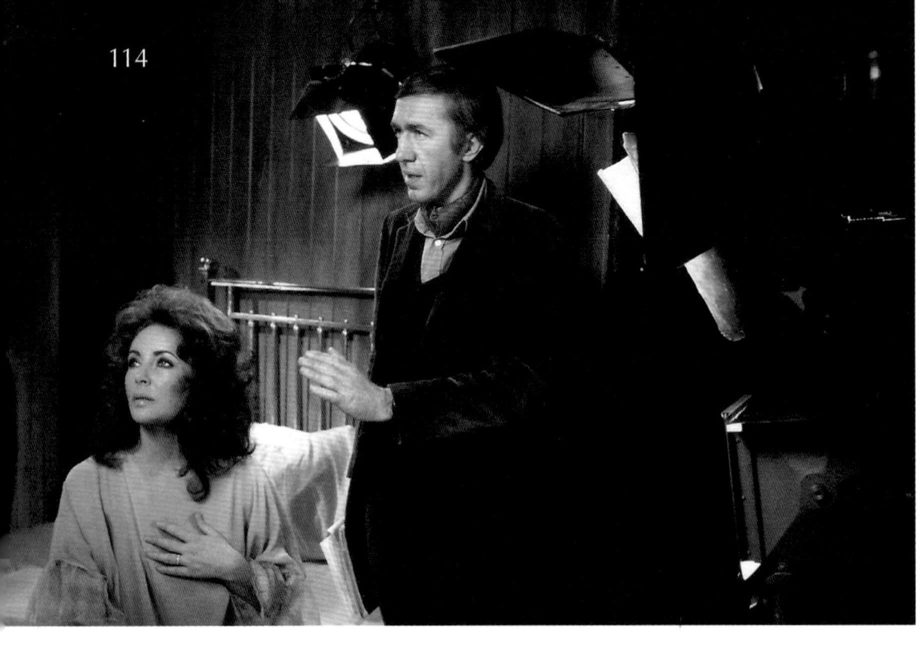

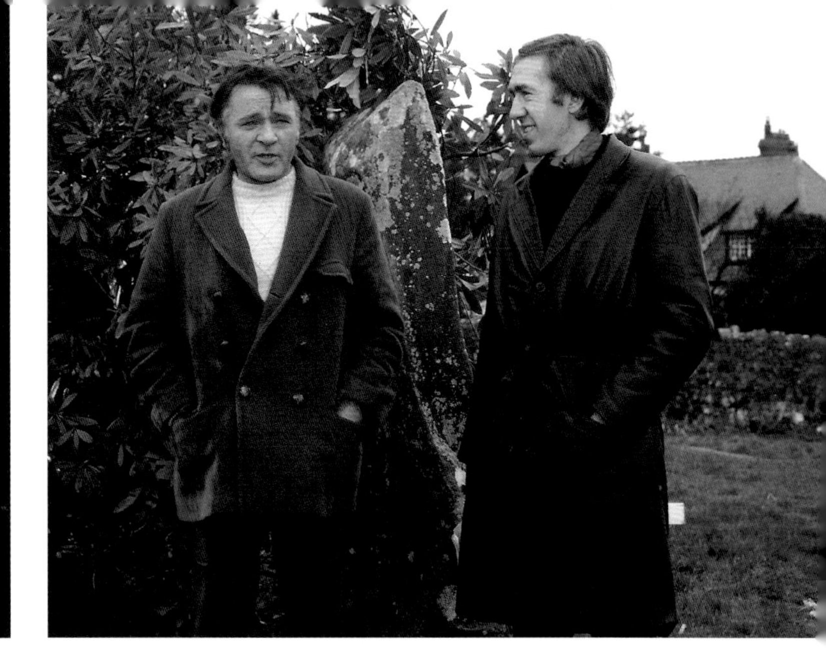

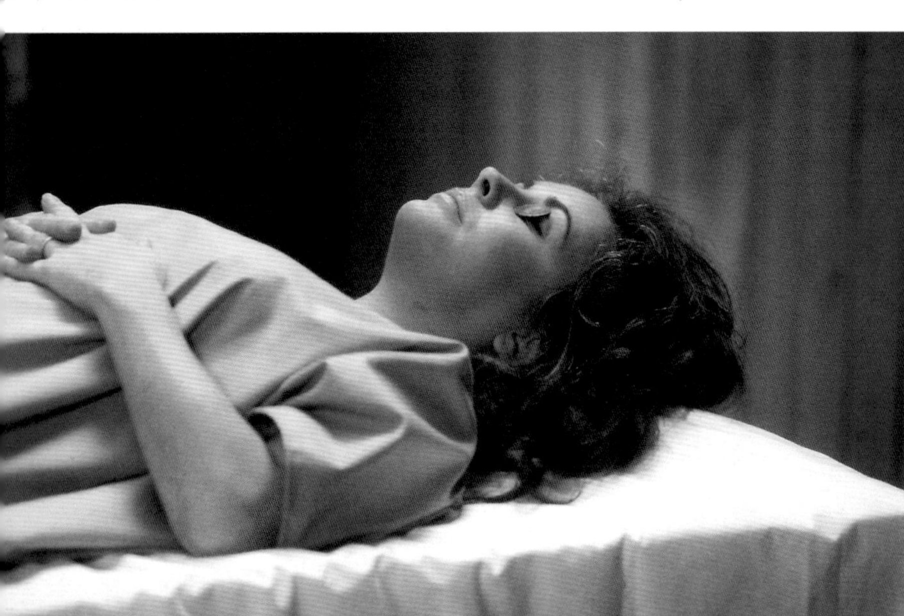

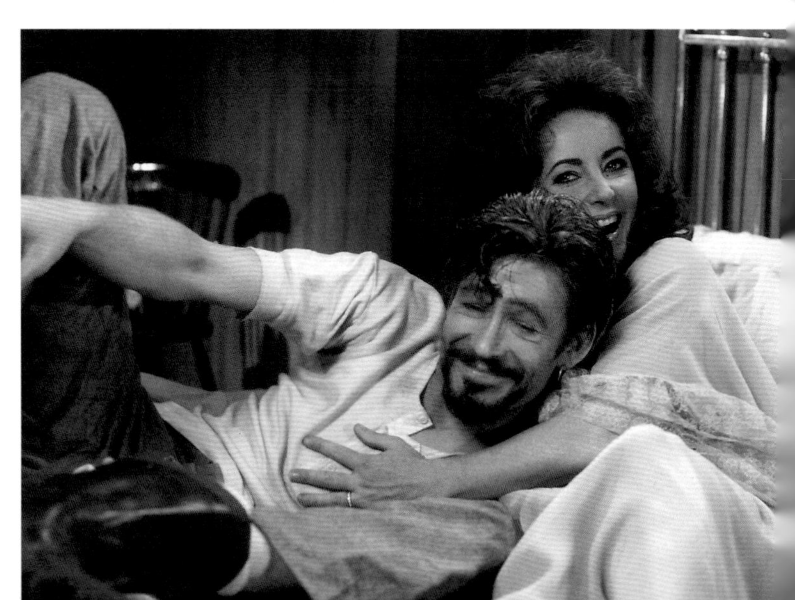

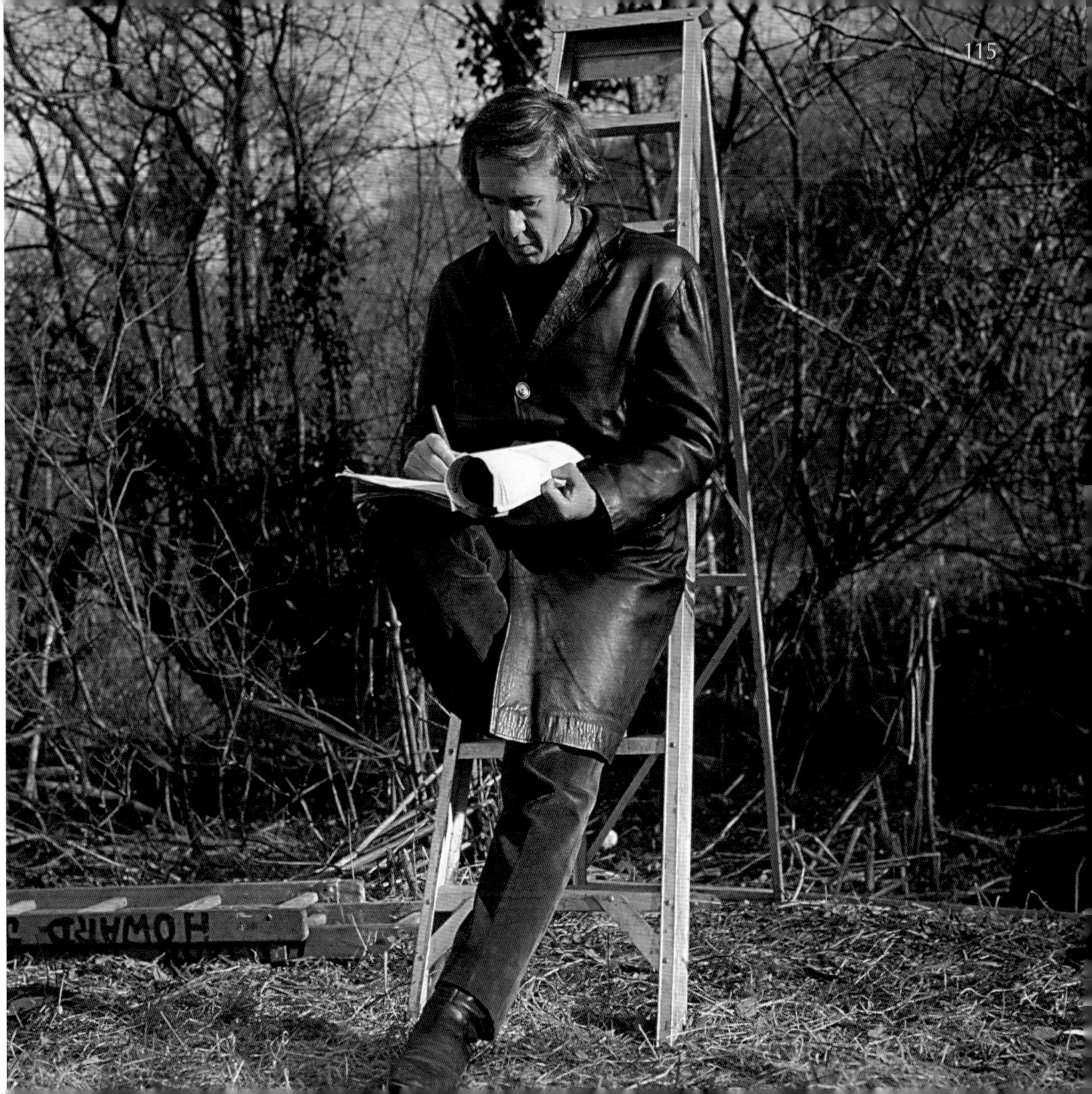

A potentially fraught day of filming with Elizabeth Taylor was salvaged by Peter O'Toole over a long, boozy lunch with Taylor and Richard Burton. On returning O'Toole told Sinclair, 'Get this shot, Andrew'. Sinclair remembered: 'He had gone away and tattooed (in biro) 'I love you, Rosie Probert' across his tummy. He pulls up his shirt and gets a laugh out of her. She's not expecting it and so there's a genuine, wonderful laugh from Elizabeth Taylor.'

session] was all over in about an hour. He was always guilty about Dylan's death.
Sally Burton: I know. They'd seen each other, I think, a couple of days before [Dylan left for America on his final tour] and they'd been drinking together. Dylan said he was in trouble and he needed money. Richard couldn't come up with the money. Dylan went off to New York and died.
Andrew Sinclair: That's actually what happened. It was only 200 quid. But actually the point, to be absolutely truthful, [was that] Dylan was earning more money than Richard.
Sally Burton: Yes.
Andrew Sinclair: Richard was earning £50 a week playing *Hamlet* at the National [sic]; that's all you got in those days. And Dylan was earning about £200 a week writing occasional film scripts, but he drank it up on the way home. It's not a sad story in its way. Richard couldn't do it.
Sally Burton: Couldn't afford it. But it was a precursor to other things because people were always asking Richard for money. Maybe in later life when he could afford he was forever giving money away to people.
Andrew Sinclair: He was a very generous man.
Sally Burton: So I think that was the first one where he couldn't deliver and thereafter he went out of his way.
Andrew Sinclair: He wasn't responsible for Dylan's death.
Sally Burton: Oh, no, no.
Andrew Sinclair: It was just bad luck that he crossed the Atlantic and said, 'I can't do another lecture tour.' But Dylan cadged all his life. He spent his whole time cadging off everyone he could possibly meet. The point was the money never got home.
Tony Earnshaw: Richard Burton always said that *Under Milk Wood* was written for him as Second Voice and that Dylan was First Voice.
Sally Burton: That's absolutely true, yes. And Richard stepped in to do First Voice [in the Douglas Cleverdon radio production in 1954].

Tony Earnshaw: How did you manage to land those three mega stars for your film? Did Burton do it out of loyalty, as a tribute to Dylan? Did he come to you with the idea or was it the other way around?
Andrew Sinclair: I managed to get to Richard and said, 'Look, O'Toole is doing *Under Milk Wood*. If you don't come to Wales, you're dead.' He was very capricious and his wife was even more capricious. Apparently, when you make a film, all you ever get is two paragraphs: if I am available I will do it for this fee. But basically the point was that Richard *had* to go back to Wales. He was the crown prince of Wales. And he loved Dylan. So if you take these two factors he had to do it. At the last moment he gypped as we were building sets. O'Toole rang me up and said, 'Andrew, I need another week on the schedule.'

'Why do you need another week, Peter?' I said.

'Well,' he said, 'the reason I need another week is Richard Burton wasn't coming. He never meant to come,' which rather did me in as I was heavily into hock at this time.

'Give me another week.'

Now, I was fully committed. I'd built the sets and all that. He was apparently coming and it was all settled. And indeed the final documents on making films in a rush are never signed until about three or four weeks into shooting but I had believed people. I said, 'He wasn't coming?' That was the ruin of my life. I was absolutely finished.

'You are so clever, Andrew.'

'What's that?'

'You set up all this publicity. He *has* to come. He's the crown prince of Wales. He can't *not* come because he's having a bad day or something. He's *got* to come.'

I'd set up no publicity. It was the publicity *his* machine set up. He was going back, he was going to do it, he was the great friend of Dylan Thomas. He was going to do Second Voice. Dylan was going to do First Voice before he died. All this and the crown prince was returning to Wales. And he was, in a phrase I invented, hoist by his own PR. I was at this point absolutely off my head. Only six days' shooting, I wanted no television crews around. Four appeared and so the film got made. But I do assure you, a publicity machine, once it gets going, can kill a star more than a director. But Richard *did* come. He came in the end because he couldn't *not* come to Wales.

Tony Earnshaw: So O'Toole, rather than Burton, was cast first.
Andrew Sinclair: O'Toole came because I've always known O'Toole. He was always going to play. Once Burton knew that O'Toole was going to play – and for nothing because he loved it and loved the part and had played it at RADA – Burton then had to play. The point was once he was there the publicity machine began happening and Richard had to go because everyone said he was going back to Wales. He *had* to go. Richard and Elizabeth come back to England. They moor their yacht opposite the Tower [of London]. They get a house in Camden. They can only stay three months because otherwise they pay in back taxes the English national debt. At this moment Richard is there. She's playing in a bad film called *Zee & Co*. He has nothing to do. I manage to get to him and say, 'The money's available. O'Toole is playing Captain Cat with or without you,' but he *has* to play it. He was Dylan's friend, there's nowhere else to go, they expect him in Wales and he goes. The worst moment of my life was when Jules Buck, who was O'Toole's manager, rings me up and says, 'You haven't got the two biggest stars in the world. You've got the three biggest stars!'

'Not Miss Taylor?' I say.

'Yes,' he says. 'You've got the three.'

'What can she play?' I said. 'Oh God, the Welsh whore, Rosie Probert!'

'You've only got her for two days at the end of doing *Zee & Co*.'

So I got her.

Tony Earnshaw: It sounds like you had your hands full.
Andrew Sinclair: Then Richard arrived and he played beautifully. He was only there six days and he was never there with O'Toole. That's all camera tricks. And we had miracles. We had sun in Fishguard in February. I was called 'Andrew the Luck'. I've always said it was the influence of Dylan. We made it for Dylan and he could even influence the weather via some mystical druid principle. It was extraordinary how everything then worked. We shot on the run. There were forty sets. We had seven weeks.
Tony Earnshaw: How did you fare with Elizabeth Taylor?
Andrew Sinclair: I never got on with Miss Taylor. Richard was told not to do it; certainly by his wife, and in the end they both

appeared very much against her will. There was a lot of tension in those days between them but he loved Dylan and he had to do it. There was the terrible moment when Elizabeth said she had a bad back and couldn't come from London so I had to go down to Lee Studios, which certainly there was no budget for. Talk about budgets! For the whole budget of the clothes we had £1,200. Elizabeth took £600 for three nighties from Paris for her brief scenes! Anyway, such is life. That's making movies for you. I'll tell you another story. I'm with [Welsh comic actor] Ryan Davies. I've got to meet Miss Taylor off set. And Richard has decided he loves Ryan, his Second Voice, and me more than anyone else on earth that particular night. There are two cups 'From the grateful people of Wales'. He gives one to me and he gives one to Ryan. At that moment Elizabeth comes in wearing the first yellow hot pant suit I have ever seen and a mink coat with nine tails dripping on the floor. Then a row begins. I look at Ryan. Ryan looks at me. We put a cup each back in Richard's hands and we skedaddle! I always said Dylan made that film, we did not. We were only interpreting it in our own terms. It was all made for the love of Dylan. Nobody got more than two hundred a week. Not Glynis Johns, not Victor Spinetti.

Tony Earnshaw: The supporting cast is particularly fine. You had people like Glynis Johns as Myfanwy Price and Victor Spinetti as Mog Edwards, also Vivien Merchant as Mrs Pugh and Siân Phillips as Mrs Ogmore-Pritchard. Can you reveal how you landed such significant guest players?
Andrew Sinclair: Glynis Johns came to my door in Soho. She came up the stairs – I'd never seen her before – and said, 'May I have a part in your film, Mr Sinclair?' I said, 'Any part you like. I've been in love with you since I was eighteen.' Once it was being made there wasn't a notable Welsh actor who didn't have to be in it. They'd never made a major Welsh film before. It's that first film. It was *Under Milk Wood*. And it was Dylan Thomas. I did have a marvellous casting director called Miriam Brickman and I did go down to Cardiff. I spent two days casting there. None of these people had been heard of. Many of them became great later, like David Jason who plays Nogood Boyo. It was David's first film. I also went round the whole Welsh coast for a fortnight [seeking locations] and only Lower Fishguard was there. One of the Dylan Thomas trustees, Wynford Vaughan-Thomas, held part of that land and it's now a national park. So I preserved the last old bit of Welsh coastline by making that movie. It's the only virtuous thing I've ever done. These things are great graces but in making films I would say that magic descends once in ten times. It is not within your control. This one worked and it was for love of Dylan, because we were all trying in certain ways to make this work.

Tony Earnshaw: It's also a time capsule.
Andrew Sinclair: Wales isn't like that anymore. Richard's style of acting is gone. It has disappeared. They don't do this sort of thing anymore so in a way it's a sort of time warp. The reason it works – and it was sold in twenty countries from Poland to Taiwan – is because it's like your grandmother's memory. There's that perfect village, you know who they are – the butcher, the baker, the candlestick maker – and these are people in every seaside village in the world. Everyone remembers that although that whole way of life has gone. So they will see it in very odd countries now. But what Dylan did was the myth. He got the

myth of that sort of life and people's seaside memories, and it is worldwide. Richard's performance is one of the greatest things. I think it is forever.

Tony Earnshaw: Richard's performance in *Under Milk Wood* came during a period of turmoil in his life and a run of mediocre movies in the early 1970s. Did he ever watch his old movies and if he did, what did he think of this one?
Sally Burton: Certainly in the years I was with him he didn't watch his films and I don't think he'd watched them for quite some time. He'd always say, 'You go into a film, you read the script, it sounds great, it's in a good location, you're working with people you might want to work with, the director's good... you never know. It feels right on the set but you don't know what's going to happen in the cutting room.' That was his take on those years and those films. But I think you're absolutely right. The marriage [to Elizabeth] was in turmoil, he was drinking a lot. He went through some very dark times. I think that he had emerged through that and particularly with *1984* he saw a way ahead with that film because he was not the lead. He was second. It was a low budget British film. Andrew's was a low budget film.
Andrew Sinclair: £300,000.
Sally Burton: Yes. It was wonderful for him to be on those films, certainly with *1984*, to be back with creative people making a film rather than [this notion of] he was the big star who was arriving. I think directors very often stood back because they'd got Richard Burton 'so just let him do it'. He enjoyed *1984* by being directed and responding to direction.
Tony Earnshaw: Did he respond to your direction?
Andrew Sinclair: I'll tell you how it is with a great star. You always have to go through tests. He knew I lived in a big house. They had a house in Hampstead as well as the yacht. On the walls [were] apparent Cezannes, Matisses, whatever you want. I thought they were all forgeries. He looked at me and he said, 'Don't I have some very impressive pictures?' So I said, 'Yes, they're very impressive indeed.' He said, 'I've got better ones on the yacht.' He was testing me. To which I replied, 'Oh, I see. These are your *travelling* pictures?' Now I got a grin. Then he put me through the test and this was the most difficult. He said, 'You know, I am the greatest actor in the world.' Now, if I said yes he would walk over me. If I said no he might leave the film. So I looked at him, grinned, and said, 'Bleagh!' He laughed and I was through. You go through these tests to see whether you can direct them or not or whether they'll walk over you. Richard was very humorous about it. He was a very literary man; he wrote extremely well [and] I have all his short stories. He destroyed more than he wrote. He was very particular about it and threw most of it away. And he really did want to be – if he'd not been an actor – a writer or indeed a Don, as I was. It just wasn't the way his life had gone. O'Toole was the same. He wrote two excellent volumes of autobiography. He had a first class mind and was a very, very good writer. Miss Taylor didn't like that literary side of [Richard]. She absolutely loathed it.

Tony Earnshaw: Is it because she wasn't very bright?
Sally Burton: No, I don't think it's because she wasn't very bright. I don't think she was well educated. She knew that. And it tapped a nerve.
Andrew Sinclair: She was just very jealous. If it was something

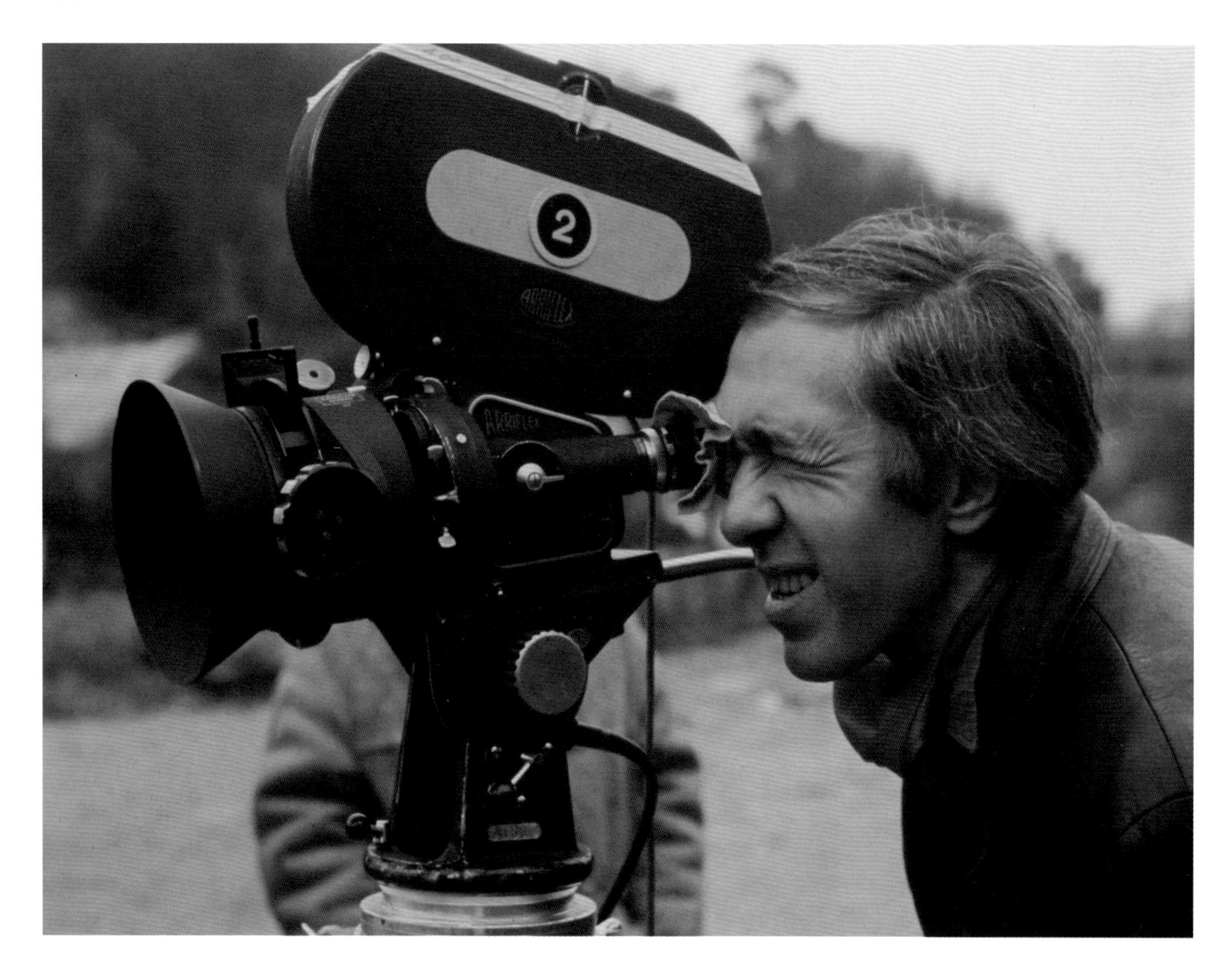

Left: Andrew Sinclair at the camera.

Right: 'Captain Cat, the retired blind sea captain, asleep in his bunk in the seashelled, ship-in-bottled, shipshape best cabin of Schooner House dreams of...'

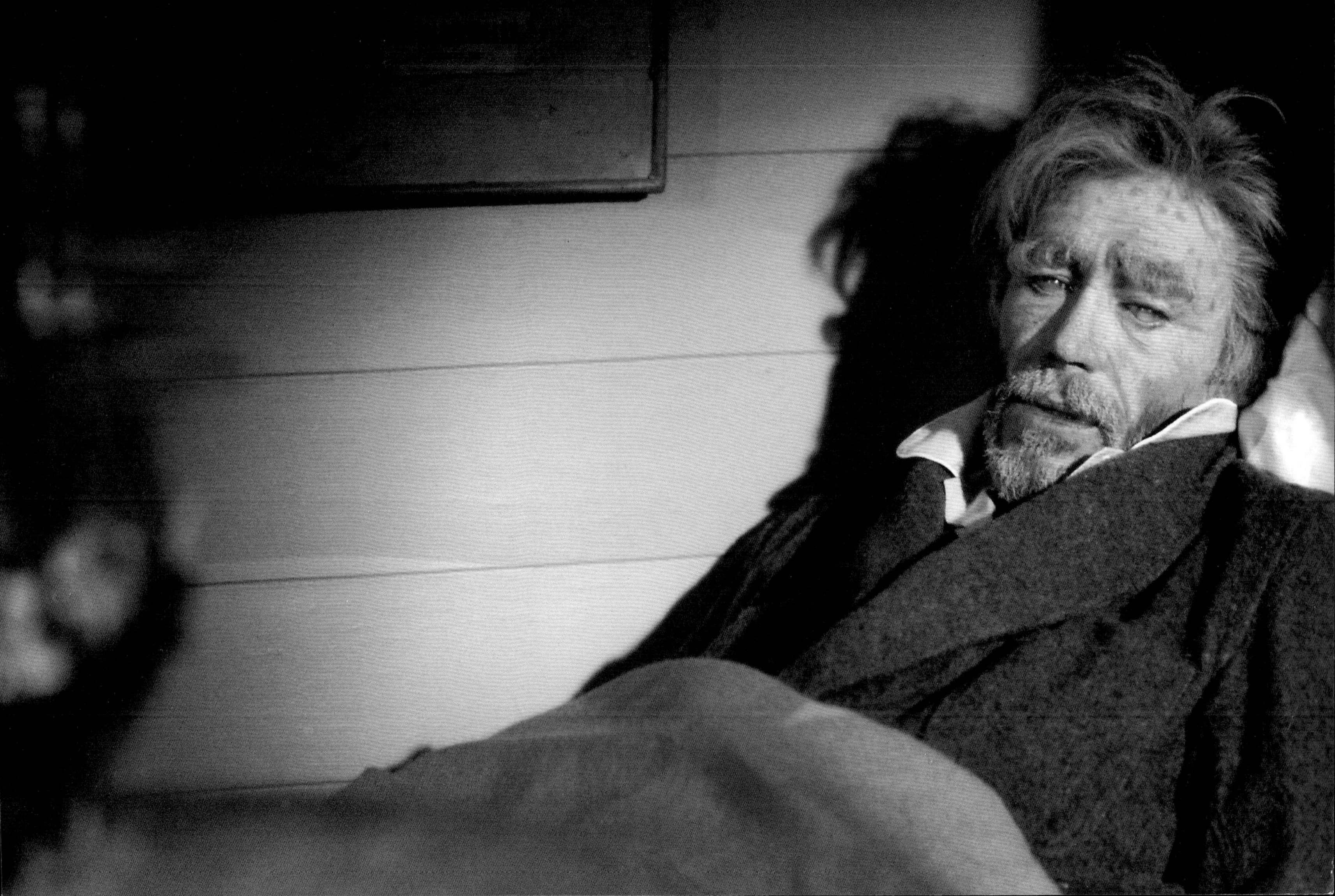

she couldn't do [then] she absolutely hated it. She didn't like any side she didn't control. I've known it in other marriages.
Tony Earnshaw: Richard recorded all his dialogue for the film before the shoot so in in essence what he was giving was a mime performance. How did the two of you approach that?
Andrew Sinclair: He had given this perfect rendering and, to be quite honest, he was not reliable in those days in terms of his acting performance. To be absolutely frank [we did] close-ups nine to eleven [in the morning], medium shots 'til lunch and thereafter on his back or in the distance.
Sally Burton: [Laughs]
Andrew Sinclair: He wasn't in the best of states. O'Toole, on the other hand, who was equally a drinker, was incredible about it because he put these [contact lenses like] soup plates in his eyes. He said that Captain Cat had had syphilis and therefore was blind from his early whoring days. He put these soup plates in and he was literally blind. And he didn't touch a drop. He was absolutely professional. The most professional man I've ever worked with. He insisted on these soup plates in his eyes, [but] they were hurting so much in the last four shots that I had to take him from the back or from a distance because he couldn't wear them anymore. He nearly went blind on the performance. I must say O'Toole is my hero in this particular case. I will now tell you another story. I had a hell of a row with Miss Taylor. It was only a two-day shoot in Lee Studios. I even bought her an Egyptian gold bracelet – 500 quid at Sotheby's – and slammed it on the desk. It was only a two-day shoot and I'd gone in at nine and she was putting on make-up as Cleopatra.

I said, 'You're not Cleopatra. You're a Welsh whore of the 1920s. They didn't look like Cleopatra, I promise you.'

Then, bang!

'I always appear as Cleopatra.'

So she didn't appear until twelve. One and a half days' shoot. Appears as Cleopatra. I said to the cameraman, Bob Huke, 'Grease the lens. She's Captain Cat's wet dream. What can we do?' Three close-ups before lunch. She loathes me by this time, to a degree. Then they go out to lunch – she, O'Toole, Burton. Long lunch. O'Toole comes to me, but O'Toole really likes me. He says, 'Andrew, for what I am about to do for you I deserve the Victoria Cross and Bar!' Then he leaves. So they have a long lunch, they come back and they're all a bit gone by that time. They prop her up between them and she reads all her lines off. She did them very well, actually, because O'Toole and Burton had been flirting with her and she's in a good mood. Of course I lie her in the bed again. This is the wonderful thing about stars. She hadn't walked off the set, which she was liable to do after lunch. All O'Toole told me was, 'Get this shot, Andrew.' He had gone away and as he suddenly is not the old man but the young man has tattooed (in biro) 'I love you, Rosie Probert' across his tummy. He pulls up his shirt and gets a genuine laugh out of her. She's not expecting it and the whole point of a true star is 'Get that shot.' It's shock. It's not scripted. And so there's a genuine, wonderful laugh from Elizabeth Taylor. That is why you value people. Richard was the same. Richard at that particular lunch had got Elizabeth going. He'd got her back into the film and he was always to me an excellent actor, totally professional in every way indeed. There is some sort of magic in that film because it could have gone so wrong so often and somehow it got done and done pretty well. I learned so much. I learned from working with Richard and Peter the sheer professionalism of people. Also, it's an odd thing. The professional actors, they do nothing. You say, 'You move from here to here,' and what's the size of the lens? And they give exactly that size of performance. Whereas the rest of the cast, the Welsh, who were all marvellous actors, I would have to say, 'Look, please don't overact. If I have a long shot showing you naked upside down, nobody will see it. But if you wink in front of a close-up it will look like the most lecherous thing on earth.' You'd have to teach the size of the performance but not to Richard or Peter, who knew the size of the distance of the camera or the lens. It's a privilege to work with people like that. The rest... it's not that they're not great actors but you've got to get the size of the performance. The best thing about *Under Milk Wood* was the children. They were local Fishguard children, absolutely marvellous, and all the Welsh are the best actors in all the world.

Tony Earnshaw: Some of Richard's biggest movies – *The Night of the Iguana*, *Who's Afraid of Virginia Woolf? Equus* and *Under Milk Wood* – were based on plays. Did he naturally gravitate towards theatre plays that had been transformed into movies or was it just the scripts that landed on his doormat?
Sally Burton: In all the films you've mentioned he gave marvellous performances and I think it's because of the words. He always said, 'The words are the most important thing.' So those particular scripts would have appealed to him enormously. In *Virginia Woolf* he turns in a magnificent performance. He was a very generous actor and one sees it in *Virginia Woolf* more than anything.
Andrew Sinclair: It's the only time he pulled Elizabeth through a movie. He did beautifully on that. It's an extraordinary movie and the best movie the two of them ever did.
Sally Burton: It was always words that appealed to him. And then there were just scripts that came in: 'Well, I might as well do it.' All actors have this insecurity that they're never going to work again. Very few of them say, 'I'm going to take two years off.' So some scripts I readily admit were not good. You were very clever to have picked up on the fact that some of the best ones were plays, because they were just beautifully written. Richard came to English as a second language and I notice it with French people – they play with it and it's so attractive. It's so beautiful. They're so intrigued with the words and the way the language goes together. But Welsh people have a delight in language – their own and other languages.

Tony Earnshaw: You mentioned actors and their insecurities; Richard Burton did not come across as insecure. But was he quietly, secretly insecure?
Sally Burton: I would have thought the manifestation of that was buying diamonds and yachts, the physical things.

Tony Earnshaw: Was that insecurity part of not wanting to watch himself on film, or did he just not watch movies?
Sally Burton: Oh no, he did watch movies. But the job was done. Early in his career maybe he did watch them and he would have gone to premieres. He would have done all of these things. But when I was with him that was it: the job was done, let's move on.

Tony Earnshaw: Were there ever opportunities for you to work together again that perhaps didn't come off?
Andrew Sinclair: No. It was very odd, chiefly my war with Elizabeth. It really was such a set-to with her [that] they left the set and I never

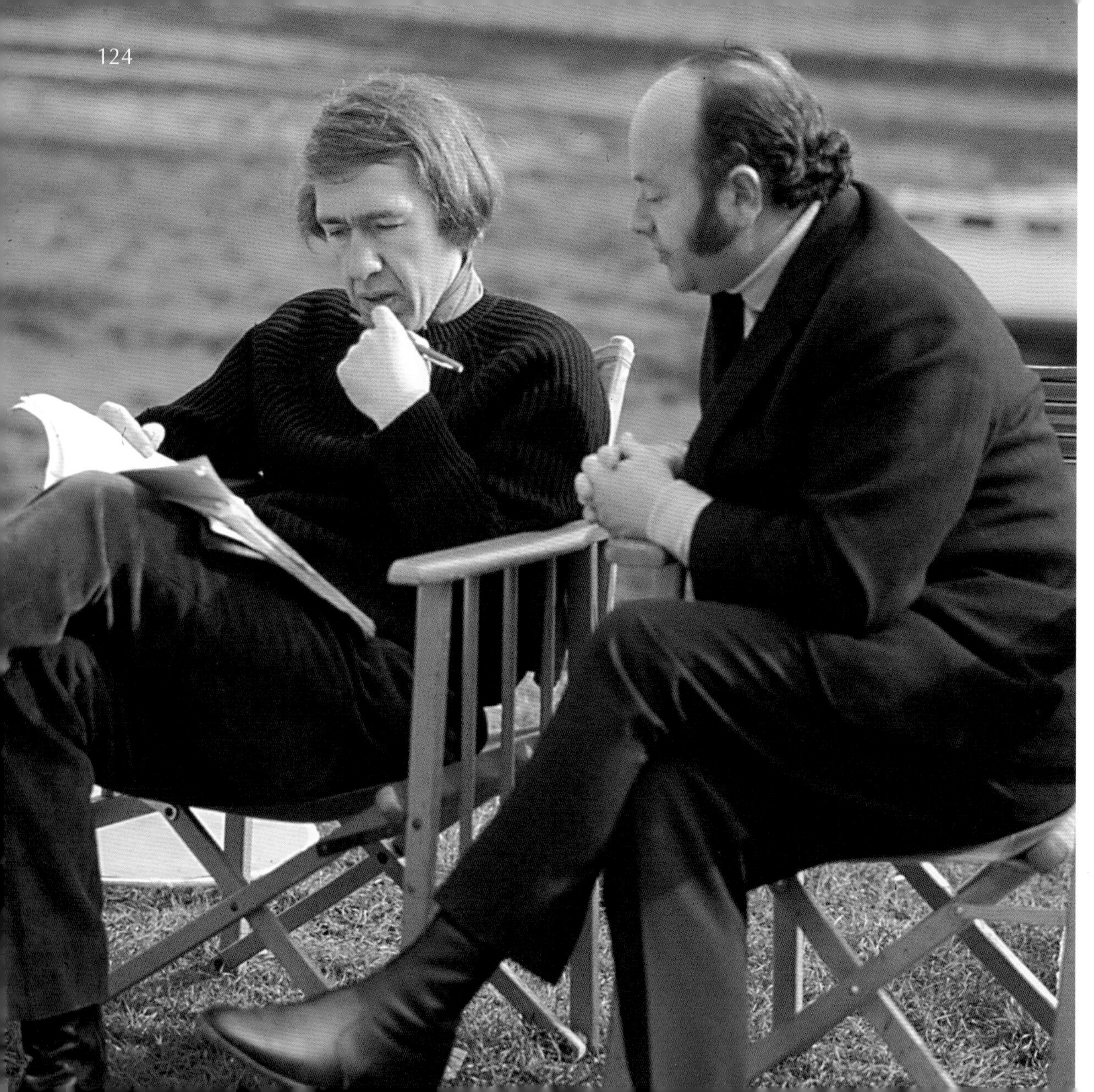

Writer/director Andrew Sinclair on location in Fishguard. Behind him on the Quayside can be seen Schooner House, a magnificent piece of production design that was created especially for the film.

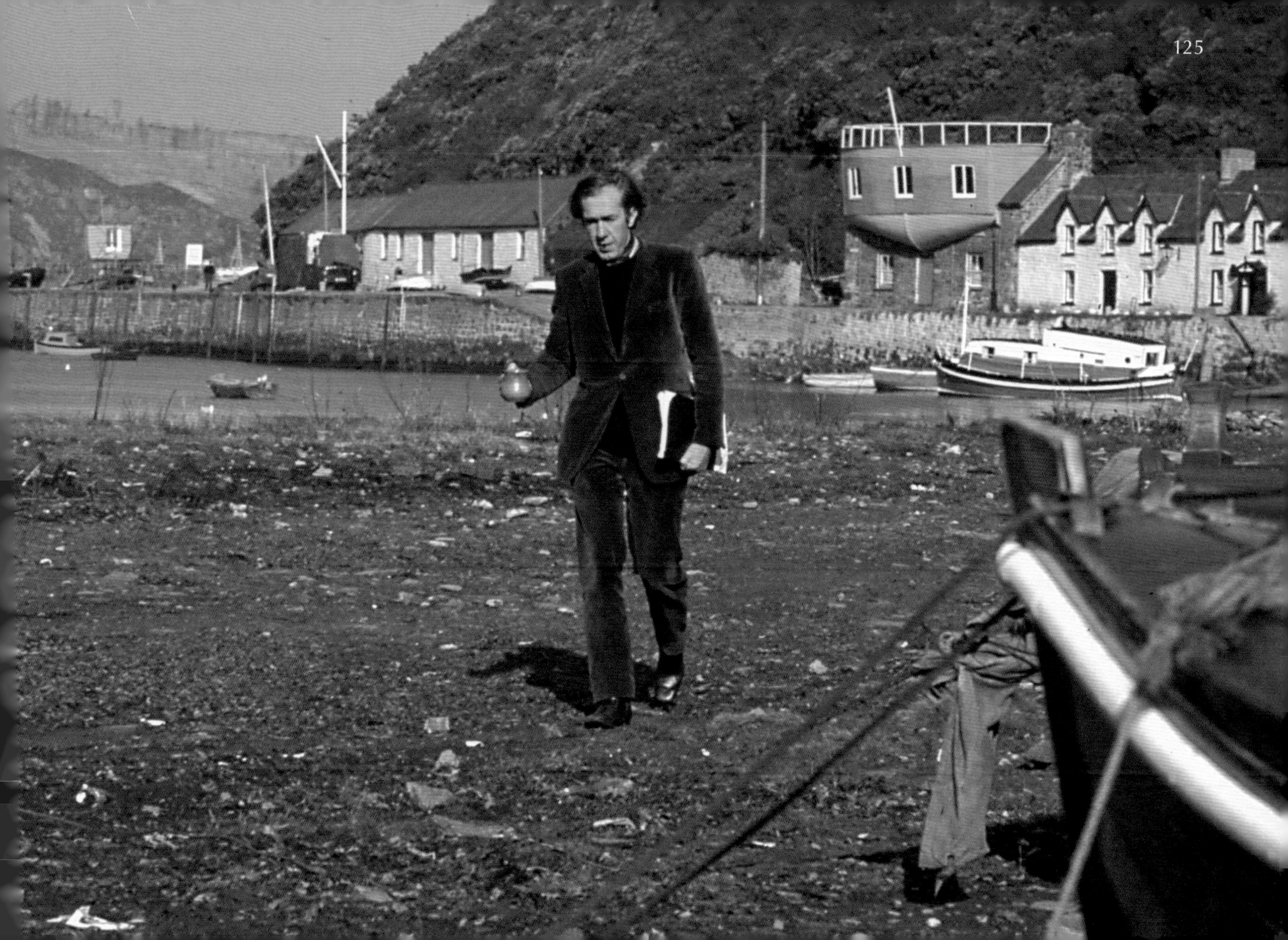

saw them again. It was all Elizabeth. I really had quite a spat. Whereas O'Toole remained one of my great friends. I really couldn't deal with her. Instant dislike. She didn't want his Welsh past.

Tony Earnshaw: What was the reaction from the Thomas family, and from Caitlin?

Andrew Sinclair: She loved it. Basically the reaction was they got for the first time in their lives £20,000 – worth about 200 [thousand] now. They never received more than twenty pennies in their lives. Caitlin married again, a Sicilian, so I really made them all rich for the first time in their lives. I put them all through college. She came to the premiere and absolutely loved it. She came to me and said, 'This is exactly what Dylan would have loved.' I think there was also the first sentence you read about it – she actually thought I had done a good job.

Tony Earnshaw: Why have so few films been adapted from Dylan's works? There haven't been very many.

Andrew Sinclair: Dylan made ten war documentaries for Strand Films. Then he wrote about three scripts for Strand Films. To me they're some of his finest writing. He had a rather clotted, surreal style in the Thirties. Doing these ten war documentaries he refined his style - he had a mass audience – without losing his lyric quality. And his poems from the war onwards are the famous ones. The first eighteen poems are very difficult to read. I think curiously enough [that] most writers are ruined by writing for films. I think it cleaned out Dylan's act a great deal in certain ways. It did him nothing but good. The actual act of screenwriting does make you get rid of all your long words and various other things. In *Under Milk Wood* I had to go with that radio play and everything else. It only survives by a trick of camera. Burton was never there with O'Toole but you'll never know that. Burton looks up to a dark window, O'Toole looks down. It's all done with sliding cameras. It works because I didn't cut the words. You couldn't. All the words flow and the camera flows with the words – between dream and reality and the living and dead.

Tony Earnshaw: Did Richard ever contemplate any of those other scripts as actor or even producer or director? Did he ever want to do anything else of Dylan's?

Sally Burton: Certainly he never talked to me about it. He just loved the poetry and whenever he did a personal anthology it was always Dylan who was in there, and particularly 'Fern Hill', which was one of his favourites. I think it was the poetry that he connected with. It was quite extraordinary because he could just do them, like that. 'Fern Hill' or any part of *Under Milk Wood*. Out it would come. Just like that. He didn't see himself as a producer or developing projects. That was not for him.

Tony Earnshaw: Have you had a hankering to do more?

Andrew Sinclair: Only what I've done, which was *Dylan on Dylan*. I optioned afterwards his other great radio play *Return Journey*. Didn't manage to make it. I optioned it for three years. I optioned *Adventures in the Skin Trade* to make. Again I couldn't manage to make it. The gap between optioning something and getting it made is total. I would say in film terms of a hundred scripts ten reach pre-production and one gets made. The wastage is phenomenal.

Tony Earnshaw: Was there a genuine chemistry between Richard and Dylan or was it more about being associated with someone who was more like the person you want to be?

Sally Burton: In the fact that Richard so loved writing? Yes, he had infinite respect for Dylan in those terms and I know that he absolutely thrilled that he discovered the poetry and then meeting Dylan in London and working with him. It was a truly valued friendship and I think that's a very interesting point – that Richard wished he could write like that. Though Richard could. He wrote some wonderful things. [They did have a rapport], absolutely. There was the Welshness for a start. There was the love of life. They were both robust and drank a lot and rollicked around. Yes, a good match.

Tony Earnshaw: Since Dylan was no longer around to read his own work was Richard the voice of Dylan's words?
Andrew Sinclair: There was a poll on Radio 4 and the question was asked of the great audience, 'If you think of Wales what describes it best?' and the answer is always '*Under Milk Wood*'. That is to the whole of consciousness. If you think of Wales you think of *Under Milk Wood* because it has this mytho-poetic quality. It is the essence of Wales.

Tony Earnshaw: Richard's involvement with Dylan went through his life and beyond. When he died his daughter Kate read, 'Do not go gentle…' and a copy of Dylan's verse was buried with him. Was that something you had ever discussed?
Sally Burton: It was instinctive. It was just so much part of the man. It had to be 'Do not go gentle…' and a book of Dylan's poems absolutely went with him, yes.

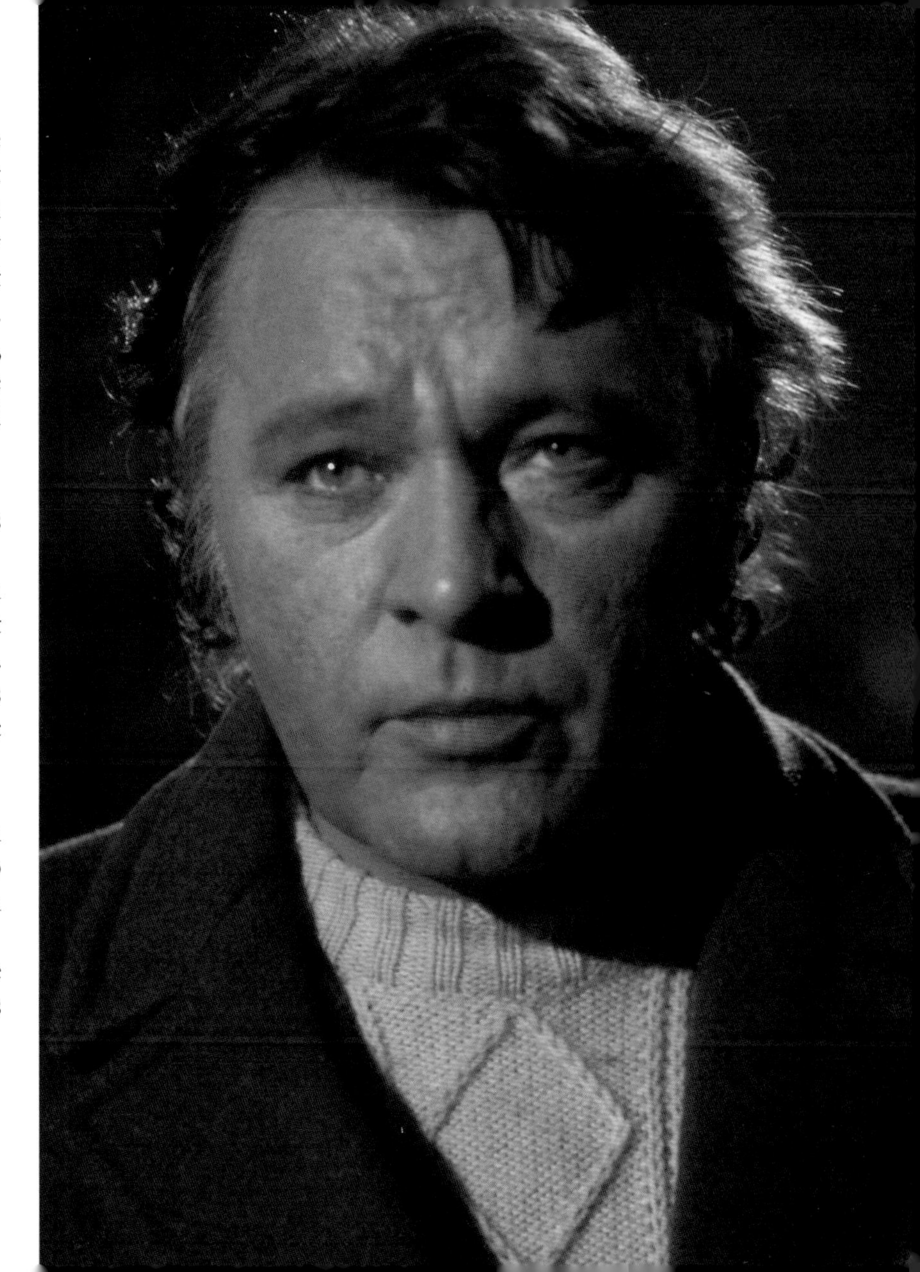

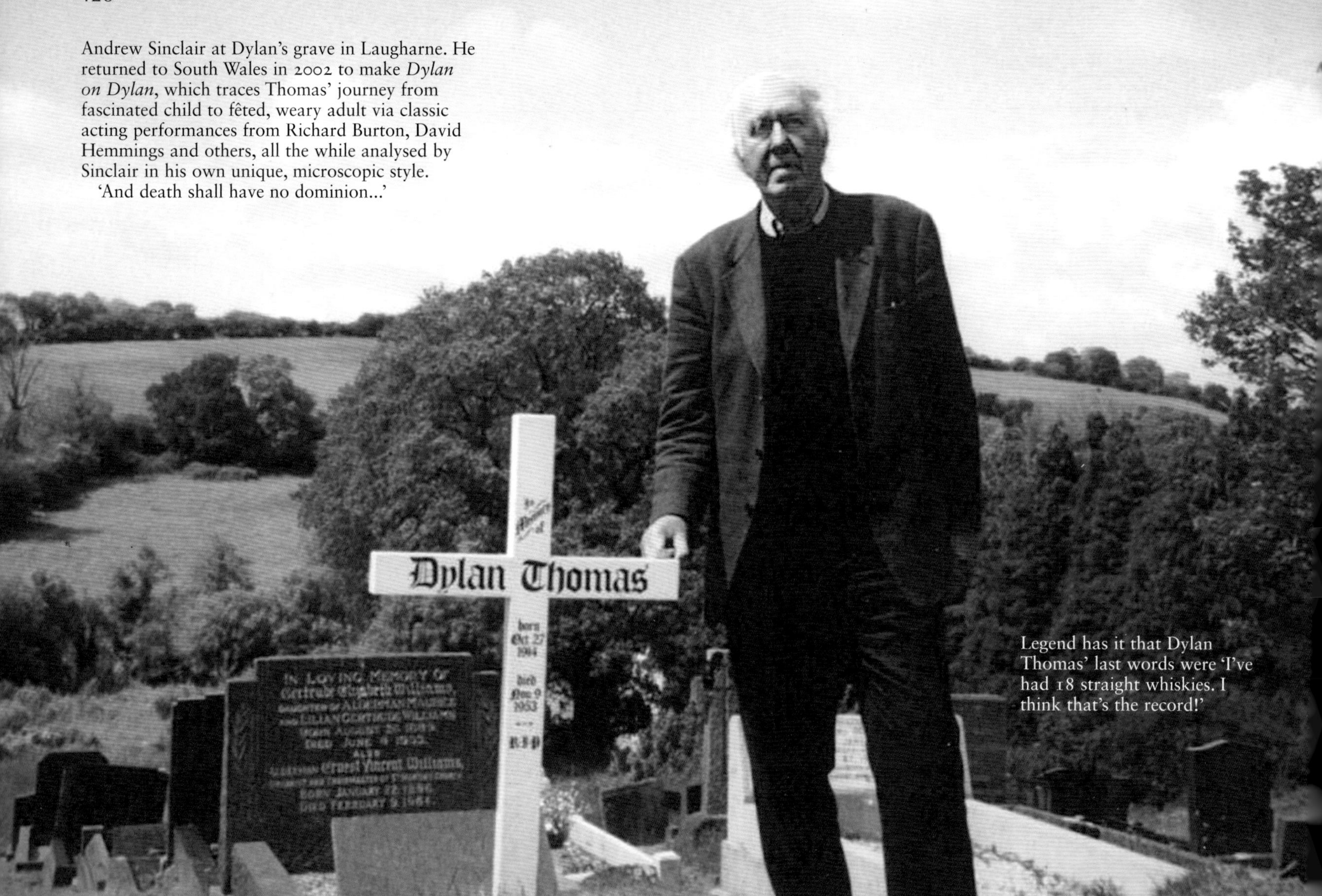

Andrew Sinclair at Dylan's grave in Laugharne. He returned to South Wales in 2002 to make *Dylan on Dylan*, which traces Thomas' journey from fascinated child to fêted, weary adult via classic acting performances from Richard Burton, David Hemmings and others, all the while analysed by Sinclair in his own unique, microscopic style.
'And death shall have no dominion...'

Legend has it that Dylan Thomas' last words were 'I've had 18 straight whiskies. I think that's the record!'